THE
NOBLE
BREED

THE
NOBLE
BREED

BILL COSGROVE

Rutledge Books, Inc. Danbury, CT

Rutledge Books, Inc.
107 Mill Plain Road, Danbury, CT 06811
1-800-278-8533
www.rutledgebooks.com

Manufactured in the United States of America

Cataloging in Publication Data
Cosgrove, Bill, 1945 -
  The Noble Breed

   ISBN: 1-58244-063-8

   1. Chicago (Ill.) -- Biography.
2. Fire fighters -- Illinois -- Chicago -- Biography
920/.71

Library of Congress Catalog Card Number: 99-65960

This book is dedicated with love and understanding
to the widows who truly know loneliness after the
loss of their husbands.

I would also like to dedicate this book to the many
children of firefighters who lost a parent
in the line of duty.

THE

Emphasizing one of a group, or type, as the most outstanding or prominent.

That's a Fireman!

NOBLE

Having and showing qualities of high moral character, such as courage, generosity, or honor.

That's a Fireman!

BREED

To develop new or improved strains in men, having consistent and recognizable inherited characteristics developed and maintained.

That's a Fireman!

From:

The American Heritage Dictionary, Second College Edition

ACKNOWLEDGEMENTS

IN THE COURSE of gathering all the material for this book, interviewing firefighters, and collecting the photographs, I had invaluable assistance from my uncle, Jack Gallapo. I would also like to thank: Larry Kasonski, the captain of Truck #15, for the times I needed to read the old journals; William Kugelman, the president of Local #2, for the wonderful video; Mike Hein for his many newspaper clippings; Phil Lamm for always being there to help; and my brother, Mike Cosgrove, for all his knowledge of the fire department and the ambulance service. A special thanks to Lewis Buick for the encouragement to push this book forward during our backyard meetings.

A very special thanks to the person who was able to sort through all my handwritten pages— my good friend Margaret (Peg) Campagna, who put this story into type. I will always be thankful.

Whenever I was stumped about a time or a date when an event occurred, I always had a way to call and find out the correct answer. For all the help with misspelled words and improper grammar, I owe a very special thanks to my friend, boss, and chief, William C. Alletto, Deputy Fire Commissioner, Chicago Fire Department.

As always, I could not have made it to first base without the love, understanding, and encouragement of my lovely wife, Suzi. After working all day in downtown Chicago, she would come home, sit down at our computer, and help me straighten all of this out.

My sincere appreciation to the Chicago Fire Department Photo Unit for all their help and to Fire Commissioner Edward Altman for permission use the cover photo for the book.

A special thanks to firefighter Raymond N. Moran, who was able to take the cover photo.

Contributions will be made to:
The Fireman's Annuity and Benefit Fund of Chicago
Ende Menzer Walsh Retiree's, Widow's, and Children's Assistance Fund

THE ENEMY

I AM MORE powerful than the combined armies of the world. I have destroyed more men, women and children than all the wars of all nations. I massacre thousands of people every year. I am more deadly than bullets, and I have wrecked more homes than the mightiest guns.

In the United States alone, I steal over 500 million dollars each year. I spare no one and I find my victims among the rich and poor alike; the young and old, the strong and the weak. Widows know me to their everlasting sorrow. I loom up in such proportions that I cast my shadow over every field of labor.

I lurk in unseen places and do most of my work silently. You are warned against me, yet you heed me not. I am relentless, merciless, and cruel. I am everywhere, in the home, in the schools, in the factory, on land, in the air, and on the sea.

I bring sickness, degradation and death, yet few seek me out to destroy me. I crush, I maim, I devastate-I will give you nothing and rob you of all you have.

I AM YOUR WORST ENEMY-
I AM RAMPANT FIRE.

Unknown Author

INTRODUCTION

THE SHOOTING OF *Backdraft* was completed in December 1990. The director, Ron Howard, called the last wrap. The crew with all their trucks and trailers filled with special effects left Chicago.

I didn't hear from Bob for a while, but every day I thought about him and the way movies were made.

On Christmas 1990, Todd Dickison had returned to Chicago from Fort Lauderdale, Florida. Robert DeNiro hired him on as his driver on the movie Cape Fear. He told me that Bob had a gift for me, and he would drop it off. It was great to see Todd. He told me how much he was enjoying working with Bob in Florida. The movie Backdraft was over and I had received gifts from Billy Baldwin, Ron Howard and now a personal delivery from Robert DeNiro. He had sent a bottle of "Cog Delamain" champagne and a handmade cigar from the Dominican Republic. It was a great year, 1990.

January 1991 started out slowly. Just another cold Chicago winter, up until January 21st. It was Monday morning, and it had snowed a little the night before. I was cleaning the snow off my 1986 Dodge van while it was parked in the driveway. My wife Suzi and I rode to work together on my day shift at the Office of Fire Investigation (O.F.I.). I would drop her off at the corner of

Michigan and Jackson. She worked for the CNA. Insurance Company. Suzi was the manager of the mailroom. There were six thousand people in the building and she had a hard job getting the mail out. As we started going north on Pulaski Road that morning, the traffic seemed light as it was Dr. Martin Luther King's birthday. The streets were wet and people were driving slowly. Driving on the Stevenson expressway was hard because traffic had slowed to almost a stop. Once you got into your lane, the speed picked up. I always went to the inside lane because it led to Lake Shore Drive. The traffic was now moving and as we cruised at about 55 mph, on my right was an eighteen-wheeler semi-truck two lanes over. At first, it appeared that the truck was moving out to the left and would be using the Martin Luther King exit as many trucks did. They did this in order to get to McCormick Place. In a split second the truck crashed into the right front door on Suzi's side of the van. Now, speeding together, we crashed into the concrete wall at Halsted Street.

I was thrown through the windshield of the van, and I landed under, or next to, the very truck that just ran over me. Diesel fuel was pouring out of a split in the truck's fuel tank and I was covered in this volatile material. At this time two men from another car had pulled me out and carried me to the guardrail and hung me by my arms. I yelled to my wife. One of the men gave me a rag and told me to hold it over my ear because it was badly cut and was only attached by a small portion of skin on the bottom of the lobe. I called for Suzi!

I called for Suzi again. I asked God to please help us. I knew I was hurt bad, and I asked God why. Why did this happen to me? As I hung over the steel guardrail, blood was dripping down my face from my ear into the white snow on the side of the interstate.

As I looked back at my van everything started to look black, and I was losing my concentration. I started to look back at my life. I was just a little boy. I remembered a sunny morning when I was four years old. The day was May 31, 1950.

CHAPTER I

THIS WAS THE day of my father's funeral. There were strange people in our home. My father was a Chicago fireman. They said he was a great fireman, and had a hell of a reputation on the job. I don't know a lot about the time he devoted to the fire department, but I do know he had about twenty-two years on the job. He was promoted to Lieutenant in 1944, and assigned to the Fire Prevention Bureau. On June 30, 1944, he was transferred from the Fire Prevention Bureau to Squad Company No. 8.

Edward M. Cosgrove was only forty-six years old when he died of a heart attack in his home at 2508 W. 113th Street in Chicago on May 29, 1950. He did not die in a fire. He died because of the various physical ill effects that were associated with long-term smoke inhalation like so many firemen. In those days there were no self-contained air masks to protect firemen.

Edward Cosgrove was the father of nine children when he died. Eleven days after his death, the tenth child was born. My mother was the wife and now the widow, of a Chicago fireman. She was very proud of that fact. She always would say to her five boys and five girls that she was lucky to have a fireman's widow annuity of $45.00 per month and $10.00 per month, per child until the age of 18 years. There were some very hard times, but

Steam pumper pulled by horses were a major improvement over the hand pumps formerly used.

all Mom talked about for years was that our father was a great fireman. She talked of the great Chicago firemen who risked their lives. My mother told many stories of the fires that our father had worked at while he was a member of the Chicago Fire Department. She talked of the horses that pulled the engines and the hook and ladders.

In 1871, the Chicago Fire Department consisted of 216 men manning seventeen engine companies and four hook and ladder companies. The population was 334,000 and there were thirty-six square miles and 60,000 structures. Most of the structures were wooden framed buildings.

The firemen were the proudest men in Chicago. In 1871, there were fourteen weeks of drought and hot, scorching winds from the southwest. At one point during this drought, the Chicago firemen fought fires throughout two days and two nights. Many had not eaten and had virtually no sleep.

A fire department watchman was stationed in the cupola in the courthouse tower. Upon sighting a fire, he would, via a voice tube, give the location of the fire to the telegraph operator in the alarm office. The telegraph operator would strike the appropriate fire alarm box and ring the courthouse bells. A fire occurred at 558 W. Dekoven Street on Sunday night, October 8, 1871. The fire raged until the morning of October 10th. When it was over, Chicago lost 300 people, 18,000 buildings, and three square miles of earth were scorched. One hundred eighty-five million dollars of property was lost and 100,000 people were homeless.

Chicago's firefighters formed the Independent Fireman's Association in 1901. They had many problems with city leaders. They did not want firemen to organize, but by 1917, sixty-six other local unions had been organized across the country. The Chicago Firemen's Association would thereafter be known as Local #2. It was necessary to create this organization for the improvement of working conditions and the reputation of the profession. The fire department expanded in the years after the Chicago fire, and so did the city. The Chicago Fire Department's largest loss of life occurred on December 22, 1910, when twenty-one men in the department were killed in the stockyards fire.

The firemen of the 4th Division responded to a private fire alarm box at the Nelson-Morris Meatpacking Company known as section 7, and located at the northwest corner of 44th and Loomis Street. The fire was discovered by a watchman in the northeast corner of section 7, between the basement and the second floor. The firefighters began attacking the fire from a long, loading dock. The fire was burning in a confined space under conditions which generated large volumes of gas, and generated products of combustion, not wholly consumed due to a lack of sufficient air supply.

The sudden opening of the door allowed fresh air to reach the seat of the fire so the rate of combustion was suddenly increased, which created a pressure sufficient to cause the east wall of section 7 to come crashing down burning the firefighters and crushing them beneath the rubble.

On that bitterly cold morning about fifty minutes after responding to this alarm, firefighters now began the gruesome task of recovering the twenty-one bodies of their fallen comrades. At this time, there were no death pensions for widows and orphans, and disability allowance did not exist in Chicago.

By the 1920's the old, one platoon system was abolished. Now firemen worked twenty-four hours and a second platoon was added, decreasing the work week down to only eighty-four hours!

The prosperous twenties were followed by the Depression in the thirties. Chicago was broke, but firemen still did their jobs. Firemen were paid in "scrip" IOUs and were met with payless paydays, but Local #2 fought back. The union aggressively campaigned to protect its members. In 1931, a new pension act was secured from the state legislature that offered death and disability benefits for firemen. For the first time, firefighters won a major voice in the administration of their own pension fund.

By the late thirties, Local #2 had succeeded in reducing the work week to seventy-two hours. Few of the city's fathers could argue with the fact that firefighting had become a very learned and practiced art. World War II arrived in 1941, and the fire department was quickly drained of men and equipment. The firemen took a stand and worked with what they had until the war was over, but not without losing eight firemen in 1943, to a building collapse at 419 W. Superior Street.

The end of the World War II signaled a profound change in the Chicago Fire Department. A change summed up in one word, "veterans." They flocked to the fire department for job security. Most of the fire trucks were old and worn out and had to be replaced with new and more modern, efficient equipment.

By 1945, the salary of a first class firefighter had only risen to $300.00 per month. Local #2 continued to fight for shorter hours and better working conditions.

In 1952, the Chicago Fire Department put the first radios into the fire trucks and the call letters "KSC 711" were first heard, and now could be dispatched out "on the air." In January 1955, a third platoon was adopted, and firemen now had one day in the firehouse and two days off. This was to reduce the working hours of firemen. "Daley Days," like the "Kelly Offs" of the thirties and forties, was put into effect, but the danger remained the same. It has been the constant factor in a fireman's life since the days of the bucket brigades. He may ride a more modern apparatus, learn new fire suppression techniques, enjoy shorter hours and more pay, but a fireman must always live in a world of smoke and flame, falling walls, and ice-covered ladders.

On a gray, winter day in December 1958, one of the deadliest fires in American history took the lives of ninety-two children and three nuns at a Catholic elementary school on Chicago's west side.

The 5-11 alarm blaze at Our Lady of the Angels school shocked the nation. Many firefighters that were there to rescue and extinguish the blaze were deeply affected by the tragedy, but they did the job as they always do, and now must live with the sorrow and the hurt of that terrible day. The statistics are frightening, yet how many people know anything about the one service dedicated to halting this death and destruction. Many people associate firefighters with lungs of leather and Dalmatian dogs as mascots. Neither image does the fire service justice. There is always another fire call and we go again the hopes that this fire will be much easier than Our Lady of Angel's fire.

CHAPTER II

EVER SINCE I was a small boy, I always wanted to be a fireman. Probably because of the influence of my mother, and the many stories that she told her ten children about their father. As the years went by, all I thought about was when I would be old enough to get on the Chicago Fire Department. In 1965, my older brother, Jim, was called by the city to be a fireman. I remember how envious I was of him. He was assigned to Hook & Ladder Company #14. They were located at 19th and Peoria. I recall going to his firehouse and playing handball in a make-shift handball court on the third floor. In the days of the horses, the third floor was where they stored the hay to feed them. When the horses were replaced by a mechanized department, the men on Truck #14 put all their talents together and made a handball court out of the hayloft. It was small, but good, and many great handball games were played by players who really excelled at the sport. Truck Company #14 was a FWD tractor, with a tiller man in the rear, that looked like it was 100 feet long to me. I was given the tour by my brother Jim, and he showed me the basement where the candidates, or the lowest man, kept a fire going in the coal-burning boiler and the coal-burning hot water tank all day and all night. In order to gain access to the third floor of this old firehouse you had to climb a winding staircase made of steel and painted high-gloss black.

The kitchen of Hook & Ladder #14 was very small with a gas stove and a refrigerator along one wall and a round table in the center. The most unusual thing that I just couldn't get over was that the ladder from the truck, the main ladder, went right through the top of kitchen wall and over the round table.

The bunk room was on the second floor. The beds were all made and were along the west wall. There were bunker boots at the foot of the beds all ready to go to the next fire. The floor was old, made of wood planking. It had varnish under the beds, but there was no varnish on the area where a path was worn, leading over to a 3-inch brass pole. When you got close to the pole, you could see your reflection. That is how shiny the poles were.

The captain of Truck #14 had his own room with a desk, a bed, and a fire pole. This fire pole led him down right next to the officer's door of the hook & ladder. All he had to do was climb into the cab. Fast push out was the most important thing to the captain of Truck #14.

Many major events took place in the years to come, but one thing was for sure: no matter what they sent the firemen to do, you know they were going to give it their best. They never left the fire scene until the fire was out, no matter how many days it took!

Just two years before I got the job, firemen were trying to win benefits for its members. Local #2 drafted proposals on pensions, benefits, and hospitalization plans.

By 1968, many departments across the nation including Local #2, had moved to drop the "No strike" clause from union by-laws and contracts, but the fires just kept coming!

On January 16, 1967, one of the largest structures in Chicago was totally destroyed by fire. McCormick Place was the showcase of conventional halls, but on the night of January 16th, it was hell on earth for the firemen that battled the fierce winds and subzero temperatures on Chicago's lakefront. They picked up in service and were ready for the next one.

Firemen of Chicago were put to the test again. January 27, 1967, the city was buried in snow. The fire commissioner ordered a general recall and all off-duty firemen were ordered to the nearest firehouse. Fires were almost impossible to get into because the snow was so deep. Engine lines 2 1/2-inch and 3-inch were dragged some two blocks to the fire. Firefighters also carried ladders for rescues and stretchers for the removal of injured citizens. Among their firefighting duties, they now helped with street cleaning of snow around hydrants and provided shelter for stranded citizens. People were removed from their stranded autos and brought into firehouses all around Chicago.

In 1968, a fire and explosion rocked the Chicago Fire Department. This fire was called the "Mickelberry Fire." On a cold afternoon, February 8th, Captain Fischer and firefighters Bottger, Leifker, and Collins, of Truck Co. #18 were killed in the line of duty. Many firemen and a few civilians were injured as a result of this explosion.

At last the announcement that an examination for the job of firefighter was issued by the city of Chicago. I remember, as I'm sure all firemen who took the exam remember, that the school that we went to for the exam was C.V.S. High School located on the southeast side of Chicago at 87th & Anthony. We took the test with about 2,000 other men. I found out one thing: after you take the test, the wait is something that seems like forever. There are stories that many firefighters have told me about waiting to get on this job that truly amaze me. I don't care who you are, you have some type of story about getting called, not getting called, or when the next class is for this job.

My friends were asking why I wanted to be a fireman after the Mickelberry fire and the snowstorm. They didn't pay us for the overtime. I answered that this was the only job that I had ever wanted, but they were right, there wasn't at that time, any provision for overtime compensation. Firefighting is unique in that you have no control over the working environment. Even with protective gear (helmets, heavy fire coats, and hip boots, etc.), there is still no protection from collapsing floors or falling walls. The Chicago firefighter's injury rate is almost 7.5 times greater than the employees in the overall work force and the fatality rate is over 3.5 times greater. In 1965, 2 1/2 times as many firemen were killed on duty than policemen and six times as many were injured.

The assassination of Dr. Martin Luther King on the night of April 4, 1968 clearly set off disturbances and riots. It was very evident that trouble was developing. By noon on April 5th, fifty-five alarms had been received from the street boxes, forty of which had come from school locations. By 3:50 P.M., a still alarm was received for a fire at 2235 West Madison Street. In rapid succession, additional alarms were sounded for this location until a 5-11 and three specials had been called. The fires along West Madison Street in the 2100 through 2400 blocks were deliberately set, by arsonists throwing a hand-held incendiary device (molatov cocktail), into buildings on Madison Street, Roosevelt Road, and many other streets in Chicago. The violence, arson and looting continued to build. The situation had deteriorated to the point that at 5:10 P.M. all off-duty firemen were called back to work. All off

Squad Company #1 taking cover during the riots in 1968.
From left to right: Kevin Fitzpartick, Rich Hickey, Joe Baldwin and Mike Schoenecker.

days were canceled. West Side firemen were ordered directly to the fire area. All other firemen were ordered to the fire academy.

Shooting at firemen and constant harassment of responding companies was getting out of control. Fires were raging all over the West Side of Chicago. Engine #77 and Engine #39 reported that they had run out of gas right in the middle of it all. A cadre of heavily armed police officers escorted fuel trucks into the area. Suburban fire companies, through a mutual agreement, were covering Chicago fire company calls. After three days of constant fire duty, the firemen were released, but the working shift remained on duty. Again, as many times before, the firefighters held on to protect the city of Chicago from the marauding arsonists. They prevailed!

When it was all measured up, the riots of 1968 destroyed

about 700 buildings and thirteen people lost their lives, and there was more than ten million dollars in total damage, not to say anything about how the rioting affected the firefighters mentally and physically.

In what seemed like a century of time that went by, I received my letter from the Chicago Fire Department. It stated as follows:

"Your name has been reached for certification and appointment to the position of firefighter. Please report for a physical examination on 2-5-69 at 9:00 A.M. sharp at 54 West Hubbard Street, Chicago, IL 60601."

On February 16, 1969, I started as a candidate firefighter at the Chicago Fire Academy. I was so excited; I could not believe that I was now on the job as my father and brother before me. Getting this job of a fireman was one of the best days of my life. My wish had come true and now I knew it was worth the wait.

CHAPTER III

IF YOU ARE a Chicago fireman, or if you were a Chicago fireman, there is a strong possibility that you went through this great fire academy, because we all started in the same place. I am sure that we all remember the flame at the entrance, the red-glazed brick walls that surround the academy, and the many artifacts that are encased on the walls of the first floor. In particular, these artifacts included the names of the many heroes that received the Lambert Tree and the Carter Harrison Awards for exceptional bravery. The inscription in the floor depicts the alleged point of origin of the great Chicago fire. Legend has it that his was the location of Mrs. O'Leary's barn. We should all remember the drill hall with the many ladders, fire escapes, and the fire hydrant, as well as the classrooms that were filled with fire protection material and equipment: building construction, wall hydrants, stand pipes, sprinkler systems, smoke detectors, and fire extinguishers, etc. If you did not receive your training at this fire academy, then you were trained at the old drill school at 720 West Vernon Park Place. The Chicago Fire Department Academy has the vital function of converting youthful firefighter candidates into safe, and knowledgeable and experienced firefighters.

The first day we were told everything to do over and over. We filled out forms for insurance, residency, birth certificates, family tree, military discharge papers, you name it. We were told how to park our automobiles in parking lot #6 on Union Avenue across from the Dan Ryan Expressway. We were told that we would be in the fire academy for a period prescribed by the fire commissioner. During this period, training consisted of physical education, military drilling, first aid, and extensive drilling in the basic firefighting evolutions. I think there were 107 guys in my class when we started.

DUTIES AND PROCEDURES FOR CANDIDATE

Roll call was at 7:30 A.M. sharp. We would answer roll call at the fire department gymnasium except on Saturday, when classes were held at the fire academy. Immediately after gym class we will report to the Fire Academy for drilling in the basic firefighting evolutions and procedures.

The first day I arrived at the fire department gym which was located adjacent to Navy Pier at Grand Avenue. There were a few other guys walking around in what appeared to be the same type of clothes that I was wearing. They must be candidates, I thought. I walked over toward them when I heard someone yell that the "roach coach" was in front of the gym if we wanted coffee. We all called it the "roach coach"-meals on wheels. All I knew was the coffee was hot.

One of the guys asked how the coffee guy knew when the class was going to be here and someone answered, "This guy can get you a transfer order if you want one. He is a brother of a fireman on Engine #42., and that is where the Fire Commissioner Quinn plays handball."

Suddenly the front door of the gym opened and the instructor started yelling, "Get rid of the coffee and smokes boys. We are going to run your asses off. Now get in here!"

I was not paying attention to the size of this building from the outside, because when I entered the gymnasium, it was so large that it took my breath away. I think it was about 200 feet across and 800 feet long with bow string type trusses that went from the floor level up some thirty feet at the cross and back down to floor level. There must have been some forty basketball courts. Also, there were mats rolled up along the side walls and a boxing ring on the south end of the gym.

THE GYM

They split the class in half and started one group on the east side and one on the west side. Marching in cadence, we walked around learning the instep calls that were being yelled out. On the fifth time around, we ran in cadence. It was hard to stay in step, but even a man like me can learn. I was not in the military service! When we finished the run they gave us a ten minute break. We all ran to the washroom and locker room to grab a smoke (just what you need after a five-mile walk and run).

We were again told to get into line, and they began calisthenics for about 1 1/2 hours: push-ups, sit-ups, jumping jacks, and anything else they thought of. Then to the showers and back to the fire academy before 13:00 hours. All candidates were dressed in gray sweatsuits and gym shoes. We were given instructions about never to have a dirty gym outfit or shoes, or we would be given a detention; the chip system. Each chip you received, the closer you came to getting kicked off the job. We lined up the same manner every day. Your name was called and you will answered, "Here sir". You talked only when spoken to. You then began to run in the two designated groups. The instructors told us what routes to take back to the academy. We had no time to mess around. By the time you parked the car and ate your lunch, there was no time left to grab a smoke outside in the drill yard.

13:00 HOURS. ROLL CALL IN THE DRILL HALL

Line up! Line up this guy was yelling his ass off. He was one of our instructors. His name was Lieutenant Frank Gargione and later would be nicknamed "The Zip," from someone in our class. Academy instructors are seasoned firefighters charged with the responsibility of preparing the candidates for the rigors they will encounter.

Lieutenant Gargione had been a fireman in Chicago for a long time. He was on Engine #48 for many years, and as a result, Lt. Gargione had a stroke. He returned to work and was placed in the academy as an instructor. Although he had a slight speech impediment, when he yelled you got the picture. The instructors were well aware that all this training might someday save the life of one of these future firefighters through discipline and teamwork.

We were now placed into groups according to alphabetical order, about sixteen guys per group. Then we would count off and have a roll call. Ladders were raised at different floors: 50' Bangor ladder, 35' three section, 38' extension, and of course the six-story, straight frame ladder that went to the roof of the drill hall.

I was in awe at the size of this drill hall. It was five stories, with concrete floors like the outside of a building. Ladders were placed into the windows at the first, second, third, and fourth floors. There was a fire escape on both ends of the drill hall. We were given instructions, per group, to start up the ladders and fire escapes. At first it was a little shaky, but after about one hour we got better and we continued to practice every day.

We had a ten minute break and were told by group where to go, and who the instructor would be. Three groups went to classrooms and three stayed in the drill yard and learned basic evolutions in the ladder raises, hose drills and the use of tools and equipment.

The classrooms were where we learned first aid, use of fire extinguishers, fire alarm systems, fire telegraph system and signatures of the fire department equipment. At the end of each day we would all meet up in room 203 for almost a half an hour. The in-structors tried to instill the mental awareness that the candidates needed to know, so we could react instinctively under extremely strenuous conditions by telling some war stories that all tie in. We all enjoyed listening to the stories and could not wait to be a part of them.

In three weeks we were getting in step and in shape. All except for someone in class who made sounds like "EEE-OOO" at the worst times. Like when Curtis Volkamer, the chief fire marshal of the department was congratulating candidates. I think it went like this: "Men you, as firefighters, can be great emissaries or salesmen in what you say, in what you do, and in what. . . ." "EEE-OOO".

A screeching sound echoed off the walls in the drill hall. Chief Volkamer's mouth was still in the open position for two minutes, then he said, "Who made that sound?" No one said anything and the chief walked out, really pissed off. We drilled that day. The instructors made us carry three-inch hoses that weighed eighty lbs. to the top floor many times, but no one said anything about who made the sound.

There were many days that went by before it happened again, but sure as shit "EEE-OOO" comes out again. Now the instructors were on our ass to find out who was making that sound. No one said anything. We were eight weeks into our training, we were running at a full gate in cadence, and we were in good physical condition. We could lead out hose and raise ladders, spanners strapped over shoulders; jump into nets; climb pompier ladders; slide ropes; and we wanted out of the academy because we thought we were ready to get out there and put some fires out.

At the last class in room 203, two men dressed in suits came to tell us about Local #2, the Chicago firemen's union. Jeremiah McElligott was the captain of Hook & Ladder #14, my brother Jim's company. He had been a member of the department and the union since 1936. It was told to us that 99% of the men in the fire department had joined the union just like us, because Local #2 stood up to the city and demanded better wages, pensions, and working conditions, and are among the highest in the nation. Captain McElligott said our wages of firefighters should be comparable to those of other skilled AF of L workers. We all joined Local #2 that day.

We were sent to Kahouts clothing and uniform store. They fit us in helmets, fire coats, and boots. Also, we were all custom fitted in dress blue Class "A" uniforms. Even if I was not a fireman, I would say he was still the best looking in a uniform. At this time we had no money to pay for all of our equipment, so Mr. Kahout set up financing by monthly payments. We all paid for our own uniforms and fire gear. No clothing allowances at that time would cover this amount!

The word came down that Mayor Richard J. Daley and Fire Commissioner Quinn were going to review the Class of '69 at the gym. It was a sure sign that we were getting out. We were all happy to know we would be assigned to a fire company soon. I was almost certain that there would not be any "EEE-OOO" with the mayor present, but you never knew.

ROLL CALL 07:30. THE BIG DAY

At that time, Felix Kolk was the fire department trainer, and ran the fire department gym. It was my second time to see or hear him in weeks. He stated that after we started to run, more like at the end of the run, Mayor Daley and Commissioner Quinn would be there. At that time he would raise his hand and give the signal. That would mean one more time around the gym and come to a stop, and line up in formation same as we would during roll call. "Do you understand," he asked, and the whole class replied, "Yes sir!"

Well, we started out at a good pace being led by none other than Will "The Squire" Danaher. We were singing in cadence, and as we approached the north end of the gym, there was the mayor and the commissioner standing there. Felix Kolk was next to the commissioner with his hand up on the last lap. Will said we were not stopping. We showed them we were the best class that ever came out of the academy. We didn't go around just once. We, the best class, went around three more times before we stopped!

We lined up and stood in formation, Felix jumped out of his skin and the commissioner said to Mayor Daley, "How do they look, Mr. Mayor?"

He replied, "They are a good-looking bunch of men, strong and healthy." The commissioner said he was right, but they were stupid, and he took two steps forward and yelled, "They don't know how to stop when they are told to, and they will stay in the academy for two more weeks." The mayor nodded, smiled just a little, and then turned and walked out of the gym. They didn't know what to do with us anymore. All the training was about over and the incident in the gym had been taken in good taste by all, including the mayor. We heard, because much on this job is rumor, we were now part of the rumors on the Chicago Fire Department. From the top chiefs on down to the candidates, a lot is rumor. As the saying goes, "Telephone, telegraph, tell a fireman!"

In the first few days in the academy, we were told that if any of our father's or grandfather's badges were available, we might be able to get it for ourselves. Lt. Gargione approached me on an afternoon at the academy and informed me that they thought that they could get my father's badge for me. He would let me know soon, but there was going to be a charge for the badges to be repaired from damage over the years. I could not wait to tell my mother. She cried out loud and hugged and kissed me. She was so happy. Dad's badge. If it happened, I would be so honored, but I couldn't get my hopes too high. Toward the end of April 1969, one of the instructors was able to get us a private tour of the Chicago filtration plant. Anything that would get us out of raising ladders was fine with me. They took us to the filtration plant in buses, and a tour guide met us; a nice man who was truly impressed with the fire department.

He informed us that on this tour we would see firsthand where our water comes from when fighting a fire. While we were there, this crazy guy yells "EEE-OOO." The poor guide's head cocked a little to the left, and he continued with the tour. My sides were breaking because I was laughing so hard! The two instructors that were with us were white as ghosts and they were pissed. The tour continued and we were taken down into the area where the water intake ports were, and then into a room with large piping. The tour guide was explaining where the water goes from this point and again, "EEE-OOO" came out loud and clear. The guide told us that this tour was over, and he was done, with the "EEE-OOO" shit and walked away. By the time we reached the front of the filtration plant, so did Fire Commissioner Robert J. Quinn. Lights and sirens were blaring and was he really pissed off at us. He made us run down Lake Shore Drive in cadence and back to the fire academy. I think we could still hear the fire commissioner yelling two blocks away. He was madder than hell!

One week later we were given our badges and assignments. There were no good-byes; no graduation. I did not get my father's badge, but Lt. Gargione assured me that the badge was being repaired. He also informed me that it was going to cost me $16.81, and I gave him the money. Lt. Gargione asked me if I could give him a ride home. He knew I lived in Roseland near his home. I was given a spare badge until my father's badge was ready. They said I would be notified. As I was driving this man home, I knew that he was almost done with the Chicago Fire Department, and I was just beginning the job. As I drove, he enlightened me by telling me that he and my father went through the old drill school on West Sebor Street. It had wooden floors with balconies on two sides where the ladders were placed from floor to floor. Candidate firemen were not allowed to use the stairs. They had to climb the ladders to go from floor to floor. I thought we had it bad because we were not allowed to enter the academy through the front door. The fire academy training, however, was good for me. I was twenty-four years old, and for the last three months, I had been training to be a fireman and now we had been transferred to fire companies. We were all happy to get out. We stopped for a few cold ones at a local bar, and told each other where we were assigned. I was assigned to Hook & Ladder Company #24, located at 10400 South Vincennes Avenue.

Chapter IV

On my first day I met with Captain Jack Sheehan, the company commander. He informed me that he did not think that Truck #24 would get a candidate, let alone two candidates. At first, I didn't think he liked me, because all I was to him was more paperwork. My good friend, Myles Hasty (Mick), was also assigned to Truck #24. He went on the 2nd platoon and I went with the captain on the 1st platoon. Captain Sheehan told me he was not sure why he got me as a candidate, because he was retiring in a few years, but he would teach me what he could. We didn't get many fires, so in the next two work days this was all we did: we sat in front of the "joker stand" and listened to the sounder that is located on it. Please let me explain:

THE JOKER STAND

Captain Sheehan was an old-timer on the job. Old-timers listened all day and all night long to the sounder; this is what the captain was going to teach me. With his pipe in his mouth, sitting back on his chair, we listened to the sounder, and listened and listened. The sounder is a telegraph key that makes a "clicking" sound, and this clicking in succession relates to a code of signals.

Each fire company has its own signature. Engine Company #45 for instance, would be four clicks followed by five clicks. Hook & ladders had their own signature, and every other piece of equipment on the Chicago Fire Department has a signature. From the mayor of Chicago: 4-3-1, right down to the light wagon: 9-1-6.

The Code of Signals: each piece of equipment that moves in or out of the station where it is located must use this code. These are some of the more common codes.

3-3-5	Returned to quarters in service
3-3-2-4	Company out of service
3-3-4-1	Unit responding to special duty
5-5-5	Unit responding to a still alarm of fire!
4-4-4	Unit responding to an alarm while on the street

Also, on the joker stand is a register, and it is located on the left side in a clear, plastic box with a wind up key on the right side. The bell inside the register would ring, indicating that a box is being struck, and give a number like 2-5-3-0 on a tape. After looking up this number in a card file, it gives the location, for instance, 63rd & Western Ave. If your fire company was on that card, then you responded to that address. A box that is being struck can be heard around the city in every firehouse.

It was very hard for me to learn the telegraph and radio systems of the fire department, but Captain Sheehan told me not to worry. He said that I'd learn. I sure did learn, because I had to sit up in the front by the joker stand about ten hours a day.

Truck #24 was a sixty-three foot 1956 FWD truck, with an eighty-five foot main ladder. It had a tiller wheel in the rear where somehow the driver and tiller man managed to maneuver in and out of this narrow firehouse. The tools that were on this truck consisted of axes, pike poles, life net, salvage covers, and the hand pumps. There were also many ground ladders: a 50' Bangor, two 38' extension ladders, a 26' straight ladder, and roof ladders with curved hooks at the top. These were used to hook over the peak of a roof, or on a window sill.

Truck #24 firehouse was long and narrow. The kitchen was on the second floor, and also the bunk room. Each work day the firehouse was cleaned and washed. All beds were made up by 10:00 hours. The heating plant was a gas-fired boiler that was new, but the hot water was a coal-fired unit that needed to be stoked and more coal added at intervals throughout the twenty-four hour shift. The captain did not like it if he was showering and the water was cold, so we made sure that this never happened.

Days went by slowly and there were no fires in our district, but there are fires all over Chicago. By now I was learning the code of signals, and I knew who was going to fires, and who was not: me!

It seemed like the same fire companies were doing all the work. Every time the register started to ring, I would check the card file and tell the captain where the fire was located. Captain Sheehan knew that I was a young man, and should be in an area where there were some fires so that I could learn how to become a fireman.

One afternoon in the summer of 1969, Engine #93 was given a still alarm. This is the first call of a fire, and means that two engine companies, one hook & ladder company, and a battalion chief will respond to a given location. After hearing 5-5-5 on the sounder, and then being followed by 93, the captain looked up from his book and said, "Get that," and the speaker opened up.

"Truck #24, follow Engine #93 to a fire at 1305 W. 103rd Street," the alarm office yelled.

As I answered the fire alarm office, I could see through the window a large amount of smoke to the east. Captain Sheehan said, "We got a fire." Finally, after almost two months out of the fire academy, I was going to a fire. To ride on the running board of the hook & ladder, you had to hold on to a rail that ran the length of the truck. I could not keep my eyes off of this enormous cloud of smoke. We pulled up to the front of the building and the Captain jumped out of the front seat and yelled to me, "I want you on my ass at all times during this fire; do you hear me?" We took a second line off of Engine #93 and stretched it into the vacant lot to the west. The captain yelled, "Send the water on 93's three-inch line."

Fire was billowing out every window on the second floor. After what seemed like forever, we got our water, and put out a lot of fire with the three-inch line. To get water you somehow had to communicate with the engineer to send the water. Most of the time you yelled, "Send the water!"

It was hard to hold on, and the captain told me to spanner in with my truckmen's belt. One wrap around the hose with a leather belt, and I put it around my shoulder. It was now much easier to hold the hose line. Once the fire was under control we went inside with the tools. The first time I was inside the fire building, smoke was everywhere, and the chief yelled to Sheehan, "Where's that candidate; we need the ceiling pulled down."

The captain led me into this hot, smoky room. I was trying to stay low, but the chief kept yelling, "Get this goddamn ceiling down. What the hell is the matter with you?" I was getting mad because I could not get the ceiling down fast enough. Then finally, I got the hang of it and I was pulling that ceiling down. Captain Sheehan was gone from my side and then someone was yelling to hold on. I just pulled and he yelled again to stop. I pulled all the lath and plaster right down on the chief's white helmet. Captain Sheehan said to me, "Oh shit, that's Chief Ambrose, now we're in trouble."

Most of the fire was out, and we were overhauling when Chief Ambrose yelled, "Who pulled that ceiling down on my head?"

I said, "I did Sir. I'm sorry." He said, "Good job kid. Teach me to get out of the way," and he showed me how to strip a window with my axe.

Chief Francis Ambrose was the chief of the 17th Battalion in Roseland, Engine #62's firehouse. Chief Ambrose was a disciplined military-like fire chief, and was very respected by the firemen. He knew who I was because of my father and mother. He lived in the same neighborhood and his wife taught me to swim when I was a boy. Rose Ambrose also worked at the corner snack shop with my sister Bette, and after swimming she would give me a free ice cream cone.

The fire was now out, and we were ordered to help the engine companies to pick up their hose lines and then return to our quarters. The days past slowly and I wanted to see more fire duty, but it just didn't happen.

During the various seasons of the year there was a uniform inspection. My first uniform inspection was not on my shift day, but you were required to be inspected by the second deputy chief fire marshal in full dress uniform and your fire gear. All three platoons were inspected on the same day, and you were ordered to be present without pay.

After being inspected, Captain Sheehan told me that I had a

Marshal line call. The Marshal line is an interdepartmental phone line. After answering the Marshal line, the chief asked who was calling a candidate on that line. I related that it was someone from the fire academy, and they wanted me to report to pick up my father's badge; that it was all ready. Captain Sheehan was impressed that I was going to get the badge that my father wore when he was a fireman, and said to get down there. I was in my dress blues, and I felt good about getting Dad's badge.

I drove down to the fire academy. This was the first time that I was allowed to enter through the front door, because I was no longer a candidate in school. I went to the third floor, the personnel division, and explained who I was and why I was there. The chief of personnel said he did not call me, but maybe it was C. H. Hanson, the badge company that made the repairs to my father's badge. He gave me the address of Hanson's Badge Company and said to try over there. The person at the badge company said they did not call me and the badge had gone to the fire academy. A little frustrated, I now returned to the fire academy and talked to the chief of personnel again. He told me to wait down in the coffee shop until he found out what was going on. In a very short time he called me back up to the third floor, and said that the badge was in the fire commissioner's office in Room 105 at City Hall. He also informed me that they said to get down there right away.

City Hall, Room 105, was full of uniformed chiefs, captains, lieutenants, and firemen. I gave my name to the fire commissioner's secretary, Sharon Murtaugh, and she told me to be seated. I sat down next to a Lieutenant Horton, and he said to me, "Are you a candidate?" I stated that I was a candidate. Lieutenant Horton informed me that I probably would not get in to see the commissioner today, because of how many men were in front of me, and since I was a candidate, I would be last. The commissioner's secretary called my name next, and I just shrugged my shoulders as I walked past everyone sitting in the waiting room.

As I walked toward Commissioner Quinn's office, there was complete silence in the waiting room. Once inside the commissioner's office, I was told by the commissioner to be seated across from him. He stated that he was very impressed with the effort that I had made to obtain my father's badge. Now I was shaking in my boots because Fire Commissioner Robert J. Quinn was "the boss," and there was only one big boss in the fire department in those days. Commissioner Quinn was about sixty years old at the time, but he was in great physical condition. He had been a fireman for some forty-five years, and had come up through the ranks. In 1934, he won the city's highest award for heroism: the Lambert Tree Award. Later in World War II, Quinn was decorated for his heroism during a fire aboard a burning ship while in the Navy. I was in awe looking at all the awards that were hanging on the walls of his office. There were trophies, plaques, certificates, and photos on every wall.

Richard J. Daley, then the mayor of Chicago, appointed Quinn to be his fire commissioner in 1957. Here I was, sitting in this office talking with this great man. He said that he knew my father well, and that they had worked together at many fires, and with that he stood up with a small box in his hand. The fire commissioner said,

"I would like to pin your father's badge on you."

I responded with, "I would be honored sir," and stood up. After the pinning, I made a statement that it was worth the money to have his badge.

Quinn replied in a loud voice, "What money?"

I told him that when I was in the academy, there was an

announcement that anyone with a father or grandfather whose badge was available, could request that badge, but the repairs had to be paid by the candidate.

With that he started yelling, "Who told you that!"

I did not want to get anyone in trouble, so I told him that I wasn't sure who had said it.

Quinn said, "Who did you give the money to?" in a very loud voice. Now I knew he was pissed, and I replied that I wasn't sure again, because I wasn't going to take Lieutenant Gargione down; he had gotten the badge for me.

Commissioner Quinn picked up a phone from his desk and with a loud voice to whoever was on the other end he said, "Get in here!" Within a second, a uniformed fireman entered the office. Quinn told this guy that I paid for my father's badge and asked why was that.

He said, "Sir," with his voice quivering, "Let me check, sir." Within a minute he was back in the office, and stated to the commissioner that the badge had to be restored by C.H. Hanson, and it cost $16.81. The fire commissioner informed this guy again, in a very loud voice, that firemen had to buy their own helmets, boots, fire coats, and class "A" uniforms, but the city of Chicago pays for, and owns, the badges. "This young man went out of his way to try to get his father's badge."

Quinn told this guy to get $16.81 for me, and he exclaimed that he couldn't. Quinn said, "Then take it out of your own pocket."

The guy said, "I will see if we have it in petty cash."

After the guy left the room, the commissioner said, "There is about $4,000 in petty cash!"

While this guy went to get the money, the commissioner

asked me how I liked Hook & Ladder #24. I told him the guys in the house were great, but I had only been to one fire since I was assigned there. Quinn said, "Your father was a great fireman, and if he knew you were on that company he would roll over in his grave. Where would you like to go to? You name the company."

I said ,I" don't know but I would like more action."

The commissioner said, "You just watch the next transfer order."

I said, "What do you have in mind?"

He replied, "Just watch the order."

The fireman returned with the $16.81, I shook the commissioner's hand, thanked him, and I was out the door. I went to see my mother to show her my new badge. She was so proud of me that she could not hold back her tears. We both cried in the front hallway of her home; the home where I was born.

The next day I was back at Truck #24 and could not wait to tell Captain Sheehan all that had happened. He was very happy for me, but said, "Did he tell you what company you were going to?"

The only thing the fire commissioner said to me was, "Watch the transfer order."

As the next few days went by Captain Sheehan said he heard that they were going to put the squads back in service, but they would be called "flying manpower squads." He said, "I bet that is where you will be assigned. We will see when the order comes out. In the meantime, don't tell anyone that you went to see the commissioner or about the transfer. We don't want the chief to know." I agreed.

In that same time the summer of 1969, the fire commissioner created operation "Splash-Down." In the afternoon, during the hottest part of the day, firemen all over the city of Chicago went to a scheduled location, set up a fog nozzle on the end of the fire hydrant, and sprayed the children, and some adults, with the cool water. Splash-down was not very popular with the firemen, as a matter of fact they hated it. Firemen fight fires, rescue the trapped, assist the troubled, and now cool down Chicago's youths in the hot, summer months until the schools open back up. Listening for calls on the radio that could come at any moment, we now sat and babysat children. Some people would drop off their kids and tell us that they would be back in a little while.

August 31, 1969, Captain Sheehan said that the transfer order was out and told me to get it at the 29th Battalion headquarters, which was located at 95th Street and Charles, but not to say anything. The chief of the 29th Battalion wanted to know why I was being transferred, and I told him that I did not know why, because Jack Sheehan, my captain, told me not to tell him about my meeting with the fire commissioner. The chief insisted that I tell him, because nothing went through his battalion without him knowing about it.

Although I was nervous, I stuck to my guns, and said I did not know, and I asked him where I was being transferred to. With the order in his hand, he threw it across the table and said, "Is that your name?"

I replied, "Yes, sir." He said, "Do you know where that company is located?"

Looking at the order I could see that I was being transferred to Hook & Ladder Company #15.

The Chief yelled at me in front of about five firemen. "Do you know where that company is?"

Again, I played like I had no idea what was going on and now

I was getting mad. He said that Hook & Ladder #15 was the worst firehouse in the city, and the only firemen that went there were those in some kind of trouble. "So Candidate Cosgrove you are going to tell me what you did, or whose toes you stepped on, that they would send you to this shit hole," he said. "Was it the Alderman or someone at city hall? You have to tell me. I am the chief," he said in a very loud voice.

I said nothing, and he said, "Get out of here."
By the time I got back to Truck #24's house, Captain Sheehan was waiting for me. He had a big smile on his face. "You didn't tell the Chief."

I said, 'No, I didn't."

We both laughed. Jack Sheehan said the chief had called him after I left and said that I was disrespectful by not telling him why I was on the order. Captain Sheehan said that this guy was never on a fire company in his time on the job and was politically heavy. That was why he was a chief, and had been a pain in his ass every since he had been assigned to the 29th Battalion.

The transfer order was effective September 1, 1969. That would have been the next day, and I did not know where Hook & Ladder #15 was located. Captain Sheehan was very surprised that Quinn would send me there. It just happened to be the hardest working hook & ladder in the city of Chicago. Truck #15 responded to 3,312 fire incidents in the year of 1968, compared to Truck #24's fire incidents of 462 runs. Captain Sheehan said, "This is the fire area that you will learn how to become a good fireman." He also stated that many of the fire calls were false alarms, but there are many fires, and you're sure to get what you have been looking for.

The Marshal line is a red phone on the joker stand, and it is for official fire department use only. The chief of the 29th Battalion called and demanded to talk to me. Captain Sheehan said not to tell l him. I answered the Marshal line. The chief told me that if I was to tell him what happened that he could stop the transfer. Again, I explained that I was only a candidate and I did not know what was going on here. The chief said that he was going to file charges against me if I did not tell him.

Early the next morning before our shift was over, the bell rang. We all ran to the front of the firehouse and sure as shit here was this chief of the 29th Battalion. He told me and Captain Sheehan that if we did not tell him what happened, that he was going to have to file charges on the two of us. Captain Sheehan is a very mild man, but I think this chief pressed the wrong button. He walked up in his face and said, "This candidate has been here for three months, and you haven't even talked to him, but now all of the sudden he has become the most important event in this battalion. Now get out of my firehouse, and if you want to put charges on me then go ahead." The chief left and I never saw him again.

Captain Sheehan had taken the leather shield from my helmet while I cleaned out my locker. I thanked him for what he had taught me and I left for my new assignment at Hook & Ladder Company #15 at 4600 South Cottage Grove in the heart of the so-called black ghetto.

Chapter V

September 3, 1969, was a very hot morning as I parked across the street from my new assignment. The firehouse was located on the corner of 46th Street and Cottage Grove Avenue. This fire station held Engine Company #45, Hook & Ladder Company #15, and was the headquarters of Battalion #16. This firehouse was the busiest in the city of Chicago. Engine #45 went to 4,438 alarms in 1968 and the chief of the 16th Battalion responded to 4,966, mostly in this Kenwood-Oakland community. This community was one of the largest ghettos in Chicago. It is called Engine 45's still-district, and its boundaries are 39th Street on the north to 51st Street on the south; Lake Michigan on the east to the Dan Ryan expressway on the west.

As I walked into my new firehouse there was only one fireman sitting at the front desk. It was Firefighter First Class Norman Doolan. He stood up and introduced himself. He also informed me that he was the chief's driver. Norm had a short-sleeve fire department shirt on with the emblem on the shoulder. The shirt was faded, but it was crisp like it was recently pressed.

I told Firefighter Doolan that I was just assigned to Hook & Ladder #15. He replied, "I know." He asked me if I had any relations named Cosgrove that lived around 51st and Halsted. I assured him that I did not know any of my relatives on the Cosgrove side nor where any of them lived.

Doolan said that was funny because I looked a little like Dave Cosgrove who hung out in the tavern at 51st and Halsted. Again I told him that I did not know Dave Cosgrove. Norm Doolan then said to me, "Well you won't mind if I call you Dave." Rather than saying any more about the subject, I just let it go with a shrug of my shoulders and said "okay."

As I walked away from the front desk, Doolan told me to put my fire gear to the side by the hook & ladder and get some coffee.

As I was walking away the speaker cracked, and in a very loud voice the dispatcher said, "45, Engine 45 you have a rubbish fire at 4410 S. Greenwood." Doolan picked up the one arm phone and repeated back the address, and at the same time rang the bell four times.

The dispatcher said "That's right Norm, just the engine." I was looking at Doolan wondering how he knew that Norm answered. Then I heard the doors to the pole hole open and two firemen slid down buckling their pants. Out from the back came Captain Ed Fox and Engineer William Marshal. Within what seemed like a second, they were roaring out the front door of the firehouse with their siren screaming and lights flashing. I was standing to the side thinking to myself that they got a run already, and it wasn't even 07:30 in the morning.

I was back by Doolan when he introduced me to Lieutenant Foran, the officer of Hook & Ladder #15 on the third shift. Lt. Foran was about six foot tall, his white hair was all over the place and sticking straight up. He had on a white T-shirt with yellow water stains all over it. His arms and hands had loose-fitting bandages on them as a result of being burned sometime the day before in a basement fire where a natural gas meter re-ignited.

Lieutenant Foran looked at me and said, "So you're the new guy on the truck."

I exclaimed Yes, Sir."

He said, "Well, let me tell you sonny boy if you came to this house to go to funerals, wakes and retirement parties, just to tell them and brag that you're on the busiest truck in the city, then get your shit and get out of here. I stood there in awe wondering why I was sent here. Lieutenant Foran started to walk away and Norm said, "Don't worry about him Dave, he just likes to hear himself talk. Here comes your lieutenant on the first shift today . . . Lieutenant Jack Gallapo, 4th Division Relief."

Jack Gallapo was walking up to the front asking Doolan where the engine went and Norm replied, "To a rubbish fire."

Doolan said, "This is our new man, Dave Cosgrove," and with that, Lieutenant Gallapo put his big hand out and shook my hand.

He told me to put my gear on the side of the rig and then said, "Let's have some coffee."

I said "Yes, Sir."

He replied very seriously, "Don't ever call me 'sir' again or lieutenant, I am your Uncle Jack. So come on punk, let's have coffee and I will introduce you to the rest of the first shift." I found out later "Uncle Jack" Gallapo was the recipient of a silver star, a bronze star and three purple hearts while serving with Baker Company, 1st Battalion, 7th Marine regiment at the Chosin Reservoir in Korea in November-December 1950. Additionally, Lt. Gallapo was the recipient of the Lambert Tree Award in 1960, Chicago's highest award for bravery. At forty-three years old, and

6'3", 220 lbs., this new "Uncle" was a "natural man," no doubt about it! The smoke from the exhaust of the engine just now settling and I was able to look around. This firehouse was not at all like Hook & Ladder #24 where I had been assigned. There were newspapers, cans, bottles, fire clothes, and boots strewn all over the place. It was filthy, but I didn't say anything.

Hook & Ladder #15 was a 1956 FWD. rig, with a manual eighty-five foot aerial ladder. Lt. Gallapo told me that this was a spare rig and that our regular truck was in the shops for repairs.

After meeting the men on the first shift of Truck #15 and Engine #45, we had coffee and one of the firemen, Jim Nolan, who I had come on the job with, showed me around the firehouse.

The firehouse was about fifty-five feet in width. Behind the engine bay was the first floor washroom. Anyone that walked down Cottage Grove could just walk in and use the washroom.

Next to the washroom was the hose tower. After returning from a fire, dry hose would be dropped down and re-bedded on the engine. Then the wet hose was connected to a 3/4" rope and pulled up into the tower and hung there to dry. The closet around the corner was where the officers would hang their fire gear. It was very small with just enough room for their gear.

The hook & ladder was backed all the way to the west end of the building and the chief's car was in the front. The aerial ladder extended over the table where we ate our meals. In the corner there was a telephone. This is where we received our calls from home.

The "hub" of this firehouse was the kitchen: a small room with another table and two benches partially covered with a vinyl material and the rest with silver duct tape.

The main TV was located just above the kitchen table encased in steel angle-iron, bolted into the wall. Jim said, "When we leave for a fire they steal everything." The other side of this room had wooden cabinets with padlocks, one for each shift. The other part of the kitchen was the galley where the stove, sink and refrigerator were. All the meals were prepared there. "The walls are dirty with carbon from the exhaust of the firetrucks, but we make the best of it," Jim said.

The cook that day was a fireman by the name of Jack O'Brien. He was an older man and said he knew my father when he was on Squad #8, but never said much more about it and then collected $3.00 from each man for the meals that day.

Fireman Nolan told me to get my sheets, he would show me what beds were open in the bunkroom. Once on the second floor, you entered a locker room with some forty lockers that were about seven feet high. A double door entrance led to the bunkroom, which was a large open room with about ten beds around the outside walls of the room and two beds located in the middle. Once inside, there was a smell of smoke and fire in the air. The pillows were stained with an almost oil black color and the mattresses were all contoured; when you laid on one, you just fell into the middle. The windows were covered with dark green, pull down, canvas shades that were also mended with silver duct tape. There were three brass fire poles in the corners of the bunkroom that were all in need of brass polish. In front of the bunkroom were two other rooms: one for the officers of the truck and engine and the other was for the chief of the 16th Battalion. There was tile on the floor, but it was hard to tell what the color was because it had so many coats of wax. It was shiny black, except where it was worn out.

Jim Nolan was assigned here right out of the fire academy. He said, "We are not real big on housework, but the house is clean for how busy we are. The work we do is out in the ghetto. There are fires . . . lots of them." I could tell in his voice that he loved this job. Jim told me his grandfather was a fireman right here in this house. With a very proud voice, he said, "He was the pipemen on Engine #45 back in 1909."

Back on the first floor I asked Lt. Gallapo, or now my "Uncle Jack," about obtaining a truckmen's belt and an axe, and a big laugh came out of the guys sitting at the table behind the hook & ladder. I explained that they told us at the Fire Academy that axes and truckmen's belts would be supplied by the company officer. Again they laughed. Gallapo said, "We don't have any and, if you want one, you somehow get them yourself."

One guy stepped up and introduced himself. "I am Jasper Neal, and I am on the truck," he said. "I have an extra belt you can use until Captain Wilson gets back from furlough."

Jasper was a black man, tall, but thin. He told me not to let the guys bother me. "They laugh at everything that's not funny, but they're good firemen; we take care of each other." Jasper also outfitted me with an axe and said, "Don't lose it because it was given to me by a fireman on Truck #11. We are going to show you how to raise the aerial ladder as soon as we can, because O'Brien is cooking, so it's just Gallapo, Wagner, you and me," Jasper explained.

When I returned to the apparatus floor Gallapo said, "Come on punk, were going to raise the main."

Richard Wagner was the driver of the front end of the truck and Jasper Neal was the tiller man who steered the back end of the truck. Firefighter Mike Vinci, one of the fireman that was on the engine, was stopping traffic on Cottage Grove.

Fireman Wagner pulled out onto Cottage Grove Avenue, swung the rig around, Jasper turned the wheel in the back and the rig was almost parallel to the firehouse. The move was almost effortless. They were good and knew what each other was doing. We placed the jacks or stabilizers to the street.

The next move was to disassemble the tiller by pulling a pin. The steering wheel came right out, they swung the windshield out of the way, and the main ladder was ready to be "kicked off."

Standing on the turntable of the rig, Rich Wagner said, "See that pedal on the floor? Step down hard on that pedal to release the ladder."

After Wagner stepped on the pedal, there was a loud bang, and up this spring-loaded 85' ladder went, almost to about seventy degrees. Wagner said, "You have to hold on to this handle to stop the ladder from raising. So, don't pull the handle until you want the ladder to stop being raised!" Then we turned the raised ladder into the building by rotating the turntable. It took two men to extend the fly and set it onto the structure.

After repeating this maneuver two times, Gallapo said, "Let's put it away before we break something." Back in the firehouse you could smell something cooking and I wondered what we were having for lunch.

When the speaker opened up with a loud voice, the dispatcher called, "Engine #61, Truck #15, Engine #45 respond to a building collapse at 4853 S. Indiana. Lt. Gallapo answered the office and they again said, "That's right Jack, and take the buggy with you".

The roar of the engines starting up was enough to make my adrenaline flow, and we were now traveling down Cottage Grove. We turned west on 47th Street. Firefighter Neal had the back end of the rig a little cocked so that the traffic would get out of the way. I was standing on the running board of the right side of the rig. All the people stopped to look at this great big firetruck racing down the street.

We pulled up behind Engine #61 and Gallapo jumped out of the front seat and yelled, "Get your tools, punk." Together, Gallapo and I entered the structure through an overhead door. Inside the building, the roof was caved in in the middle, and the sprinkler system had gone off with water spraying all over. What had happened was a man backed up an ice cream truck and hit one of the pillars, knocking it over and causing the roof to cave in. The chief called into the Englewood fire alarm office to tell them what had taken place, we shut down the sprinkler system and evacuated the structure.

"Please notify the building department, and were all returning in service," the chief told the Englewood office.

As we made our way back to the firehouse through the crowded streets, Engine #45 was behind us. All of the sudden Engine #45's lights started flashing and their sirens were blasting. The engine passed us on the left and our lights and siren started. Uncle Jack was waving his arm out the window trying to tell me and the tiller man that we had another run. There was no way that I could find out where or what type of alarm we were going to, so I just hung on to the bar that ran the length of the hook & ladder. This was my second run in twenty minutes and I had no idea where I was because everything was different. Engine #45 was an FWD. pumper and was smaller than our truck. They made better time, but we were moving fast. As we rounded the corner at 43rd and Drexel, I could see a light amount of smoke emanating from a vacant storefront. Lt. Gallapo jumped out of the cab of the truck, looked back at me, and said, "Get the pump, punk, and come on."

I jumped off the side of the truck, put my axe in my belt, grabbed a pike pole and the hand pump, which was filled to the top with water, about five gallons which weighed about fifty-five pounds. Now, I was trying to keep up with Lt. Gallapo into the smoke filled store. There was garbage strewn throughout, and most of the garbage was on fire. There was a lot of smoke and visibility was bad, but I could hear him yelling in a sharp, serious tone "Come on punk."

I was saying, "Here I am, Lieutenant."

He would reply, "I am your uncle, not your lieutenant."

He uncoiled the hose from the hand pump and started saying, "Pump! pump! Come on." As we extinguished the fire, Uncle Jack was talking and talking about God only knows what, because none of what he was saying had anything to do with fires. He really had a great sense of humor . . . but behind that facade was a highly intelligent and well-educated man. This fire was now out, the smoke was lifting, and as I looked around, we had about four hand pumps working. Fireman Rich Wagner, the driver, and Jasper Neal, the tiller man, were on the other side working their hand pump. For a second I stopped pumping and my "uncle" yelled at me, "Don't stop pumping." So I started to pump again, but my new uncle had the hose tip pointing at Fireman Nolan and Fireman Guttillo and water was now hitting them so I stopped pumping and he said, "Keep pumping, punk," so I did what was told. The next thing I knew they were squirting water at me and calling me all kinds of vile names. We all started laughing. I now could sense the camaraderie that these men had, and I liked it. I wanted so much to be a part of it. Norm Doolan, the chief's driver, entered and said the chief wanted us to pick up

Both hand pumps were being directed at Fireman Doolan. He

said to Gallapo, "You get me wet and I will shoot you, you M __ F__." We were roaring with laughter.

Out in front of the building we were putting our tools and pumps back on the rig, and I was looking at Firefighters Neal and Wagner and Uncle Jack. None of them had fire clothes on, just their leather helmets and firehouse clothes.

The fire was at 43rd and Ellis Ave. It is very hard for me to describe the filth and destruction of the buildings. Burned out structures with people living in them! It made a new "punk" like me gasp in horror! Standing in this street it seemed that I was the only one that was looking around, and then Norm yelled out, "Did everyone meet the new guy? His name is Dave."

Backing into the firehouse, the engine and hook & ladder blocked the traffic on Cottage Grove, and after guiding them in by stopping traffic, we all went in the firehouse. I thought to myself, we had a building collapse, a fire, and it isn't even noontime yet!

The cook yelled, "Set the table," but Gallapo said to me, "Fill both hand pumps first, punk." He told you in a way that was a joke, but you also knew he meant to get ready for the next fire first, then set the table.

As we sat down to eat the meal, I noticed that the chief was not there, nor Norm Doolan, his driver. I asked my new uncle why were we eating without the chief and Doolan. Gallapo replied that he was on a "special diet," and they eat at Engine #60's house. I ate my spaghetti dinner and didn't give it much thought because I was hungry. When the meal was over the cook, Fireman Jack O'Brien said, "Your name is Dave?"

I said, "No."

He said "I don't care, but you're on the dishes."

With what seemed like a thousand dishes, pots and pans, my

Fire fighters and officers at the 46th and Cottage Grove

name was officially on the dish card, "Dave." Chiefs, captains, and lieutenants think you're officially on the company because of rosters, journals, and transfer orders. Firemen know that you are on the company because of the detail card and the dish card, and it carries more weight with them. I am not sure where all the firemen were now, but I went up to the joker stand. The officer of the engine was Lieutenant Edward Steed. He was a black man about six foot tall and kind of heavyset with a barrel chest. He was about fifty years old. Lt. Steed was always in a good mood and was always dressed in a white officer's shirt.

"Hello Engine #45" the speaker cracked. Lt. Steed jumped up from his chair. "Engine #45 — Truck #15 there is a fire at 3939 Lake Park on the 7th floor." The dispatcher called, "Engine #19 you are the second engine".

Lt. Steed repeated the address and rang the bell, one long

ring. Everyone was running to their rig and donning their fire clothes. The next thing we knew, we were flying north on Cottage Grove and I was again holding on to the side of the truck. We pulled up to a sixteen-story brick high rise public housing project building. Gallapo was out and moving fast. In the hallway, in front of the elevators we waited until the elevator arrived. There was only enough room for about six firemen. Gallapo said, "Bring the hand pumps and the rest of you get the next elevator."

We got off on the sixth floor and walked up to the 7th. Someone yelled out, " It is the incinerator."

There is a chute in the center of the structure where people throw out their garbage, which leads to the incinerator on the ground floor. Very often the chute gets clogged up, and someone ignites the garbage thinking it will burn off and fall, but usually it fills the floor with smoke. Once we push the garbage down the chute, the smoke clears and vents out the top of the chimney.

Back in the firehouse we sat around the table, behind the truck, talking about the "ghetto." I was getting to know the guys better. Uncle Jack called me up to the front. He said, "I have to make out a form #2 on your personal history; name, address, date of entry, and your file number." Everyone that comes on the Chicago Fire Department gets a file number. It is very much like a social security number, which identifies you.

Uncle Jack said, "Open the truck door, punk, the chief just pulled up in front of the firehouse." As the door opened, the 16th Battalion car backed in and Norm got out and walked around the front of the car. Chief Deneen sat in the front seat with his hands folded on his lap in front of him and didn't move. Norm walked over to the joker stand, pushed the guide over, and in rapid succession, banged the 16th Battalion "back in service at quarters" on the telegraph key, 3-3-5 -2-4-6.

Norm said to Gallapo, "Next time you see me pull up, I expect you to put us in on the key before I back in. You got that?" Gallapo said in a joking manner, "The only thing that I'll put in, is this size twelve shoe in your ass, boy."

Doolan looks at the Chief who was in the car laughing hard. "Ha, ha," Norm said to the chief. "Have you met Dave yet?"

I walked over and shook his hand. He said that he knew Jack Sheehan and had talked to him. My old captain from Truck #24. The Chief continued saying that Captain Sheehan said I was a good, hard worker. We needed hard working firemen, there was plenty of work in this area.

Chief Thomas Deneen was about fifty-five years old with white hair and a heavy-set build. He lived on the north side, but he was born on the south side in the Visitation Parish, around 55th and Halsted. Rumor had it that he had a disagreement with Fire Commissioner Quinn and was sent to the busy 16th Battalion as punishment. I think he likes working here as the Chief. He has Norm Doolan as his driver, and Norm takes good care of him.

Rich Wagner, a fireman on Truck #15, asked me if I would like to see the basement where they sharpen the axes. I said sure, I would get my axe or the one that I got from Fireman Jasper Neal.

The basement was small. It was only the back half of the firehouse. The front was a crawl space with a broken door hanging half off. There was a sandstone wheel that was used for sharpening the axes and a motor that ran the two wheels. One was wire and the other was for polishing the axes.

They called him Rich Wagner "Wags," and he had been on Truck #15 since he was a candidate. Just talking to Wags you could sense he was a good fireman and had done plenty of fire duty since 1967.

In the basement we heard the speaker "45, Truck #15, a fire." The bell sounded and "Wags" said, "Let's go, that is our fire."

We arrived at 4210 Berkley Ave. The fire was issuing from a window on the west side of the building. Gallapo yelled, "Get the pump." People were screaming hysterically. We went up the front stairs to the second floor. Smoke was throughout this floor, and was getting heavy. I started to get down when Gallapo yelled, "Get that pump in here."

I pushed the hand pump across the floor to the doorway and he took the nozzle of the hose and said, "Start pumping, we have a mattress." I was choking on the smoke. I didn't know if I could take any more. He said, "Get in here, punk. There is no smoke in this so-called bedroom."

I was pumping a lot better now because he was right. There was no smoke. You could breathe a little better. He said, "Give me your axe and stay down on the floor." Gallapo knocked the rest of the window out and I could see Lt. Steed, Guttillo, and Nolan with the other hand pumps, working the water on the burning mattress. Now Gallapo said to me, "We have to roll it up, and throw it out the window." I was trying to help get the mattress over to the window, but it was heavy and burning!

The next thing I knew, Wags and Gallapo had the mattress out the window and we used the hand pumps to wash down the other things that were burning. This fire was out, and I was exhausted from the heat and smoke. We cleaned up the rest of the room. "Put your tools on the rig, but bring your axe." As we all went around to the back, Jasper Neal who they called "Rocky," was now pulling the mattress out to the street and it was still burning.

Waiting by the fire hydrant was a fireman from Engine #45 named Cliff Armstead. He opened the valve as we pulled the burning mattress under the heavy flow of water from the red fire hydrant. After thoroughly soaking the mattress, it was finally extinguished.

On the way back, Wags explained that the only way to extinguish a mattress fire is to put it under the hydrant. Then, and only then, did you know the mattress fire was fully extinguished. As we backed into the firehouse, you could smell the roast that was most likely over-cooked. We were all hungry. The food was ready for us to eat right away. "But first fill the hand pumps, punk," Gallapo stated.

After sitting down, we began eating and talking about the fire on Berkley. The pumps almost didn't make it. We should have led out a 1 1/2" hose. "Don't be silly," Gallapo said looking at me. "We had a half a can of water left in our pump. Right Dave?" I replied, "Oh, sure," as I kept buttering my bread. "Anything you say, Uncle."

The speaker opened up again, "Engine #45, Truck #15, check the box 4537 S. Drexel." Lt. Steed jumped from his seat and ran for the front to answer the Englewood Fire Alarm office. Everyone was putting a piece of meat on their bread to take with them. In forty seconds or so, we were pulling out the door onto Cottage Grove.

The box was only one block away from the firehouse. As we pulled up, Lt. Steed told Gallapo to hold the rest of the units, it was a false alarm. We started back towards the firehouse and the office was calling "45" on the radio.

"Check the box 4351 S. Drexel." The lights and sirens are on again. Around the corner on 43rd Street, there were about six boys standing on the corner. The engine pulled up. Lt. Steed yelled to Gallapo, "Hold the rest of the responding units, outside false."

Back in the firehouse someone asked Lt. Steed, "Do you think they know when were eating?" He looked up and just laughed it off. The food was cold, but I ate it anyway.

After dinner dishes were washed and put away, we drew for watches. It was new for me, because I had it easy at Truck #24. Watches were set by the captain. He always took the last watch. Here in this firehouse we had a Chief and he followed Engines #16, #19, #60, and #61 if they were called to a fire. The only way you would know was on the sounder telegraph key. You had to listen for the signal "5-5-5," which meant a still alarm of fire. Then you listened to the engine company on the key, 6-1. After hearing that, you picked up a phone, called the "talker" and you got the address of the fire and repeated it to the fire alarm office. After writing the address down, you would ring the bell twice for the chief. It was a "no, no" if you sent the chief to check the box when it was only for Engine #61. The guys decided that I would take student watch with Wags. He had first watch from 22:00 hours to 01:00 hours. Wags showed me our still district and the chiefs. It was a long three hours. The register rang and you had to count the rings. Then you had to look it up in the box card file cabinet to see if any of our companies were on the box that was ringing in. All the time you had to hold down the back button on the joker stand. If you let the button go, all the bells would ring in the firehouse and everyone would slide down the pole thinking that we were going to a fire. You did not want to wake anyone if it wasn't our fire. If the register repeated the same number of rings, two dots and eleven dots on the register tape, then you would know that it was a 2-11 alarm somewhere in the city. Our watch was over, and finally I got into my bunk for some much needed rest.

"Hello, Engine #45, Truck #15 and Battalion #16. Take a fire." The bell was now ringing. The pole hole doors were opening as we got dressed, and in a minute we were pulling out onto Cottage Grove. Getting out of the firehouse fast was the most important action of every fire company. It is the pride of every fire fighter to have a "fast" push-out. Within sixty seconds, we were out the door.

As we rounded the corner of 47th Street, I could see Gallapo waving his arm out the window. Up the street I could see people all over dressed in night clothes in front of the building. Engine #45 was leading out a 2 1/2" line up the front stairs. Gallapo yelled to me to help Jasper with a ladder to the second floor where a woman was yelling for help. We threw the ladder up with the help of Lt. Steed and I climbed up to the woman who was now almost out on the ladder. I am not sure what I said to her, but we carefully made our way down to the ground. "Let's get this thing ventilated" the chief yelled. He told me to get back up the ladder and pop those windows. Standing on the top of this ladder, breaking windows on a burning building, the adrenaline was flowing.

I was able to get two windows from my position, and Jasper was on a ladder next to me taking windows to the east. More glass was breaking on the west side of my ladder, and then I saw a fireman sticking his head out the second floor window. It was Gallapo. He said "Hey, punk, if you're done playing around out there get in her and get the ceiling down."

Once inside, the smoke was very heavy. I could not see a foot in front of me, but I could hear Wags yelling at someone to get out of the way so we could get the ceiling down. I crawled my way

Fire throughout the third floor and the roof of the burning structure.

over to him, only to find out that he was standing up in this heat and smoke.

"Come on Dave, they want the ceiling down." I wasn't sure if I could stand up, but then my new uncle grabbed my arm, and I was up next to Wags pulling down hot embers and plaster onto my helmet. We made our way across the room to a window. We were both hanging out the window getting a fresh breath of air, and it felt good.

All the time the engine was directing water at the fire in the hallway. Jack O'Brien came in from the back where he opened the rear doors, and broke all the windows for adequate ventilation. Now the smoke was lifting and the fire was almost out. Gallapo said, "Why did you guys lead out? We could put this out with hand pumps."

Someone yelled out, "Your mamma could have put it out with hand pumps." We all laughed as we overhauled the four rooms on the second floor that were destroyed by fire. All in all, only a small half of the second floor was destroyed and twelve people were taken out safely.

Standing on 47th and Vincennes at 03:30 in the morning, putting the hose back on Engine #45, I thought to myself, who would believe it if I told them how great I felt being here with these outstanding fire fighters.

Back at the firehouse Engine #47 had changed quarters and Truck #52 was also in our firehouse. Any time that we had a working fire, someone would change into our house because we were so busy and they never wanted to leave this firehouse empty.

The second shift began to relieve us, and my tour of duty at Trwck #15 was just about over.

Wags said, "We take our fire gear home with us because if you leave it here, there is a strong chance it will be gone when you come back to work."

The firehouse is always open and if your personal things are left out they will be stolen. There is something missing almost every day; shoes, shirts, tools, and even the dishes!

As I was driving home, I thought about the fires and the new firemen that I now worked with. What a change from my old firehouse!

Later that day, I stopped by Truck #24's house to see my friend Mick Hasty, who I had gone through the drill school with. He was cleaning out the supply room where all the extra axes and house supplies were kept. We went up to the kitchen for a cup of coffee, when Truck #24 got a run. We said good-bye and I told them I would close the doors to the firehouse.

The front door closed automatically at Truck #24, so all I had to do was close the back door and lock it up. Out of the corner of my eye I saw the supply room was still open. I now knew that I would have my own ax and Truckmen's belt, because they had many extras.

It was 07:20 when I returned to 46th and Cottage Grove. I had to park my car down 46th Street because there was not enough room by the fire station until the firemen on the third platoon pulled their cars out. Then we put ours in the back yard. There is only room for six cars in the yard and the rest are parked on the sidewalk next to the fire station. To my surprise, as I walked into the station, the fire trucks were out. Jack Gallapo was sitting at the table having coffee, and he informed me that the third shift was still working at a 3-11 alarm fire that they caught last night at 4824 S. Champlain. He said, "Get a cup of coffee. As soon as one more guy gets here, we will take my truck over to the fire to relieve the third platoon."

We pulled up to 48th and Champlain where the streets were all blocked off by Chicago police cars. We pulled our fire gear out of the back of Gallapo's pick-up truck and started getting our boots, fire coats, and helmets on. There were engines connected to hydrants with hoses stretched down the block to the fire. Truck #15 had the main ladder raised to the roof and Snorkel #3 was in front of the building directing a large stream of water into what looked like the remains of a three-story brick building. There was still a large amount of smoke in the rear.

We met up with Firemen Henderson and Sobieski of the third platoon. They told us about the fire when they arrived on the scene, and that four people were rescued, but also two people died in the fire. I introduced myself and they welcomed me into the ghetto. As we approached the burning structure, there was another fire fighter directing a stream of water into the front windows of the burning building. His face was blackened from smoke and heat. Uncle yelled, "Hey, Gep, how are you doing?"

"I'm fine now, but we had a major problem a little while ago when we first arrived."

Uncle Jack said, "Gep, meet Bill Cosgrove. He's a new man on Truck #15."

Then Gallapo said, "Punk, this is Don Goeppner from Engine #61."

Don extended his free hand. In his other hand he was holding a 2 1/2-inch hose that was secured to itself by a spanner. A spanner is a leather strap used by enginemen. In a low, rough voice, Don Goeppner said, "It's good to meet you Cosgrove. We need more young men around here."

We went right into the burning building and started pulling ceiling and sidewalls. Soon all the rest of our shift was on scene. We started working and it was great!

The fire had destroyed two floors of the building and the roof had collapsed into the third floor. We chased the fire throughout the building, extinguishing small fires in all the nooks and corners, and we were back in the firehouse about 11:30. Most of the hose that Engine #45 used at the fire we put back on the rig wet, because there were only seven lengths of hose that were dry in the hose tower. Two of them had burst at a fire the day before.

By the time the engine was back in service, it was already past noon. When the cook got back from shopping, we had pork and beans with hot dogs for lunch. We were hungry and they tasted good! It is hard to cook on days when you have a fire in the morning. By the time you shop, get back to the firehouse and prepare the food . . . well, it's just hard.

While we were eating, I found out that Jack Gallapo was a

trustee on the board with the Local Union #2, and also the chairman of the blood bank. This guy was involved with more things. The phone never stopped ringing for him. You'd think he was a bookie. At one time he could have calls on the Marshal line, the front phone, and the rear phone. Wags gave him the name of "Phone Dick."

We had a few more runs that afternoon. Most of them were checking street boxes. We were standing around in the front by the joker stand when someone said, "The third platoon sure worked their asses off yesterday with only four guys on the engine." In the company journal it showed that they had twenty-two runs, a 3-11, and a still and box, and also three other lead outs at still alarms!

As a result of their busy day, they lost three people to fires. Chief Deneen looked at all of us and said, "The first company to arrive at the scene of a fire has to make rescues and lead out hose, so that we can get water on the fire before it gets any larger. Most of the time we do not have sufficient manpower to perform either function as fast as necessary. Many lives are lost and property is destroyed as a result."

The speaker opened again: "Truck #15, release the elevator at 3983 Lake Park," the dispatcher said, "and take the buggy with you." The bell rang three times for the truck and twice for Battalion #16. With lights and siren we headed north on Cottage Grove.

The building at 3983 Lake Park is a sixteen-story Chicago Housing Authority building. Also known as a "project building" by the people who live in them. There were little children playing all over the front of the building in what used to be grass and was now black dirt and broken glass. As we entered this run-down, low rental apartment building, whose facilities and maintenance barely meet minimum standards for living, it bothered me, but I had a job to do.

The lobby was full of people standing and waiting for the elevator. Some kids ran up to us and told Gallapo that people were stuck in the elevator on the sixth floor. We tried to explain that one elevator was still running and we needed to take it to the sixth floor. Now everyone was crowding up, saying they didn't care about anyone on the elevator. Yelling started, we had no radio, and I didn't like this at all.

Rocky was a black fireman, and he tried to relate to these people that we needed to help the victims in the elevator. The door opened to the elevator and people started pushing and shoving. Once we were inside the elevator, we couldn't move. Those who did not get in the elevator called us names, mainly at Rocky: you "Uncle Tom," and "Nigger." He laughed it off and the door closed.

Two people made it inside with four firemen and one guy said, "You can get whoever after I get out on the tenth floor." The car stopped on the third, fourth, and then the sixth floor. Wags and Rocky grabbed this guy and threw him out of the elevator and he turned back. Rock had an axe in his hand. Wags said, "What are you going to do partner, it's your move." After calling some choice names he headed for the stairs.

We could hear the people calling for help in the stuck elevator next to the one that we were standing in. Wags said, "Who's got a light?" Jack Gallapo aimed his light through a small space between the two elevators, and with a small, thin broom stick, Wags pushed a release lever. The door opened and there, right in front of me, were about eight people inside this elevator. The car was about three feet lower than the floor. One by one, we pulled them up out of the broken elevator. They were all very thankful because they were in there for about an hour.

Back in the firehouse I was telling Nolan and Guttillo about what happened, and they laughed. "Get used to it, Dave. It happens every day."

Jim Guttillo was assigned to Engine #45 from the fire academy, and had about two months more time on the job than Nolan and I. As you must now know, there are nicknames for almost everyone on our shift. Jim Guttillo's nickname is "The Monk."

It was a hot night in September and people were outside sitting around on cars and the sidewalks. Curtains were hanging out of the windows of apartments because residents could air them out and not worry about being robbed at this time of the night. However, with the late night that follows in the ghetto, you don't leave the doors or the windows unlocked. As Lt. Steed would say, "Frankenstein or the Wolfman will get you. They lurk everywhere in the ghetto at night." I soon learned that he was very serious about Frankenstein. He takes from anyone that is not looking, and he is dangerous.

The bell rang one long ring. "Everybody!" Doolan yelled. We all ran to our places and started to get our fire gear on. At the same time the register started ringing. Most of the firemen knew that it was our box that we were responding to. Over the roar of the engines I could hear Gallapo yelling to me, "We have a fire. Pull your boots up."

As we rounded the corner of 46th and St. Lawrence you could see the smoke and fire billowing out of the second floor window. People were screaming for help on the other side of this six-unit structure. Gallapo yelled, "Get a 38' foot ladder right now!" As we attempted to pull the ladder, another command, "Get the life net!" We stopped pulling the ladder out, and instead pulled the life net from its compartment on the truck. We started to unfold the net and I heard the worst, most unforgettable, sound of my life. Just in front of us, as we approached, two victims hit the concrete sidewalk with a "splat," and then the third victim landed on top of the first two. I said to myself, "Oh my God!"

The windows on the fire floor were breaking and glass was falling down upon the lifeless victims that lay on the sidewalk. Norm was on the radio calling for ambulances as we pulled their bodies away from the burning structure.

Wags was now raising the main ladder to the roof with Rocky, and Gallapo ordered me to get to the rear and ventilate the back of the building. Now more firemen were arriving on the scene, but I was all by myself in the rear. There were people in the back saying that more kids were on the second floor. Once I reached the second floor, the rear door of the kitchen was open. I started to make my way into the smoke and I met another fireman. He said they wanted another line on this floor.

I informed him that there might be more kids up there, and he replied that they looked through and did not find anyone. I said I would get to the third floor by way of the back. As I climbed the stairs, I could see the side of the building next to this fire building.

Reflection of the fire was lighting up the gangway. With my axe I broke the windows that were in the door. Heavy black smoke and heat rushed out at me, knocking me backwards. I banged away at the lock of the door until I was able to break it loose, pushing it open. I now tried to enter on my hands and knees. The heat was too much. I had to back out. I was still all by myself. I started to break the windows in the area next to the door.

Heavy black smoke was now billowing out of the door and windows.

Finally, I heard voices. Firemen from Engine Company #60 had made it up to the third floor with a 1 1/2" hose line. I returned to the front and found Uncle Jack. He said, "Where were you? Did you go for coffee or something?"

I told him where I was. He said, "Get your tools; we have to get some ceiling down for the engine on the second floor." I looked over to where the victims had been lying and they were gone, but I could still hear that sound of them hitting the cement. I followed Gallapo up the stairs to the second floor.

The water that was flowing down the stairs was unbelievable. It was like a waterfall. Once we were on the second floor, we made our way toward the rear where Engine #45 was working their line. We needed to get the ceiling down in this room. Engine #45 shut down their line so we could enter. It was hot and smoky. Uncle said to get against the wall, and we would pull it to the window. Once my pike pole was into the ceiling, I started pulling down hot plaster and wooden lath. Sparks were all over and Gallapo yelled, "Don't stop until we're at the window." By the time we made it to the window, not even a minute had passed, but now the entire ceiling was on fire. While we were pulling, I kept hearing him talking, but what he was saying didn't make any sense: "How's your moo-moo and your auntie?"

Uncle said, "Punk, let's get out and let the engine hit this with the line." The cold water hit the fire and it was out, but the hot steam made it almost impossible to see or breathe. The snorkel worked on the third floor and the roof, and we pulled the ceilings room by room until the fire was out. Picking up our equipment and putting the ladders back on the truck, Norm came over and said two of the victims had died as a result of jumping out the window.

Norm said that the third one, a young boy, was in serious condition at the Provident Hospital. I later found out that Norm had picked this boy up, put him in the back seat of the buggy and raced him to the hospital.

We re-bedded the hose on Engine #45 and returned to the firehouse. The change companies were Engine #65 and Truck#52, and by the time they left and we got back into the firehouse it was 02:45. My arms, legs, and whole body were hurting and I was only twenty-four years old.

The next few days had bothered me, wondering if we could had been there a few minutes sooner. Could we have saved them by catching them in the net? I was on my Daley Day. That means I had five days off and I needed the time to catch up on some rest and get some things done around my new house. The only thing was my fire gear was in the back of my Ford station wagon, and the smell of smoke won't let me forget the other night on St. Lawrence.

Man has now taken the first steps on the moon with the greatest space feat ever. July 20, 1969: Apollo 11 with Neil Armstrong landed on the moon, and we could not save those people with our 1956 FWD fire truck. I couldn't get it out of my mind. We have the funds to send a man to the moon, but the fire trucks are so old that we lose victims in fires every day. Something was wrong with this picture.

Driving into the firehouse I now wondered what was in store for us that day. The Dan Ryan Expressway was never without problems. Cars were always along the side of the roadway. Police and fire trucks had traffic all messed up, and it seemed that the gapers' block was worse than the accident.

Traveling east on 55th Street I knew that for the next twenty-four hours I would live in the ghetto. There are many burned up buildings along Cottage Grove, and the poor and the homeless live in some.

As I parked my car and started getting my gear (boots, helmet, firecoat, ax, and truckmen's belt with my light) out of the firehouse, the engine responded to check a box.. After a fast "hello" to the guys drinking coffee, I took the fire gear of my partner that I was relieving, off the truck and put mine on. I checked my hand pump. I told my partner that I was in service, and he was now relieved of duty.

Uncle Jack introduced me to Relief Lieutenant Bill Alletto, who was permanently detailed to the 16th Battalion. He would be on Engine #45 today. As I watched him talk and the gestures that he made with his hands, face and eyes, I knew he had been a part of the 16th Battalion and the fire department for a while. He knew his way around the division and relieved on all 16th Battalion companies.

Lieutenant Alletto is not your typical fire department officer. He wore a white shirt with the C.F.D. emblem on his shoulder, but the blue pants were not fire department issue, more like Sears Roebuck, and the shoes were not fire department issue for sure! They were combat boots, army type. The leather was dried and cracked, but they were shining. His pants were cuffed like he was in a flood, but you had a clear view of his boots, which were laced up to the top. Lieutenant Alletto was not a tall man, but his black hair and barrel chest, and rock hard arms, more than made up for any height loss. Uncle Jack always said, "Billy Alletto is "street wise, tough as nails, and well-educated, and fits real well in a busy firehouse." I learned from guys who knew him as a young fellow that they called him "Billy Barbells" because he liked to work out. He loved the bantering back and forth in the firehouse, but when the bell ran, he was all business! He was very physical and you wouldn't want to mess with him on a serious note.

As the officers entered the roll call in the journal, the firemen started the housework and checked out the rigs. The cook checked out the supplies in the first shift's food locker. He always needed coffee. Within a twenty-four hour shift, we prepared about twenty pots of coffee. First we used the big electric pot, which makes forty cups, when the shifts were changing, and the rest was prepared in a twelve-cup percolator. Firemen drink a lot of coffee, and always did, all the way back to the days when my father was a fireman and even before that.

The speaker cracked. "Engine #61, Truck #15, check the box 4926 S. Wabash," the dispatcher yells, "and take #45 with you." Lieutenant Alletto repeats the address back to the Englewood Fire Alarm Office.

At 4926 South Wabash is DuSable High School. Engine #61 responds to this box about sixty times per month, and it is almost always a false alarm. The problem of increasing numbers of false alarms is currently being experienced in most major cities. In Chicago, the practice is to dispatch one engine to check the box alarm, unless it is a school box alarm, then two engines, one truck, and a battalion chief will respond. Engine #61 held up the responding companies, and we all returned to our quarters.

Sitting around the table in the back of the firehouse, there were strong rumors of changing the on twenty-four hours and off forty-eight hours by the city. Gallapo, being a union trustee, said, "Whenever the city wants to upset the rank and file they always start the rumor of changing the work hours." In 1967, the union worked very hard to get a reduction in working hours to 47 1/2 hours per week. This was accomplished by getting every sixth work day off, which was and still is, called a Daley Day after Mayor Richard J. Daley.

The twenty-four hour shift had its origin way back in the days when there was a two-platoon system, and we worked eighty-four hours a week. Gallapo said, "We are not about to lose what we have."

"Set the table," the cook yells from the kitchen. Setting the table meant to wash the soot from the exhaust off the dinner table, and to put the salt and pepper, ketchup, mustard, and all the other condiments out. Today's meal was a meatloaf that had a lot of fillers and the guys were not too happy with the cook, but we ate all the same. We used a lot of catsup.

The day passed and we checked the school box a few more times. Most of the firemen tried to get some rest in the afternoon. It was a little insurance to get a nap just in case the night was busy, and we were out all night. The bells rang again for a fire in the project at 4414 S. Cottage Grove. Lt. Alletto reported a fire on the 8th floor. Smoke was billowing out three windows on the east side of the building. As we entered the bottom floor, the janitor informed us that the elevators were out of service. This was no surprise; we often had to climb the stairs in the projects because the elevators were out of service.

We took the stairs, dragging all the hose and all the tools. As we made our way to the fire floor, one man led a 3" inch hose to the standpipe on the outside of the building because the pumps had been out of service in this building for a long time. To walk up eight floors with just your fire gear on, helmets, boots, and the heavy fire coat is one thing, but then to carry all the equipment up is a task. Once on the fire floor you must prepare to catch your breath, and enter this hot inferno of heat and gases.

The concrete floors and ceilings are like an oven. Alletto led Nolan and "The Monk" into the fire. I was on my knees. They were working the line on the ceiling, trying to cool it down. Gallapo yelled that we had to get the windows open. Wags crawled into the smoke-filled room and disappeared from view. All of the sudden, the smoke started to lift, and the engine advanced the line into the fire room. The steam was so hot that was burning my face.

Two more windows were broken out and now we could stand up. With one swing of my axe, I knock the frame of the window out.

"Let's get these mattresses out the window," Alletto said, and in a matter of minutes the fire was out. "The Monk" directed the pipe toward the open window and adjusted the nozzle to fog, which pushes the heat and smoke out of the apartment.

As we rolled the hose up, and picked up all the tools, we could see that this fire affected many of the firemen. The people who lived in this building just kept on doing what they normally would, like nothing happened, because they are so used to fires. It was like "oh well".

Backing into the firehouse, I noticed the firecoat on Lieutenant Alletto. It was ripped and torn and had been mended many times with silver duct tape. The fire helmet on his head was twisted and distorted from heat. This guy has been in a lot of fires, I thought to myself. Engine #45 went out to check the box about four more times that evening. We all got a couple of hours of sleep before we responded to a 2-11 alarm fire at 49th and Princeton in Engine #50's fire district. Three wooden two flats in a row. The fire fighters called the wooden structures "battleships."

October 6th through the 12th is Fire Prevention Week in Chicago, and the last three classes that were in the fire academy were ordered to City Hall for a graduation ceremony. Mayor Richard J. Daley, out in front of City Hall on LaSalle Street, swore us in. It was also a day for new fire trucks. Some forty engines were lined up on LaSalle Street, and one of them was Engine #45.

Fire Prevention Week got its start back in 1922, to proclaim a special time to commemorate the importance of fire safety. Here in Chicago, fire prevention is also a time when firemen are honored for heroism.

Back in the firehouse, October means that Captain Wilson's annual furlough was over, and at last I got a chance to meet and work with the captain of Hook & Ladder #15.

Thomas Wilson was about forty-three years old, medium build, and was highly respected by all officers and firemen. He was very strict and knew a lot about fires, and his motto was "don't make waves and do your job." Captain Wilson was one of the first officers on the "Snorkel," which proved to be one of the most successful pieces of fire equipment in Chicago.

There were two other firemen that returned to Truck #15 from their annual furloughs: Donald Staskon and James Ward. Truck #15 was heavy with firemen, and Captain Wilson had to make some changes in the roster in order to balance the manpower. Jack O'Brien was put onto the third platoon and Jim Ward was now our new cook on the first shift. Don Staskon was a tillerman, and went to the roof with Wags when we had a fire.

October was a very busy month in the 16th Battalion, and was also the beginning of winter. Captain Wilson did not want me on the roof of fire buildings until he was sure that I would know what to do when I was up there.

I learned how to work the ladders on Truck #15 very well, because we raised them every day at fires. I learned to use many of the tools for rescue work. We were making about 16 runs a day. We were called to boats sinking in Lake Michigan off of 39th Street; auto accidents on Lake Shore Drive; and Captain Wilson taught us how to carefully extricate victims from motor vehicles, and place them on stretchers so they could be transported to hospitals.

One afternoon in late November, we responded to 51st Street CTA "El" train station where a man had been hit by a "El" train. Somehow he had climbed up onto the tracks at about 50th Street and tried to jump on the passing train. His head and a portion of his upper body remained at this location and the rest of him rode the train into the 51st Street "El" station.

When we arrived on the scene all you could see was the bottom portion of his legs under the second car of the train. In order to remove him from under the train we first had to have the power cut off in both directions. Wilson also placed a heavy chain across the rails just in case the power was turned back on. This would blow the circuit and most likely save our lives. With two twenty-ton hydraulic jacks and many wood blocks, we lay on the tracks, and jacked the second car on the train up until the victim's body was released.

It was one of the worst looking incidents that I have ever seen. Captain Wilson had a way of encouraging us as we slowly, in the cold weather, removed the twisted body. Back in the firehouse, some two hours later, Wilson showed us some new ways to work on the tracks in case we ever had that type of situation again.

Dinner was ready and Jim Ward asked us to set the table. I did not have much of an appetite, but you had to eat. The bells rang again, a still and box alarm 4410 S. Greenwood. The smoke was already about one hundred feet in the air by the time we arrived on the scene. Wags and Staskon went to the roof. Wilson and I went with the engine to assist them with leading out a 2 1/2" line around the back.

The rear porches were fully engulfed in flame. It was another abandoned building. How the hell does a fire start in an abandoned building? Captain Wilson was yelling at Wags to get off the roof. I could hear him calling the Englewood Fire Alarm Office: "Truck #15 to Englewood . Emergency! Give us a 2-11 with a blast of the siren."

The fire had communicated to the structure to the south. Chief Deneen arrived on the scene, and ordered Norm to get a 3-11 alarm. All of our efforts were now directed toward evacuating the occupants of the structure to the south.

More firemen were arriving. Hose was being stretched in every direction. People were screaming for help. The fire building was a three-story brick, approximately 50' by 75' with fire on all three floors, and when it was occupied, had six rental units.

Snorkel #3 was positioned in front of the burning building and 2 1/2" fire hoses were being connected to the snorkel that were stretched from blocks away by arriving engines.

The roof of the structure had fallen in towards the rear. Captain Wilson ordered Wags to put the main ladder on the building to the south. He informed me that we were going to the roof, and told me to get my axe and an eight-foot pike pole, and the stripping ladder. I followed Captain Wilson and Wags up the 100-foot aerial ladder to the roof and we went right to work on the skylight.

Breaking the reinforced glass down into the building and

Opening the roof at 4410 So. Greenwood

releasing the hot smoke and gases, Wilson showed me how to pull the wainscoting inside the skylight with a pike pole. The plaster and lathe was falling down on the men below in the stairway, but the smoke was billowing out of the cockloft. Wags was cutting a line with his axe into the flat roof. Captain Wilson told me to start chopping at ninety degrees from Wags, and he showed me how with a few swings.

Swinging the axe into the tar-coated roof in a straight line took some doing, but I got the hang of it, while Wags made the third cut. Wilson took my axe and showed me how to swing the pick of the axe through the roof to lift the first boards back.

I swung this 8 1/2 pound axe as hard as I could, because smoke was now billowing out of the corner of the hole and right into our faces. Wags brought back the stripping ladder, which was about twelve feet long and was constructed of wood, just as I finished pulling the first board. He dropped the two hooks into the hole and the three of us pulled back the roofing and the 1' x 8' wooden boards that were nailed to the rafters.

Coughing uncontrollably, we moved back from the four by four foot hole, and the captain said, "We have to push the ceiling below in with the stripping ladder." Fire was now starting to issue from the hole as Wags pushed the ceiling down on the third floor, and the smoke and heat, almost like hundreds of pounds of pressure, was released from the burning building.

We moved away to catch a breath of fresh air toward the side of the roof. Wilson said, "After you catch your breath we will get another hole over here." We started chopping again in an effort to relieve the hot gases from the upper floors so the engine could advance their hose lines.

After making two large holes in the roof we could hear firemen on the third floor yelling up to Captain Wilson, "Good job, truck," and the captain gave a small grin of satisfaction.

Standing by the coping on the roof we could see fire engines in both directions and firemen pulling hoses into the fire buildings. There were about one hundred and ten firemen and about thirty-five pieces of fire equipment on the scene. The captain said, "Finish your cigarettes and bring down all the tools." He climbed down the aerial ladder to the street below. "There is still a lot of work to do, Cos," Wags says, "so lets get down to the street."

Captain Wilson said to us, "Let's get a cup of coffee from the canteen truck around the corner." The 5-11 club and the Salvation

Army disaster service provided us with warm gloves, coffee, doughnuts and cigarettes at all big fires.

"If you are going to donate money to anyone, don't forget these guys," Wilson said. "They're the best!"

We finished our coffee and headed back into the buildings to overhaul and release the water from the floors. It took a lot of manpower to extinguish a fire of this size. We broke the toilets off the floors of the bathrooms, and cut holes with our axes to relieve the knee-high water left from the snorkels and the many engine streams that it took to put this fire out.

Back at the firehouse everyone had a job to do to get back in service, and I think that Engine #45 used all the hose on their new rig at the fire. It was after 01:00 hours. before we were all back in service. Most of the firemen went to get some sleep without even getting cleaned up. Their soot-covered faces told the story of where they were.

One lonely tired fireman stayed on the apparatus floor to hold watch while the rest hit their bunks. The 2nd platoon started to filter in to relieve us, and the bells started ringing.

In the following month of December, fires raged throughout Engine #45's still district in the Kenwood Oakland neighborhood. Fifteen abandoned buildings burned during this month in a strip less than two miles long and about one mile wide. Three of them had burned twice. Namely, the Morocco Hotel at 3941 S. Drexel and the Tudor Ellis at 4300 Drexel.

Repeat fires can reduce the expense of tearing down a building like this very rapidly. In many cases in the ghetto, while a wrecking company is demolishing a structure, mysteriously the crane that is being used is moved a safe distance away before the fire begins.

There are signs, like all the metals such as plumbing fixtures and radiators have been taken out before the fire. I was too young or naive to spot it, but Captain Wilson and other officers had spotted this intriguing pattern for a long time. "This was definitely arson, and whoever is paying him is paying good, because this arsonist is a master," Wilson said.

Christmas time came and so did the sub-zero temperatures. I was off-duty at home with my family, but my thoughts and prayers were with the firemen that had to work Christmas Eve and Christmas Day.

The new year rolled in and on February 20th, 1970, I was blessed with the birth of my new daughter, Mary Margaret. My third child; it was cigars for everyone!

CHAPTER VI

WE DIDN'T HAVE a barbecue grill at our firehouse like many other firehouses. Somehow the second shift got an old slop sink out of an abandoned building. The third shift was able to fasten this concrete sink to the brick wall which was outside in the backyard. They filled the sink with bricks and put a stainless steel grate over the bricks. Now we had a very unique barbecue grill.

The cook made steak and baked potatoes for dinner and they were the best. The truck and the chief had a special duty call, a lock out at 4215 South Ellis Avenue. We raised a twenty foot ladder to the side window and I climbed up and opened the apartment. The gas stove was supposed to be left on and that is how they were able to get the fire department to respond, but the reason they were locked out was because they lost the keys. We returned to quarters.

I had first watch and most of the guys had gone to bed. At 23:18 hours the speaker cracked and the office called Engine #45 and the group. "You have a fire at 4444 south St. Lawrence." I grabbed the handset and depressed the button, repeated the address, rang the bell, and opened both doors in the front of the firehouse. Within a minute we were going north on Cottage Grove. It was mild weather and there was a slight fog in the air.

When the hook & ladder turned down St. Lawrence, we could smell the ripe odor of burning wood.

"We got a hit," the Captain yelled. The truck stopped in front of the burning building. Engine #45 was leading out their hose toward the rear of the building.

Captain Wilson said, "Get the jacks down." As I was pulling out the riggers that stabilized the truck, Wilson called again, "Come on we have a kid trapped." I went toward the captain.

There was an hysterical woman who was pulling on his fire-coat, screaming that her baby was on the third floor.

The structure was a three-story brick building with apartments in the front and rear. The fire was in the center and was burning from the basement all the way to the roof.

Engine #45 now had water on their 2 1/2" line, and was hitting the fire from a vacant lot on the south side of the structure. Captain Wilson ordered Firefighter Nolan and The Monk to bring the line in the back. Wilson told me and The Monk to try to get into the third floor apartment. We raced up the stairs not knowing what we had to face once we got up there. Monk and I were lying on our bellies just inside the kitchen of the third floor apartment. The fire was over our heads venting out onto the rear porches. It was a very dangerous place to be without a fire hose.

Side by side we crawled further into the burning apartment. There was a doorway to my left. It was a bedroom. I searched the top of the bed, but there was nothing. All of the sudden I saw a small shoe at the end of the bed. As I grabbed the little shoe, I felt a foot, then a leg.

I yelled to Monk, "I got her!" and I backed out on the rear porch. Monk yelled that we had her. Jim Nolan and Captain Wilson directed the engine stream from the ground up to the third floor, and under this water curtain we were able to get back out and down the stairs with this little two-year-old baby. Once we were on the ground, I fell to my knees. She wasn't breathing and I began mouth to mouth resuscitation until I heard a faint cry and she began to breath on her own. I carried her out to the street where Norm Doolan was all set up with the E & J resuscitator. Norm administered oxygen to the baby that we now know as Gil Jackson, age two. Chicago Fire Department Ambulance #4 transported her to Provident Hospital.

On two occasions after the fire, Gil Jackson and her mother visited me at the firehouse. There was a small article in the newspaper about the rescue.

The Chicago Fire Department had completed a study and the city now said that they were in a financial squeeze. With giving firemen shorter working hours and increased salaries, they had to start manning fire companies with only four men.

Local #2, led by our President John Tebbens, strongly disagreed with the new study of the "Maatman" report. Note: Gerald Maatman was a Fire Protection Engineer from the Illinois Institute of Technology. Together with the trustees of our union, they put up a good stand, not only for the firemen, but for all the citizens of Chicago. The union warned the city that if the "Maatman" recommendation of four man companies was implemented, the lives and property of the citizens would be endangered.

Over a year had passed since four man companies were introduced into the Chicago Fire Department, and time enough for a study of the records to be meaningful.

In 1968, forty-two children died as a result of fire. We reached that total in 1969, in just six months. These tragic figures proved the union's point. Children cannot get out of fires by themselves, and where rescue work must be done, and done immediately, four men often cannot get everyone out in time.

The life of the poorest citizen in a rat infested tenement has as high a value as that of the occupant of the executive suite of a high-rise building on Chicago's "gold coast." I believe that this is the thinking of all firemen across America who go to rescue people from the horror of fire

President Tebbens, Jack Gallapo and all the trustees strongly urged the city of Chicago to give us the adequate manpower to protect the citizens of this great city.

Local #2 and it's legislative team worked hard for its members to bring the manpower up to a standard, but they did not stop there. The fight to get the widows a standard pension based on a percentage of her deceased husband's salary was another major issue. There were 811 widows that received $50 dollars a month and my mother was one of them. Also, there were 210 orphans that only received $10 per month and I was one of those orphans.

It had been one year since I was assigned to Truck #15 and there had been many, many fires. We now had a new Mack truck with a 100-foot Pirsch aerial ladder and going to work with it was fun. We looked forward to being there, but the hazards of being a fireman were still there on a very hot afternoon on August 29, 1970.

Engine #61 was given a still alarm of a fire in a gas station at 71 East 47th Street. Upon their arrival on the scene, an automobile was on fire. Truck #15 and Engine #45 arrived and immediately led out a line. The fire appeared to be under control, when all of the sudden the auto's gas tank exploded. Five of the firemen were burned and two were in serious condition. Jack O'Brien and Ira

Washington, both firemen on Truck #15 were burned over 35 percent of their bodies. Firemen Brenden Dillon and Captain Kosco of Engine #61, were also burned. Fireman Jerry Linane of Engine #61 received minor burns.

As the shifts changed the first platoon was on duty, and as we drank our coffee, the subject was all about the firemen from our house that were burned. Captain Wilson told us all in his fatherly way, to have all our fire gear on and buttoned up before we got to the incident. He said, "I don't care how hot the weather is, protect yourself from getting burned."

The speaker opened: "Engine #45, Truck #15, respond to a fire at 4714 South St. Lawrence." Norm Doolan was the acting Lieutenant on Engine #45 for the day, and answered the Fire Alarm Office. After what Captain Wilson said, we all put our protective clothing on for this fire.

As we turned the corner on 47th Street you could see the smoke to the west. "Pull up your hip boots, we got a hit. Battalion #16 to Englewood," Chief Deneen yelled over the radio. Captain Wilson ordered us to raise the aerial ladder to the third floor. Wags was on the turntable while I released the jacks that stabilized the truck. Wags turned the ladder and extended the fly at the same time. A new man on Truck #15, Nick Tragos, who recently transferred from Engine #60, raced up the ladder and removed two victims from the third floor.

Captain Wilson and I assisted Engine #45 with their line to the second floor. We pulled ceilings and side walls on the second and third floors, and in no time flat, this fire was out in some fifty-five minutes!

While we were bedding the hose, Norm said, "That's how we did on the west side in the old days, when the fires were hotter, and the water was colder, and we rode on the outside of the fire trucks."

We all had to laugh because Norm always had a saying or a joke. He was a very witty and generous man.

Back in the firehouse we started the housework, but again the bells rang. We responded to 4535 St. Lawrence, hand pumps on mail box in the foyer, and then went back to quarters.

Besides getting a new man on Truck #15, which was Nick Tragos, Engine #45 also got a new man: Lewis Buick. He was a fireman on Engine #59. Rumor had it that the chief of the 4th Division sent him over on a punishment detail. Jim Ward was off so Louis Buick was the cook, and we ate like kings. Captain Wilson said, "This guy is a good cook." Splash down was canceled due to rain and we were glad of that, because splash down was a pain in the ass for all firemen.

Captain Wilson went to the Cook County Hospital Burn Center to visit the firemen that were burned. He said O'Brien was doing better, but Ira Washington was going to have a lot of skin grafting.

We pulled for watches and our system was round, plastic balls with numbers from one to ten, but today there were seven men in the watch card. I ended up with second watch: 0100 to 0300 hours.

Back in the kitchen the news was on, and we all sat at the kitchen table. Night after night we would watch the news about Chicago. Fires are sometimes in the news, especially if someone dies in a fire, but it is mostly about the police chasing people for murder or rape. Also, a big part of the news is who is on trial around town or America.

We sat and watched the news clips of our men in action in

Vietnam jumping in and out of helicopters, and hearing the same household words like "Demilitarized Zone" and the "Gulf of Tonkin." Then there was a commercial about toothpaste or something, and the next thing we saw on the news was students on college campuses protesting the war in Vietnam. I used to get pissed off watching the protesters burn the American flag, it almost made me sick to my stomach. I wanted to kick the shit out of those spoiled brats.

I was one who supported our armed forces. They didn't want to be there, and this war had been going on since 1963, almost seven years! I asked myself, why can't we win. We are the greatest nation in the world. We sent men to the moon. You mean to tell me that we can't beat a third world county like North Vietnam. It wasn't until many years later that I found out that our national "leaders" didn't want to win!

American troop strength in South Vietnam went from 16,000 in 1963, to a peak of 542,000 in 1969, and some 30,000 servicemen had been killed in Vietnam up until then!

Monk yelled out in anger, "They should just blow the shit out of that place and bring our people home. Fuck that country!" Monk was in Vietnam. The bell started to ring. It was a fire with Engine #61.

The fire with Engine #61 was at 4947 - 49 South Prairie. Before we got out of the house the office "boxed" the fire. As we approached the scene the whole rear of the structure on the third floor was engulfed in flames.

Wags raised the aerial ladder to the roof while Rocky and I raised a 30' ladder to the front. Norm told us that the chief just pulled a 2-11 on this. We also raised a 38' foot and the 50' Bangor ladder to the building next door. We pulled the ceiling and sidewalls on the second and third floors. After about three hours of working at this fire we were ordered to pick up and return to our quarters.

The change companies helped us get back in service and it was past 02:00 hours. I had second watch until 03:00 hours, and when I did get into my bunk it sure felt good, since I was really tired. The rest of the night was uneventful and the second platoon started a new day. As we left for home Captain Wilson said, "Don't forget to study for the exam".

Most of the firemen were studying for the upcoming lieutenants examination, but in our firehouse it was almost too hard to study and work all of the fires.

Captain Wilson still made all of us take the exam, and in the last days before the test, everyone tried to cram all this knowledge in that should be taught in a classroom. "This testing system is all wrong," Norm said. "It is not about what you know, its about who you know, right Dave?"

"Right, Norm." I have less than 1 1/2 years on the job, how can I be a Lieutenant, I asked myself. This system was nothing other than a political patronage plan, and the "good old boys." There was no real way to study because we had nothing to study from. You were supposed to read the academy notes that were distributed around to the firehouses and disappeared as fast as the battalion chief dropped them off.

Also, the test had many questions on rules and regulations, and practices and procedures of the Chicago Fire Department. That is, if you had a rule book to study from, and most of the firemen on the "Grove" did not have a rule book.

We did try to study at the firehouse in the days just before the test, but we just never had all that much time. Norm said that he got this from a very good source that the choice of the answers on this lieutenant's test to all hydraulic questions was "d", and all the true and false questions were true. Norm also said not to tell anyone else, and then everyone jumped on him, namely Wags:" Doolan, you're so full of shit, it stinks," and we all laughed.

On Saturday, September 19th, the day of the test, we went to Crane High School to take the exam. After taking the test we all went back to Don Staskon's bar at 52nd and Damen Ave. to compare our answers, and have a couple of drinks. This was the time that we were able to bring together this special camaraderie that I never had experienced before. We talked about the fires and Norm was at his best. He made us laugh until our sides were aching. At one time he came out of the bathroom and yelled to Don Staskon that he was out of toilet paper in the men's washroom. Don replied, "Thanks Norm, I will get some right away."

Doolan said, "Hey Staskon, I don't want to tell on anyone, but because you were out of paper, some low life wiped his ass on the window curtain!" The whole bar burst into laughter. At that time Rich Wagner started in on Doolan. They had a way of putting on a skit between them, and you would think, if you didn't know them, that they meant every word that they were saying.

I think it went something like this: Wags yelled across the bar to Doolan, "Why you Appalachian white son-of-a-bitch, you have the nerve to come out here and tell this man he is out of toilet paper, then try to tell him that someone else wiped his ass on the bathroom window curtain."

Doolan yelled back to Wags, "Shut up, you hook-nose bastard. I'm just trying to help this man out and don't try blaming me about the bathroom curtains or I'll shoot you right where you stand!" We laughed until we cried and the drinks helped us forget that none of us would be made lieutenants from this bull-shit promotional test.

The test was over, and we were into the end of October. Hydrant inspections were almost completed for the first shift, but the hydrant wrench was broken. Lieutenant Alletto was on Truck #15 for the day and he called the shops for a new hydrant wrench, but was told they were out of stock. Alletto got so pissed off at them for their cavalier answer, that he went to the locker of the engine and borrowed their spare hydrant wrench.

It was a very busy day and we had fourteen runs already and it wasn't even 1400 hours. Captain Wilson was the acting chief of the 16th Battalion and Norm was driving the buggy. We were returning from a fire at 643 East Oakwood when they gave us a run to 5153 S. Cottage Grove.

The radio transmission could be heard as we were responding to the fire. "Battalion 16-A to Englewood. We have a fire on the third floor of a storage building. Give us a box!"

As we arrived on the scene, you could see only small amounts of smoke emanating from the structure. Acting Chief Wilson ordered Lieutenant Alletto to get the roof open, because there were no windows in the building.

Nick Tragos and Jasper Neal went to the roof after raising the main ladder. Lieutenant Alletto ordered Monk and me to try to open the back of the building. Engine #60 was leading out a 2 1/2" line up the fire escape in the alley in the rear. Leo Kehoe was the acting lieutenant on Engine #60 and asked Monk to open the rear door on the third floor.

I had the Chicago bar, which is a very large crow bar, with one end for prying, and the other end had a half-round steel wedge. It was fabricated at our repair shops. This tool is one of the best for opening doors. As we worked on the door with our axes, and the Chicago bar, Engine #60 was waiting. Finally, we opened the door. The heat and smoke was bad, it pushed us back and down to our knees.

Engine #60 got into the third floor and one by one they inched their line forward. Fireman Bilawski, then Firefighter Beauregard came out of the burning third floor. The smoke blackened their faces and they were gasping for more air. I made my way in on the line to where Leo Kehoe was holding his own. He said, "Cos, take it for a spell, but keep your head down," as he made way toward the door.

I knew this was real bad, because Engine #60 didn't give their line to anyone, let alone a truckman! I could not see anything, no fire just smoke. If you picked your head up any higher than three feet, the heat would take your ears off. Finally, Monk was with me and we moved the line up just a little. I couldn't take any more. Monk took the line and I started out for a breath of fresh air.

On my way out, Howie Beauregard asked me if we were winning, and I couldn't answer. I had to get out. It was an exhausting and gruesome fight. One moment a firefighter would be on the fire escape, his lungs full of suffocating and excruciating smoke, and the next moment, he would be right back in, taking his turn at trying to get to the seat of this fire.

After Acting Chief Wilson saw how bad it was in the rear, he ordered Ambulance #25 to start administering oxygen to the firemen. There were so many of us that the ambulance took Leo Kehoe, Guttillo, and me, to Billings Hospital, where we were all treated for smoke inhalation and were then transported to Little Company of Mary Hospital for an EKG and X-rays of the chest.

We were all returned to duty at about 20:00 hours. What a day, and I had last watch to boot!

About 00:15 the speaker opened: "Truck #15, follow Engine #16 to a fire at 4446 S. Indiana." Lt. Alletto ordered the main ladder to the roof, and the 26' ladder to the second floor. We pulled ceiling and sidewalls of the second and third floors and were ordered back to our quarters about two hours later.

In talking to Wilson he told us that the storage place had a concrete roof and Nick Tragos cut two holes in the roof by using a sledge hammer. The reason it was so hot was that the walls were brick and the ceilings were concrete. It was like an oven! After my watch was over, I went home with my ass dragging, but I was also thinking about getting hurt on the job. It had been sixty-two days since that car explosion burned Ira Washington and Jack O'Brien. Rumor had it that Ira Washington, a black firefighter that had given the job twelve years, would most likely not return to the fire department as a result of the burns that he sustained in that terrible explosion. He was a good guy and an excellent fireman.

Truck #15 responded to 258 runs for the month of November and winter was now on its way. I was lucky not to have been injured too badly in the fire last week. In a survey during the last three months of 1969, 205 firemen were reported injured by smoke inhalation according to the International Association of Fire Chiefs.

To cut down on the respiratory problem, self-contained breathing apparatus were necessary, but the current ones were too weighty and bulky and caused fatigue. Many fire departments did not have this kind of protective gear, namely the Chicago Fire Department. To protect each fireman from smoke inhalation and the many toxic gases associated with fires would take a major effort on the city's part, but it could be done. Lieutenant Alletto said, "Some day we will all have our own self-contained breathing apparatus. Until that time comes it remains a health hazard to us all."

The radio crackled as a voice from the fire alarm office asked the 21st Battalion what they had at the still and box alarm. The response from Chief Mike Barry was, "The fire is at a fuel company with trucks containing heating fuel." Norm said to turn the radio on the main frequency and we would be able to hear. We all sat around the radio as the alarms 2-11, 3-11, 4-11, and 5-11 just kept coming in. They said there was a 75,000 gallon tank that was on fire.

Doolan said, "I don't like those type of fires. Just leave me here in the ghetto with the six flats, because I know what to do at these fires." At gasoline fires, anything can happen, but we knew that we were not going to this fire because we had our own fires, and we stayed in the ghetto; E-45 and Truck #15 were not change of quarters companies.

Engine #45 and Truck #15 almost never left the still and box district because the fire alarm office would have to change another fire company into our firehouse to cover the fire calls that were in our district. So as a result, when there were extra alarm fires in the city, we just listened to them on the Englewood and main frequencies.

The bells started to ring again: "Fire at 416 East Oakwood." We worked our hand pumps on an overheated boiler, and turned off the fuel supply. As we were returning to the firehouse I thought about the people who lived in the four-story building that we just turned off the heat to, and they would be cold tonight.

The cold wind of December was now blowing off Lake

Michigan, and winter was here. The "hawk" was out! It was common for us to respond to fires in basements of these buildings only to find out that they were out of coal in the "hopper," which is located in front of the boiler and was empty.

In many cases Captain Wilson would look at the faces of little children and return to the truck to report that we had a stoker fire to the office. Then he would ask us if we could throw a couple of banjo shovels of coal in the "hopper" so we didn't have to shut down the boiler of another building. In ten minutes we had enough coal in the "hopper" for the rest of the night.

Back at the firehouse, Norm called me over and said that the next day was his Daley Day. "I recommended you to Chief Deneen to drive the "buggy."

"I thought that Cliff Armstead, a fireman on Engine #45, usually drives the chief on your Daley Days."

Norm replied that he did, but he was off the next day on tickets.

"What are tickets?" I asked. Each year every battalion chief was given tickets to sell throughout his district for the annual high school "prep bowl" football championship between the public high school and the Catholic high school. The money would go into Mayor Daley's Youth Foundation, which was given to firemen for their heroic efforts at the Fire Prevention Week Awards.

Norm said, "You're in the car next day, punk, or else we have to detail a man out, and bring Leo Kehoe from Engine #60 to drive the chief."

I tried to tell Norm that I didn't know what to do, or where we were going. He said, in his way, "I know you can't be as good as me, ha ha, but you will make it. The Chief will tell you which way to go. He knows the district."

I still had a problem with this Fireman Armstead selling tickets, but I kept my mouth shut and agreed to drive Chief Deneen.

Fireman Clifford Armstead was a black man who told me that he came on the Chicago Fire Department when he was older, about forty years old. Before he was on this job, he worked in the steel mills. He had this saying that he always used to express himself. "Daddy," he would say, like when he poured steel. " Daddy, it was hot, and the work was hard."

I liked Cliff. He seemed to be an honest guy and he knew his way around the ghetto. He had some jukeboxes that he owned or serviced along 47th Street between Cottage Grove and South Park, and knew many of the merchants. That was how he sold the tickets for Chief Deneen.

To drive the chief around in the "buggy" for the day was not hard, but there were a lot of things to do. First you had to check the car's oil, water and fuel.

The "buggy" was also used as an ambulance and supplied oxygen to fallen firefighters at fire scenes. The E&J resuscitator was carried in the back of the buggy. It was a heavy, black box that held two oxygen bottles that must be full at all times for immediate use in case one of our men was overcome by smoke and the gases of a fire.

The chief carried the only portable radio on the fire scene. This handy-talkie had to be checked every morning by the buggy driver. After replacing the battery from the charger you would call the Englewood Fire Alarm Office for a radio test to assure that it was working properly.

By 09:00 hours, the chief would finish his paperwork and it was time to make the rounds to all the firehouses in the 16th Battalion. The first firehouse was Engine #60's house located at

1150 E. 55th. Engine #60, Truck #37, Snorkel #3, and Ambulance #25 ran out of it. It was the largest firehouse in the 16th Battalion. Then we went to Engine #61's firehouse located at 5349 South Wabash Avenue.

Engine #61 was a very busy engine company, and was always in the top ten engines in the city. Ambulance #36 also ran out of this firehouse.

In the firehouse, Chief Deneen would talk with the men and update them on any new orders put out by the fire commissioner, and also pick up their paperwork.

After leaving Engine #61, we went to Engine #59's firehouse which was also the 4th Division Headquarters, and the chief would turn in all the paperwork from our last work day. From division we drove back into our still district and on a good day, with a little luck, the chief would not get a fire call.

To respond from division, which was located at 818 West Exchange Ave. at the east side of the stock yards, all the way into the ghetto, was a long way with the lights and siren. The day was very uneventful. We had a few fire calls, but nothing big. As the night set in, we followed Engine #61 to a fire. Once we were there, the buggy driver stayed with the car for communication purposes.

This was a problem with me. I would rather not sit around for one, or sometimes two, hours until the fire was out. I would ask the chief if I could go in and help the firemen with their line. He said I had to stay in the car and listen to the radio and give a progress report to the office from time to time.

Well twenty-four hours in the buggy was just about all the time I could take on that job. I was glad to see Norm the next day at work. Chief Deneen was a nice man, and very quiet, but I preferred to be back on Truck #15.

Snow was falling in the city and the street was quiet. After only six runs we all started to file up the long stairs to the bunk room. Jack Gallapo was talking to someone on the other side of the bunk room. Norm threw a pillow across the room, hitting Gallapo, and all hell broke out. He called him "boy" and Doolan returned with, "Who are you calling boy?" We were all in our beds laughing. Norm Doolan did not sleep in the firehouse. He made his bed, but he just laid there listening to the sounder.

If he heard a company close to us go out, he would call over to me, "Dave, heavy equipment going out."
Gallapo would yell over, "Shut up and go to sleep, asshole!"

We all laughed into our pillows because if Norm knew you were laughing, he would keep you awake all night. The new-fallen snow muffled the noise from the street.

Suddenly, there was gun fire on Cottage Grove. Doolan sprang from his bed and ran to the window to see where the gun fire came from The shade was pulled down, but the window was open about six inches. Rich Wagner moved over to the window. "Can you see anything, Norm?"

"No, not now, but I saw one guy run into the alley across the street." Wags called to me to come over and now two more firemen, Buick and The Monk were also at the window. We were all standing by a steaming hot radiator in our underwear. We couldn't see anything because it was snowing outside. Wags kept pushing Norm a little closer to the hot radiator until his leg touched and we all started to laugh. Wags and Doolan got into name calling. Wags to Doolan: "You Jim Moran looking, slick hair, M.F.!" To which Doolan retorts, "You ugly hook nose M.F.!"

We all returned to our beds laughing like school children.

Doolan said to Wags "It is a good thing I wasn't packing or I would have dusted you right where you stood."

Gallapo yelled, "Shh, shh" to Norm. He returned with, "I will shoot you too, M.F.!" It is 03:20 hours, and were lucky because we slept through the night.

The next morning, as we were having our coffee, Norm came up to the table and said, "We have two details tomorrow, one to Engine #61 and one to Truck #8."

I drew #61's house and Jim Nolan went to Truck #8. The only bad thing about this detail was it was Christmas Eve. My first Christmas Eve away from my family and it would have been nice to be with my second family, the boys at Engine #45 and Truck #15. But, oh well, we lived by the dish card and the detail card and at least E-61 was in our battalion. They were a great bunch of guys. Some houses had different systems. We had the card system last detail or oldest date on the card, and we went! All firemen started the same way as we did. We did the dishes, and we took details.

My first Christmas Eve in the firehouse, and I was detailed to Engine #61 at 5349 South Wabash.

I had been a little angry for the last few days, because of all the days to be detailed-Christmas Eve.

Engine #61 is an old FWD pumper, about a "1956" model. The firehouse was small, just an engine and ambulance and had a great reputation for having some of the best firemen in the city. Before Squad #3 went out of service, it was housed with Engine #61. This was the busiest squad in the city.

The firehouse was old and the ceiling in the kitchen above the stove was falling down a little each day. The hole was about three feet in diameter, and on the second floor in the washroom there was another hole about the same size.

I already was informed that the lieutenant of Engine #61 would be Pat Durkin, a quiet man with little to say, but what he did say you listened and learned from him; an excellent fire officer!

The engineer of #61 was Matt Moran, a seasoned veteran that had been promoted to engineer.

Rumor had it that Engineer Moran knew where every fire hydrant in Engine #61's district was located. He drove that engine like he was in the Indianapolis 500. He was fast, but good.

It was cold outside and had been getting colder. By the time I arrived at the firehouse for the twenty-four hour shift, the temperature was two degrees below zero. Eight men would be on duty today, five on the engine, and three on Ambulance #36.

Lieutenant Durkin gave me a warm welcome, and told me I was the hydrant man, so put my fire gear on this side of the engine. Also, on the back step was Joe Pennman and Bernie Cooney, who were both firefighters on Engine #61. Bernie Cooney was the cook, and he informed us that we were going to eat like kings today, because it was Christmas Eve. We all put five dollars into the food club, and the cook left to shop for the groceries.

Matt Moran and I checked out the rig. Out on the apparatus floor, Matt told me how we would make the hydrant in this cold weather. He had a great sense of humor about everything, but when it came time to go to work at a fire he was as serious as a heart attack. "I know you're on a truck company, but this is an engine, so I want to show you how to make the hydrant," he said. After drilling me on the way to use the Chicago valve and opening up the hydrant a few times, we went to the bunkroom, made the bunks and gave the second floor a fast clean-up. Matt showed me to my bunk and a place to put my extra clothes, because in weather like this you always had extra warm, dry clothing with you.

The cook returned and our first meal was like brunch with a typical firehouse menu of eggs, bacon, sausage, fried potatoes, and orange juice and of course plenty of hot coffee. This satisfied the heartiest of appetites.

We had a couple of runs in the early afternoon: an auto fire and two check the box that were false. While returning from an incinerator fire in the Robert Taylor projects at 52nd and State Street, we were given a still alarm with Truck #30 and Engine #51 to 61st and State. A fire in a junk yard. As we arrived on the scene, there was a large amount of fire and smoke way in the back of the junk yard. Lieutenant Durkin hopped off the rig and checked out the fire. Matt told me to get a hydrant up the street. I grabbed the hydrant wrench and the Chicago valve, and started for the hydrant. Fireman Joe Pennman began the lead out with Lieutenant Durkin. Matt yelled to me, "Don't open the hydrant until I get there."

Soon the engine roared up to me, dropping hose along State Street and Matt jumped out. "Get the valve on. Hurry don't flush the hydrant." He put the soft suction on the other port. "Okay open it up," he said, and I started turning the hydrant wrench. It wouldn't turn, it was frozen. Matt reached down behind him on the street and brought up a plastic container with a mixture of gas and diesel fuel.

With a little homemade mop, he slopped this flammable/combustible liquid on top of the hydrant. Standing back with a flare, he ignited the top of the hydrant. I looked at him like he was nuts while the flames were now dying out. We put the wrench on and turned the valve until we heard water filling up the six-inch soft suction that was connected to the engine.

Telling them the water was coming, I ran back to help hold

the big 2 1/2 inch hose with Firefighter Pennman. The fire was burning out of control. There must have been ten autos and a hundred tires burning. We played the engine stream on the cars for about an hour before we got the fire out. The wind was blowing and we had about ten lengths of hose off by the time we picked all the hose off State Street. I was frozen. My gloves were wet and so was my canvas firecoat. All I thought about was getting back to the firehouse and having some hot coffee.

We ate dinner a little late, after we got back in service and put a dry bed of hose on the rig. There was only one phone to use, so we had to wait for a turn to call home.

The snow was blowing across Wabash Avenue in swirls, and the temperature was five degrees below zero. All I could think about was not being home on Christmas Eve with my family, especially the kids. I called and talked to the kids and told them to be good because Santa Clause was coming later, and Daddy would be home in the morning.

It was late and the television in the kitchen was on playing It's a Wonderful Life. Joe Penman and Matt were watching. I sat down at the table and tried to watch the television, but all I could see was the steel frame that was holding the television down so that it wouldn't be stolen when they were at a fire.

The ambulance returned from another run. They had done about fifteen and it was only midnight. I decided to go to bed. Matt said the movie was just getting to the good part. I told him that I had seen it before. As I lay in bed, all the windows in the bunkroom rattled with the wind. The heat was on, but it was still cold in the bunkroom in Engine #61's house.

The bells started to ring. I knew I had been asleep for a little while. I jumped up and started to get ready to go. As I slid down the cold brass pole to the apparatus floor, Matt was yelling that Engine #45 had a fire and Doolan just pulled a 2-11 alarm at 43rd and Evans. The engine started to move out, as we were still buttoning out coats. When the cold wind hit my face, I knew we were in for a long night.

Matt turned north on Wabash Ave. toward the fire, about two miles away. By the time we arrived, it was a 3-11 alarm and we were ordered to drop two lines, one into snorkel 3 and the other around the rear of the building. The rear porches were burning from the first floor through the third floor.

After making the hydrant with Matt, I went around the back to meet up with the rest of the guys on Engine #61. Lieutenant Durking said "Cos, do you have a spanner with you?"

I said, "Yes, and a wall hook."

"Good man," Cooney said.

I would have liked to take credit for bringing them, but Matt was the man who told me to bring them. The spanner is a very useful tool. The uses are innumerable, limited only by the ingenuity of the firemen, of course. When holding on to a 2 1/2 inch line for ten minutes, you were looking for the spanner. Once it was around the hose and over your shoulder, it freed your hands up so you could advance the line or climb a ladder. The wall hook's primary function was to secure a line to a tree, fence, or even to an auto if need be.

The fire raged on. Once we got some more lines in the back, the fire seemed to be subsiding. Everything was turning to ice, including the firemen. Although this was a dangerous fire, on nights like these, ice can be a greater hazard to the personal safety of firefighters than the fire itself.

We were all covered with ice and icicles hung from our heavy helmets. Engine #61 was ordered into the building, and we connected 150 feet of 1 1/2 inch hose to the shut-off pipe. Led by Durkin, Cooney, and Penman, we started to ascend up the rear stairway that had already been weakened by the fire.

Floor by floor we extinguished the fire. We met up with the guys from my house: Engine #45 and Truck #15, Wags, Buick, Nolan, The Monk, Ward, Staskon, and Rocky. We wished each other a Merry Christmas. It was good to see them, even if it was at a fire. Buick said, "What do you mean by Merry Christmas, it ain't too merry to me." We all laughed and continued putting out the hot spots in the burned out building.

As we advanced our line from one apartment to another, I could see Christmas trees with presents under them, all wrapped with red and green paper. It hurt to see this type of thing happen on Christmas morning. The men of Engine #45 and Truck #15 rescued many people from this fire. Lieutenant Jim Davin was the officer on Truck #15, and he told me that when they pulled up, there were fifteen people standing on the fire escape dressed in their night clothes with no shoes in the sub-zero cold.

I wasn't sure of the time, but we heard Norm Doolan yelling to Engine #61 to pick up and get the hell out of there, and he didn't have to tell us twice. Most of the hose was frozen to the street, but with help, we laid it on the top of the rig and left "45" and the group, because we came on the 2-11.

It was after 0700 hours when we backed into the firehouse. Cold, tired, and wet, we re-bedded the engine and left to go home to our families on Christmas morning.

As I was driving home, all I thought about was how lucky I was that I had a home on Christmas day. I thought about my kids and how happy they would be to see me. I did know one thing.

Somehow I was sure I would never let them live anywhere they were subjected to what I had just witnessed in the ghetto on the east side of Chicago that Christmas Eve!

Merry Christmas!

Chapter VII

By the time New Year's Eve rolled around, and we were back in the firehouse, the 16th Battalion had responded to some sixty runs, in just five days. There was one still and box, two 2-11 alarms, and two 3-11 alarms. Being in the firehouse on New Year's Eve was not that big of a deal, because if we did anything like going out to a party, we would have been together. Most of our time off we would go to each other's houses with our wives. Jim Nolan had most of the parties at his house over by the Midway Airport.

December 31, 1970, wasn't any different than any other day. Louie Buick was the cook, and made a large pot of oxtail soup and Prime Rib for dinner. We had about six runs during the day. A mattress fire at 44th and St. Lawrence and an incinerator fire at 4040 Oakenwald on the eighth floor.

We drew for watches. There was only the one television in the kitchen and that was where we spent most of the last night of the year. No one would go to bed because we just knew that we would be checking the box after midnight somewhere in the district.

Jim Ward had first watch from 2200 hours until 0100 hours, and it was a good watch to have because everyone would stay up, even Chief Deneen. I had fourth watch, and when midnight came we wished each other a Happy New Year. To our surprise, there were no calls and we were had been so sure there would be. Doolan bet Wags that at midnight Engine #45 would get at least one check the box. There were no calls so we slowly started, one by one, to call it a night.

At 01:07 hours we responded to a fire at 4018 King Drive, and had three more runs in a row, but no fires. They were all what we call "mistaken citizen runs."

Back in the firehouse we had a small cup of soup and, of course, two smokes and headed back to the bunkroom. Not forty minutes went by. We all responded to 4000 South Ellis to a cold box and we returned. We went back up to the bunkroom, to another cold box, and on our way back the fire alarm office sent us in on a 2-11 at 134 East 34th Street. We worked this fire for over three hours.

By the time we got back to the fire house it was almost 07:00 hours and time to go home. So much for spending New Year's Eve in the firehouse. I think we all just went home and slept the whole day.

The winter months of January and February were hard on the equipment that we used to fight fires. The air brakes on the rigs were freezing and had to be bled two times a day. It just seemed that there were burst hoses almost every day. In the month of February Engine #34 loaned Engine #45 four lengths of hose until they received new hose. That's how short of fire hose we were.

There were fires every day in the 16th Battalion. During these cold months, Engine #45 responded to 535 runs and Truck #15 had 467 runs, and of these runs, twenty-one of them were still and boxes, ten were 2-11 alarms, three were 3-11 alarms and two were 4-11 alarms.

Truck #15 had a flat tire and the siren was out of service. We could not respond to a fire because our door was frozen closed and they had to replace our joker stand. What a time!

The winter months were very hard on the firefighters. Just in our firehouse, eleven men were injured on duty. Most of the injuries were minor except for one, Firefighter James Ward of Truck #15 was detailed to Engine #60.

While working at a 2-11 alarm on January 12, 1971, Jim Ward suffered a possible heart attack and was rushed by Ambulance #25 to the University of Chicago Hospital. Firefighter Ward died on February 23, 1971. It was a great shock to all of us that one of our own from Truck #15 had died from the various side effects associated with long-term smoke and heat inhalation.

Another tragedy on the north side claimed the lives of two firefighters in an explosion. Lieutenant William Quinn and Firefighter Martin Dyer were sent to their final resting places.

We all stood as honor guards next to Jim Ward's casket for the two night wake. The first shift worked February 26th, but we were all at the funeral on February 27th. After a long twenty-four hours in the firehouse, and after two extra alarm fires, we were getting our uniforms on. Norm walked into the washroom on the second floor with a cup of coffee. Norm proposed a toast to Jim Ward, our fallen comrade, at 08:00 in the morning. Although we were up most of the night, the coffee toast made us feel good. After the toast to Jim Ward, we left for the funeral home located at 81st and Ashland Ave.

Engine #45 was out in front of the funeral home, draped in the purple and black. Inside we took turns standing by the casket as honor guards. All the dignitaries filed by: alderman, police officers, Commissioner Quinn, and even Mayor Richard J. Daley came to pay his respects. The honor guard formed a line all the way through the funeral home and out onto Ashland Avenue. As we were getting our overcoats on, in the back of the funeral parlor, Norm said, "Hey, who took my overcoat!" We all just looked around while putting on our own coats. He could not find his uniform overcoat that he put in the closet in the back room of the funeral parlor. There was no time left, we had to line up and now some of the relatives were passing through the long line. Everyone was telling Norm to stay out of the line because someone was going to say something.

Norm would not listen. He said, "I am an honor guard. Who would say anything?" Even Chief Deneen, whom Norm drove in the buggy, said, "Maybe you should wait outside. Don't worry, no one will say anything."

As the flag-covered casket emerged from the back of the parlor, the call was loud and clear: "detail attention," and we all snapped to attention. The next command was: "detail, hand salute," and the long line of firefighters raised their white-gloved hands into the salute position. As the casket passed me there was a terrible knot in my throat. Knowing that Jim Ward was just working with me on the first shift of Truck #15 in what seemed like yesterday.

Behind the flag-draped casket was Jim's wife and son, his brother and the rest of his loved ones. Mayor Richard J. Daley and Fire Commissioner Robert J. Quinn followed behind them. Then came the chief fire marshal, first deputy marshal, and the second deputy marshals. We kept our hand salute, no one said anything about Norm's overcoat, and then out of the silence some chief says, "Hey, Firefighter, where is your overcoat?"

With no hesitation Norm said, "It's in your wife's closet" and the whole line of firemen were laughing. As I looked to my right, I could see Commissioner Quinn and Mayor Daley laughing and covering their mouths.

Only Norman Doolan could have pulled that off without anything from the chief, who made the statement, "not even one word about this snotty remark." Firefighter Ward's casket was carefully lifted up onto Engine #45's hose bed which transported him to Holy Sepulchre Cemetery and his final resting place.

We were all invited to a luncheon back at the Beverly Woods restaurant. Jim Ward's brother took us into the bar, put a large sum of money down and said thank you to all of us, and that Jim loved being a fireman. "You guys gave him a hell of a tribute and a great send off."

I can only say that Jim Ward was a wonderful husband, a good father and a good fireman. It was hard to return to the firehouse after Jim Wards funeral, but firefighters are not strangers to death.

The month of March brought new firemen to our firehouse. Engineer Fred Morgan and Firefighters Jack Robin and Francis Donegan were now on Truck #15. Firefighter Frank Connors was moved from the third shift onto the first platoon. Working conditions were constantly improving on the Chicago Fire Department. We were now the highest paid fire department in the world. New equipment was being delivered every month. Local No. 2 and its president, John Tebbens, and the negotiating team were hard at work.

No matter what type of equipment we had to work with, firefighting was still the most dangerous profession. Some of the worst fires of the winter were in the Loop where a 3-11 alarm in twenty degree temperatures with forty mph. winds made it hard for the firemen in the 1st Division. There were major, extra alarm fires on the west side just before Christmas at 2401 South Pulaski Road.

There was an order in the journal from Captain Fox to the men of Truck #15: clean the kitchen and follow the work card. To impress Captain Fox we cleaned everything in the kitchen and the whole firehouse.

At the request of all the members of our house, the rodent control bureau showed up to spray quarters for the elimination of roaches. The chemicals that they used to get rid of the roaches had a bad smell to it, but the roaches went away for a while. We had wooden cabinets in the kitchen, and they were loaded with cockroaches. I know, from being detailed to other houses, that they also had a case of the roaches.

Once, Lieutenant Ed Rickard, who is on the engine, asked the man in charge of the rodent control unit, "How do you mix the chemicals into the spray cans? What is your formula?" The man from the rodent control unit said, "You put about a half of an ounce per two gallons of water."

Lieutenant Rickard was a very serious guy about this roach problem. "Dad" Rickert was his nickname, because he would treat us like we were his kids. Rickert said to the rodent control guy, "What if your poured the whole bottle into the spray tank? Wouldn't that eliminate all the roaches?"

The guy replied, "If I did that at every firehouse, I wouldn't have a job, because all the roaches would be dead and you guys wouldn't call any more."

Rickert was furious with this guy and started yelling, "What the hell is wrong with you? We want to get rid of the roaches and you are just teasing them with water. Get the hell out of here!"

and he kicked him out of the fire house along with his two workers. We loved hearing stories about things like that because it added to our day, but the only bad thing was that we still had the roaches.

The bell rang for everyone, with a fire at 3943 South Drexel. Norm reported on the scene and asked the office, "Do you have any more on this?'

The Englewood Office said there was a fire on the second floor at that address. We took our tools and headed into the building. A woman on the second floor was trying to tell us that water was leaking through her kitchen light fixture. "Hold up the second engine there is no fire," Norm yelled down to the chief.

Captain Wilson told me and Rocky to see if we could get up the back stairs and get into the apartment on the third floor. It was all locked up and we had to kick in the rear door off the back porch.

The bathtub was overflowing and water was all over the apartment floor. Norm called for the police because we had to make a forced entry. Truck #15 picked up the command from Captain Wilson. As the truck traveled south on Drexel Boulevard, I thought to myself that they always know if they call the fire department we will be there in a hurry.

Bummer had dinner ready as we returned. Tonight it was two footballs or meatloaf, mashed potatoes and green beans. Louie Buick had a way of making meatloaf with onions and green peppers and gravy.

The cook yelled out to set the table. Someone washed the table and others got the condiments from the first shift locker.

In our firehouse, when the cook yells to set the table, most everyone helps out, but for the guys that were missing from the kitchen, it was customary to hit the brass fire pole with a heavy, steel object. This way even if you were across Cottage Grove Avenue mailing a letter, you could hear the banging on the pole, and you didn't miss dinner. In the dinner line we would take some meat and mashed potatoes throw them on your plate and go sit down.

Lieutenant Steed was in line right behind me and would say, "Cosgrove, you had better take another scoop of those potatoes." I said, "And why is that Lieutenant?"

He said, with laughter in his voice, "You don't know whose roof you will be on tonight." We all laughed because Steed knew I liked potatoes, but in a way he wasn't kidding about the roof.

I had second watch from 01:00 hours to 03:00 hours. Don Staskon had first and always gave me an extra twenty minutes to sleep.

Officers maintained the floor watch during the day from 07:00 hours until 22:00 hours. Then a fireman usually took four watches throughout the night. Most firehouses would follow a watch card and your name was placed on the blackboard. When a member was relieved from watch, he would inform the fireman taking the next watch of any fires in the city, or anything that might be of some importance. The fireman reporting for floor watch must enter his name in the journal and specify the exact time he started the watch.

A firefighter on floor watch takes a look around at all the apparatus and equipment, and makes sure that it is ready for immediate use. Second watch is one of the worst, because it seems to be the longest watch. Many nights when everything was quiet and we were tired from working all day, the clock just seemed like it had stopped and you looked at it every fifteen minutes until you were relieved.

In some cases, the fire alarm office would call on the Marshal line and have the fireman on watch give a test on the telegraph key. Sometimes the Marshal line would ring and they would tell a new guy to give two taps on the key. The caller would say that he was a fire alarm operator, but it was another fireman in another firehouse that knew you had this watch. Then the caller would ask you to hold down the black button on the joker stand. The man on watch pushed the black button and nothing would happen. The caller would say, "Are you sure you pushed the button down? We did not receive it in the office." The caller now had the man on watch push down on the button again and yelled at him to push down on the black button and the red button at the same time.

The bell rang throughout the fire house and the chief and all the sleeping firemen slid the pole at 0200 hours. If you tried to tell them that the office made you do it, they all called you names as they went back to bed. Playing practical jokes on each other, made the long twenty-four hour day a little easier. Believe it or not the jokes bring the camaraderie among the men.

The Fire Alarm office is located inside City Hall, and this is the main fire alarm office, which covers the North and West sides of the city. The Englewood Fire Alarm office was located at 6361 South Wentworth Avenue, and covered all fire calls from 3900 south to the city limits.

The men who worked in the fire alarm offices, and handled the dispatching of all fire apperatus were specially trained civilian fire dispatchers. Upon taking a call, the dispatchers had to evaluate the circumstances and decide on the type and quantity of equipment needed to send to the incident. Bob Tinney, Jack Hanrahan, Rainy Byrnes, Ken Little and Bob Fleckenstein were just some of those special dispatchers that sent us to all those alarms. They also supported the firefighters in so many ways like attending parties, wakes and funerals.

The special people made many, life-saving, split-second decisions based on their knowledge and instincts. They opened the speakers in many firehouses across the city and called us. They also checked maps to see if an extra truck was needed, and without hesitation, the fire alarm office would pull the box, and send in more fire companies.

At roll call the captain informed us that Truck #15 was going to the fire academy for our annual training. What this means is that we have to get the "rig" ready. Ladders were cleaned and paint was applied to the base with our numbers. All of the diamond-plated steel has to be painted silver. The tools and the compartments on the truck had to be painted, and also the pike poles. The captain had all this work equally divided between the three shifts, but because he was the captain and we were on his shift, we did more work than the second and third shifts. All this work had to be done while we were in service.

From the time the skipper informed us, we had some sixty-seven fire calls and three of them were still and box alarm fires, with one 2-11 alarm. All across the city, fire companies had to get their rigs ready for school! By getting the truck ready on all three shifts, it brought up the morale of the firefighters. We all bitched about the work we had to do, but when your "rig" pulled into the drill yard you wanted everything to be the best it could be for the company.

THE FIRE ACADEMY

All fire companies throughout the department had to return to the fire academy annually for two days. Usually an instructor met us in the drill yard and told us where to place our rig. The first place we went in the academy was the coffee shop on the first floor. From there we were sent up to room 208 where we filled out paperwork about our personal history. This included our present address in the city, vehicle stickers, and any new children or dependents.

The companies were divided up into groups for various evolutions like aerial pipe operations, safety on roofs, and forcible entry. Other companies attended visual aid classes and lectures about high rise fires. They conducted school fire drills and first aid classes about bone and joint injuries.

All and all, the instructors tried to teach us new techniques that would make us better firemen. Before we left the academy they had to tell us about disciplinary procedures just in case you were a "bad boy." The fire academy was always a long day, and when we got back to our firehouse we were happy to be home again.

We were not back one hour when the bells started to ring: "Engine #16, Truck #15, a fire at 4334 South Calumet." Before we arrived on the scene, Chief Deneen requested a box. It was another abandoned building. Truck #15 was ordered to raise the aerial ladder to the roof and also to take a 3" line off Engine #45 and operate a stream into the first floor of the subject structure. Wags and I opened the roof, but we now had a K-12 saw which was a gas-powered saw with a twelve-inch carbide blade. The skylight was broken out in a previous fire, and the saw made short work out of this flat roof.

Engine #45 led out their line into the first floor and worked their stream on the rear area until extinguished. Chief Conte of the 4th Division at 18:44 hours, struck out the fire, and we all returned to quarters in service. We ate dinner and drew for watches, and I drew last watch. We sat around the table talking about the fire academy and all the latest rumors in the city. We had a few more runs before we got up to the bunkroom. It was a long day at the fire academy, then a still and box, and then a few more runs. I was glad to hit the bunk, only to be called for watch at 05:00 hours. Fourth watch meant cleaning the kitchen, the apparatus floor, making the coffee for the oncoming shift, and ordering fuel for all the companies in the 16th Battalion. By the time I finished all the duties that were required on fourth watch it was 08:00 hours; time to go home. Before we left to go home we had to strip our beds and put our sheets away in our lockers. If we didn't, there was a good possibility that they would be used for rags. The bells started to ring, and I know that the second shift was on duty, and this was Saturday, my day off.

By the time that I returned to the apparatus floor, the chief and engine had responded to a fire that was now a still and box alarm at 715 East 63rd Street. Lieutenant Ed Szymanski on the second shift informed me that Engine #63 had a fire, the building had collapsed and firemen were trapped under the debris of the building. We listened to the fire radio and then the 4th Division requested a 2-11 alarm. The only ones that were left from the 1st shift were Louie Buick and myself. Bummer said, "Dave, let's drive over there, because it's on our way home." Without a word we left in our own vehicles.

By the time we arrived on 63rd and St. Lawrence we met up with Jim Nolan and some of the guys from our shift. They had informed us that Eugene Craven and Harry Beilawski of Engine #63 were trapped under tons of rubble. We all wanted to help in the rescue of our brother firefighters, but we were ordered to stay back with all the other concerned citizens. As time went by, we

Drawing of a fire fighter taking a knee next to the body of a fallen comrade.

were told that they were talking to one of the trapped men and that he would soon be out of danger.

Minutes led to hours as the rescuers made their way into the collapsed building. Fire Commissioner Robert Quinn asked that all off-duty firefighters stay back. We went to Don Staskon's bar and waited for news. After many hours, Firefighter Craven was pulled out of the collapsed building. He was in extreme pain and was listed in critical condition at Billings Hospital. The search continued for Firefighter Beilawski while his brother Bill watched from under the rapid transit line that ran above 63rd Street and in front of the structure.

Soon daylight faded, but the search continued under floodlights. The word came out over the scanner radio at Staskon's bar. No one was leaving until their fellow firefighter was brought out. Almost twelve hours after the call, Firefighter Harry Beilawski's body was found lying face down and the news was now all over Chicago. Father McDonald was with the firefighters and held the long vigil on that cold wall on the side of the building. Father McDonald climbed down the ladder into the hole. He was administering the last rites of the Catholic church, and the firefighters who were down in that hole took a knee.

With their helmets in hand, and tears streaking down their sooty faces, the firemen prayed along with Father McDonald for their fallen comrade. Firefighter Harry Beilawski had answered his last alarm and after some twelve long hours, his brother firefighters ever so carefully raised him out of the hole that once was a building with an address of 715 East 63rd Street.

Safe, back in my own home, I stayed awake thinking that the trade of a tile-setter was a good, safe business. By this time I would have been a journeyman. It was the trade I was in before I became a firefighter. My thoughts went back to prayers for Harry Beilawski and his family; his brother Bill, who worked with me on Engine #60 on the first shift, and the family of Firefighter Eugene Craven, holding a vigil as he lay in critical condition in the hospital.

Why are firefighters killed? Because they fight fires and thus engage in one of the most dangerous occupations. The National Fire Protection Association records indicate that between 200 and 270 firefighters die annually in the line of duty across the country.

Firefighters are subject to extreme physical effort and psychological tension, jumping, running, hauling hose, climbing stairs or ladders, rescuing people, carrying heavy objects, meanwhile looking for flare ups, falling walls, dangerous openings underfoot and other tension making threats.

Back in the firehouse we found out that the building in which Firefighter Harry Beilawski lost his life was an abandoned building. We received the new general order #786 to all members of the Chicago Fire Department. No one was to enter into abandoned buildings. This order just wouldn't work if there was a small fire in an abandoned building. What were we supposed to do, wait until the fire got out of control before we extinguished it? There are over 100 abandoned buildings in our still district. Not to say anything about the west side and the north side of the city.

Bummer collected the money for the food club, and we started checking the rig and cleaning the firehouse. After the housework was completed, we watched television or read a magazine. Now that the weather was better you could work on your car in the backyard. The bells started to ring again; no car work today.

"Engine #45, Truck #15, a fire now at 1322 East 47th Street." There were people in every window calling for help. Wags raised the main ladder to the third floor window while we pulled the ground ladders from the rear of the truck. You could hear Norm giving the exterior dimensions of the burning building, and then Englewood emergency gave us a box, with the sound of the siren.

Engine #45 was leading out a 2 1/2" line up the front stairs. The Monk had all the 1 1/2" hose over one of his shoulders and one fold of the 2 1/2" hose with the 1 1/4 " shut off pipe over his other shoulder. Monk was a strong fireman. The inside stairway was filled with people screaming for help, and yelling at the firemen that there were children still up on the second and third floors.

Captain Wilson ordered us to do a primary search of the third floor. While the ladders were being thrown against the side of the burning three-story building by Firefighters Donegan and Robin, Firefighter Connors was now with The Monk taking out the kinks in the dry hose that lay in the stairway. Monk told Connors that Dave was on the third floor. Connors said, "I would rather be on the fire floor than above it; that's a truckmen's job and it's a greater risk."

As I returned I told them, "We need a line on the third floor. There is fire in the back of the apartment." We could hear breaking glass from the skylight on the roof. The smoke was heavy, but it was lifting as the hose started to fill. Monk cracked open the pipe, first a gush of air, then the water. Lieutenant Steed, Monk, and Frank Connors advanced the line down the dark, smoke-filled hallway. I yelled to Monk to let me see if I could get some ceiling down. You could hear the fire making a crackling sound in the walls. As I pulled down the ceiling, the hot plaster and lath hit the top of our helmets.

Frank Connors took the line and gave Monk a spell in the back of the apartment on the second floor which was all fire. I met Gallapo in the stairway and he said there were children missing that were on this floor. Gallapo and firefighters from Truck #37 searched the other side of the floor.

Back down on the first floor, I reported back to Captain Wilson that I could not make the third floor. "We have to get a line up there," Wilson said, "because there are kids missing." The screams of an hysterical woman out on the front sidewalk told us that her children were missing. Norm said that the chief pulled a

2-11 alarm; the rear porches were burning from top to the bottom. As more fire companies arrived at the fire, hoses were being stretched into the burning building from all sides. I made my way back up the second floor to pull ceiling and sidewalls for the engine guys.

"Let's try to make the third floor," Gallapo yelled as we advanced up the front stairway. The fire was in the cockloft and Wags and Staskon had the skylight out and they had cut a hole in the roof. The smoke lifted from the stairway and with Engine #60's line, we started to make headway down the long, third floor hallway.

With three lines on the third floor, we began to start winning against the fire. Then I heard the call of a fireman from a bedroom. We all moved toward the rear bedroom on the third floor.

We found three children. Two were against the west wall on the floor, and the other still was in his crib. The word was sent down to the chief on the ground floor. There was still a lot of fire to be extinguished and all the ceilings on the third floor had to be pulled. As we worked our way from room to room, pulling down the lath and plaster, the hot embers and sparks fell down upon our helmets and our water-soaked fire coats. The fiberglass insulation and asbestos was everywhere in the smoke-filled rooms.

The three body bags were brought up to the third floor and the lifeless bodies of the children were gently taken down to the ground floor. Firefighters live and work around death, but when the life that is lost is a child, it is very hard, even on a fireman.

There were four lines outside in the rear extinguishing the burned out wooden porches. The roof collapsed into the kitchen area in the rear of the structure. Norm came upstairs and told the 2-11 companies to start picking up. We overhauled the rest of the top floor and moved down to the second floor.

Chasing the last sparks around in closets and the corners of the rooms, Lieutenant Steed said, "Let's wash down the rest of this room and I will tell the engineer to shut down."

Truck #15 took all of our ladders down and put them back on the truck. We finished picking up the last of the hose and returned to our quarters. Most everyone was tired. We ate dinner and just sat around playing cards and waiting until the news came on television. The fire on 47th Street was the top of the news, because when children die in fires that makes big news.

In April of 1971, another Apollo mission took place and we were supposed to land on the moon. This mission had a major problem. There was an explosion and Apollo13 was venting oxygen into outer space. They were not sure that the astronauts would make it back to earth let alone land on the moon.

At a cost of millions of American dollars the Apollo mission was a big failure. In the ghettos of Chicago and other large cities, there was little concern about the moon or astronauts that were on the troubled spaceship. There are people that are so poor they don't have food or a table to eat from. They sleep in burned-out abandoned buildings. These are serious problems when children don't even go to school and hookers stroll the streets just to turn a trick so they can get a fix for tonight. They don't worry about a space mission.

Just think if for some reason they canceled one mission to the moon and all the money (millions) was put into the ghettos in America, to feed, house and clothe the poor people. Norm said, "Dave, you're a dreamer. It's not going to happen." Well, it was a good thought.

One night in mid-May, after a busy day, Truck #15 and the 16th Battalion were given a release the elevator at 1132 East 42nd

Place. Three young boys were stuck between the ninth and tenth floors of this project building. They had been in the broken elevator car for about two hours, and were frightened. In order to get to the boys, we had to climb on top of the elevator on the tenth floor, cross over into the elevator shaft, and jump down onto the broken elevator car. After forcing the escape hatch we finally were able to get to the boys. One by one they were lifted out to safety. Norm had come up to the tenth floor, and said, "Dave, the fire alarm office just called. You have an emergency at home." The next day, on May 15, 1971 my fourth child was born at Christ Community Hospital. Timothy Francis was 7 lbs. 4 oz., and born at 10:13 A.M. More cigars for the boys.

The summer months came in with a bang. On June 28th, it was hot and broke an all time record with the temperature reaching 101 degrees. The sun was so cruel that with all the gear on your body, the temperature was well over 110 degrees. The first shift relieved the third at a 3-11 alarm fire at 4523 South State Street.

While the third shift was responding to the 3-11 alarm fire, a group of angry citizens had thrown a rock at the rig striking the windshield on the officer's side. The glass had to be replaced.

After picking up from the 3-11, we returned to 46th and Cottage Grove. It was hot, and the one air-conditioner in the bunkroom just could not cool this large room. One of the guys said that his uncle had an air-conditioner that was used. Norm said, "Can you get it today?" In a short time we had a better unit in the bunkroom. We told the house treasurer, Engineer Bill Marshal, that we voted on the unit, because like in any firehouse you owned the stove, refrigerator, air-conditioners, and the coffee pot. The city of Chicago provided nothing for our comfort.

In August as we were watching the news, the President of the United States, Richard Nixon, came on with his usual, "my fellow Americans," and was going on about the economic problems that this country was facing. Inflation had risen to 8.3 percent nationally and in order to correct this he was forced to place a freeze on all wages across America.

At first the president's message did not bother me, about freezing all the wages, but a few days later we found out that the president's executive order No. 11615 would put a halt on progression pay increases and longevity increment also.

The president's action, known as Phase I, was by his own admission, only a temporary measure. Some of the firemen shouted that this was a crock of shit. Monk said, "You heard him, it's only temporary, and presidents don't lie, right Dave?" Yeah Right.

Just when we thought that things were looking better as the months passed everything was starting to go to hell. The city fathers took full advantage of this economic problem. It now became apparent that the city had every intention of keeping the freeze for seventeen months. The 1972 budget had no provisions for a pay grade advancement.

It was Fire Prevention Week again, but this year I was to be honored for the rescue of the little girl on St. Lawrence Avenue. I was ordered to appear at the city council for a "hero award" on Tuesday, October 5th.

The city council honored firefighters once a year. I was awarded my first honorable mention from Richard J. Daley and Fire Commissioner Quinn. They honored me to be with some sixty other firemen that were also given honorable mentions for rescues made during 1970. Also, I received a check for $100.00 from Mayor Daley's Youth Foundation. This money was the proceeds of the annual football game; the football game that Firefighter Clifford "Daddy" Armstead sold the tickets to for Chief Deneen.

It was a great day. We were able to have our photos taken with Fire Commissioner Quinn. He remembered me from the day that he gave me my father's badge. The commissioner also told me that my father would have been proud.

Back in the firehouse there was a lot of talk about working out of class. Things were changing on the fire department. It seemed like just about every day someone was acting out of rank.

In our firehouse, Chief Deneen of the 16th Battalion was detailed to the 4th Division as a division marshal. Captain Wilson was acting as the chief of the 16th Battalion; Lieutenant Steed moved to Truck #15, acting in Captain Wilson's position; a firefighter was acting as lieutenant of Engine #45; a firefighter was also the acting engineer of Engine #45. Captain Wilson said not to make any waves and roll with the punches. This practice was going on all over the city.

There was a scandal about a magazine about firemen selling adds purportedly for the benefits of firemen's widows and orphans, while in fact, the firemen's widow and orphans had not received any money from this fund raising magazine called Today's Firemen.

The Illinois Attorney General, William Scott, said, "The magazine sales presentation is designed to intimidate Illinois residents. Businessmen, through the use of veiled threats and innuendoes, created a false impression that if businessmen did not place an ad in the magazine, they would be subject to harassment by the fire department inspectors . Future inspections concerning fire code regulations will be very troublesome." The Chicago Firefighters

Union stated that this magazine was not affiliated with us in any way, nor did they contribute to our death benefit fund.

Norm said, "Hey, what the heck, these guys had a good idea, they just blew it by strong arming the big guys."

We all laughed because Norm always was looking for some way to get rich. He used to tell me, "When I make it Dave, you can be my driver." Norm's dream was to have his own tavern; a shot and beer place. Somewhere the guys could come in for lunch and get a bowl of soup, maybe a sandwich, and a cold beer. He had a great sense of humor with all of his one line jokes, and Norm had a million "one-liners" as he called them.

Back in the firehouse after a fire in a basement at 5046 South Prairie Avenue, the rig was discharging and we just made it back. Captain Wilson called the fire department shops for service. We were ordered to report to the shops and went out of service at 10:35. No one likes going to the shops, especially firefighters. I don't care what fire company you were working on that day, when they told you that the rig was going to the shops, it immediately caused the morale to disappear and gloom set in. The rig needed service on a few things. There was a bad leak in the controls of the main ladder and an alternator because of the discharging problem. The shops are located at 31st Street and Sacramento Avenue on Chicago's West Side.

The department's highly-skilled mechanics have specialized in the repair and maintenance of fire apparatus. They have the equipment and the knowledge to repair apparatus as diverse as the fire boats, fire engines, aerial platforms, or truck companies, and many other rescue units like the squads that carry many diverse tools and equipment.

Repair Shops: Chicago Fire Department

Firefighting places tremendous wear on apparatus engines and pumps, especially our rigs that were making eighteen to twenty runs per day. Wilson used to say, "Why do you think we are always calling the shops?"

The outside of the shops was filled with junk firetrucks that hadn't been moved in years, but they saved them for spare parts. The interior of the shops was this large, cavernous hall about three stories high, full of fire trucks loaded on lifts and jacks. There were no provisions at the shops for firemen who waited for hours until their rig was ready.

In fact, firemen were not allowed to go into the building or walk around the shops. We were ordered to stay in one place by the side door, and if you were caught outside, you could be suspended. It was like we were criminals, with no coffee or even a place to sit. I could not wait to get back to 46th and Cottage Grove.

Rumor had it that if you carried your precinct, you could get a job at the shops.

Four days after we left the shops, the third shift broke down again, and they brought a spare rig out to us. It was the old FWD with the tiller.

Winter set in again. The cold played hell on the firemen and the equipment. Christmas and New Year's came and went, but the fires raged across Chicago with injuries to firefighters at an all time high. The year 1971 was a bad one for the Chicago Fire Department. Eleven firemen died in the line of duty.

In December, Lieutenant Fier of Engine #16 answered his last alarm after suffering a heart attack working at a 4-11 alarm fire at 1223 South Wabash Avenue. Tony Fier was a great fireman that gave all he had at a fire. A snorkel brought him down from the abandoned building's sixth floor. Tony Fier was transported to Mercy Hospital and listed in critical condition.

Chapter VIII

DURING THE MONTH of January bitter cold temperatures posed big hazards for firefighters all over Chicago. Fire and ice were just old enemies as the firemen of the West Side in the 2nd Division fought a fire at Lake and Waller in an abandoned building.

Firefighters of the 12th Battalion fought a 4-11 alarm fire at 63rd and Stewart on Chicago's south side. Most of these fires were caused by overheated boilers that were stoked to capacity to provide more heat for the people that lived inside the buildings.

On a very cold, early morning the firefighters of the 7th Battalion were tested on a very large fire when a gasoline tanker truck crashed into the guardrail and exploded on the Dan Ryan Expressway at Taylor.

The firefighters of Chicago were freezing. Not just out in the street, but the pocketbook of firemen and their families were freezing when the city put the freeze on our wages. One freeze went through the end of 1971, and the other through the end of 1972. John Tebbens, our President of Local #2, pledged that he would end the wage freeze, but said it wasn't going to be easy.

Tebbens formed a coalition with several unions, and they met with the city boys for more than 2 1/2 hours, mainly for the purpose of negotiating payment for all the raises which came due for their members. The city finally agreed to the retroactive pay for 1971, and pledged that all money due would be paid within ninety days. Tebbens said he would recommend ratification of the agreement to the members with the understanding that the 1972 salary steps would remain negotiable. To me, this meant no step raises, now wasn't that a bitch. When we came on the job, the city said there were four step raises until you became a first class firefighter. Now those step raises had to be negotiable. Firemen were working at fires with shit equipment, freezing in the cold weather, being injured every day, and some were dying. We had to negotiate for our pay now, but they said not to worry, things would get better.

The next work day I was detailed to Ambulance #36 which was located in Engine #61's quarters. I'm not sure how other firefighters liked working on the ambulance, but in our battalion no one wanted to be detailed to an ambulance and I, for one hated, the ambulance. Ambulance #36 was a 1970 white Pontiac. The area covered by Ambulance #36 was 60th Street South between Cottage Grove Avenue and Stoney Island Avenue to 39th Street North. It was part of a federal program called "model cities." One of the only things that was good about this detail was that I was working with firefighter Mike "White Dog" Walsh.

The men of the ambulances save many lives each year in the course of responding to accidents, sick calls, and fire alarms. At accidents we administer first aid to the injured. As soon as he or she can be moved, the victim is taken to the nearest hospital for more complete care. Most of the sick calls that Ambulance #36 responded to were coronary or emphysema cases. Oxygen usually had to be administered immediately upon our arrival. Ambulance crews have basic training, and care for victims the best we can, because we are firemen. So most of our victims just got a ride to the hospital. In the twenty-four hours that we were assigned to this ambulance we had twenty-eight calls.

Included in the equipment is an inhalator-resuscitator-aspirator. It can be used to supply pure oxygen, act as an inhalator for firefighters who have taken a little too much smoke, and it can provide automatic breathing while we are transporting a victim to the hospital.

This was the best thing we could do for a victim-give a fast ride to the hospital. Norm met the ambulance at Engine #61's quarters, looked at me and said, "The last victim that you two guys took to the hospital died. Not as a result of his injuries, but from fright because of how fast you guys took him to the hospital." We all laughed at Norm. He always had to put a little laughter in, because he knew that we were already on our 14th ambulance call that day. With all the other news, some good news came to the 16th Battalion. Lieutenant Bill Alletto was promoted to captain, and on April 1, 1972, he was assigned to Snorkel #3 in Engine #60's house in our Battalion.

I was on watch and it was peaceful and quiet, almost too quiet. A time when a firefighter can look at a book and think about other places. My brother "Boots" is a real fisherman, and he had given me a magazine about the upper peninsula of Michigan. The pictures were beautiful and for a time I was there away from this!

The speaker opened: "Engine #45 - 45 and group. A fire now at 4815 South Drexel." I rang the bell, and down they came, first Norm. "Where are we going Dave?" I gave him the address and out the door we went.

Upon our arrival there were a few people standing outside. There was smoke on the fourth floor. We held hand pumps as we entered through the front door. We just smelled urine, not smoke. There were gang signs all over the entrance walls. "Panthers Run It" and "Free Jeff Fort". Norm was yelling down to us to tell the chief to hold the second units. We had meat on the stove.

Once on the fourth floor all the doors were closed, but the hall was filled with this smoke. There were about six or seven firemen knocking on doors asking if they were cooking. Every one of them said no, it was in 404 because he was always burning something. We banged on the door of 404; no answer. The smoke was very heavy now. I simply can't describe the putrid smell of meat on the stove. Most firemen will tell you that if you get a bad pot of meat, it will make you cough for hours after you are back in the firehouse.

Captain Wilson ordered us to open the door to Apartment 404, before we choked to death. Monk loved kicking doors in and with one big kick the smoke came pouring out of Apartment 404 and into the hallway. The kitchen stove was on fire. Frank Connors and Bummer hit the fire with hand pumps; the rest of the firemen opened windows.

Captain Wilson tried to awaken the cook who was sound asleep on the sofa. In a matter of minutes the fire was out and Wilson told the cook what could have happened, but he didn't care.

Back in the firehouse we all continued to cough from the piercing smoke from "meat on the stove" M.O.S. Most of the guys made their way back up to the bunkroom, while the officers put the run in the journal.

As I was walking up to the front desk to tell Lieutenant Steed that I was still on watch, I could see a cockroach crawling across his back. I yelled, "Lou, get up from your chair, you got a roach on you."

Lieutenant Steed jumped up and pulled off his sweater, and about five roaches fell to the floor. As we stepped on the roaches, I got the shivers and Steed said, "Cosgrove, I hate roaches because it represents one thing: poverty.

It was 04:30 and Bummer came up the front. He said, "Dave, I've got to get some sleep."

Bum had last watch. He picked up my magazine that my brother gave me about fishing. "Hey Dave, what's this about?"

I told Bum that my brother Boots was a fisherman and he was going up to the upper peninsula.

Bum said, "Why don't we go on a fishing trip?"

I said "Okay, when do you want to go to Michigan?"

Well, needless to say, we sat there looking through the magazine and planned a trip in mid-June. We decided to go to the upper peninsula in the Hiawatha National Forest, near Land O'Lakes Michigan. In the following months, Bum had bought a camper that fit on the back of his pickup truck Jack Robin, a firefighter also on Truck #15, said he wanted to join us on the fishing trip. "The more the merrier," we said. We had to make some trade-offs because we were on the same shift.

Bummer told me to get the beer and he would get all the food. I thought that was a good idea because he was the cook at the firehouse and he knew what to buy. We mapped out the way up to the upper peninsula and we set out at about 04:00 hours. We thought the trip would only take about eight hours, but it took twelve hours.

Chief Deneen told us that he knew a guy that lived up there and he found us a place to set up the camper with electricity. When we arrived, we met this guy who showed us where to park. We were tired from the long drive, and just sat around a fire, drank beer, and looked at the stars. The next morning we looked around the area that had been an abandoned camp for boys. We found out that the lake that we parked about ten feet away from was called Moon Lake. All we did was laugh.

I said to Burn, "Hey, where is the food?"

"It's in the cooler," he said.

When I opened the cooler there were three bags of sausage, five pounds of breakfast sausage, five pounds of Italian sausage, five pounds of polish sausage and one loaf of bread. I said, "What the hell is this? I thought you went shopping."

He said, "Dave, all you need are the basics. A little of this and a little of that and a lot of Old Style beer."

We laughed as we prepared breakfast sausage. Bum told me he was over at Engine #60's firehouse there was a firefighter on Snorkel #3 named Andy Kowolski who made the best homemade sausage you could buy. It was all handmade by him and firefighters at Engine # 60's firehouse. "So, I thought this will be good for our trip," he said.

Later that day we went fishing with my brother Boots and my brother-in-law Mike Kirby. We did not catch any sizable fish, but we had a good time just being away from Chicago and the fire-prone southeast side. This was good enough for us.

Sitting around under the starlit sky of the north woods, Jack Robin, Louie Buick, and I talked about how many fires we had responded to in the ghetto. It just seemed like nothing was being done to prevent all the fires. We all felt the same way. Every work day you put your life on the line, fire after fire. But, we were on vacation, and we weren't going to dwell on it, because we still had one more day to fish.

The three days that we fished in the lakes all around us, we never caught any big fish. Bum said, "That's it! I am not going to drive around looking for a lake to fish on when we are parked right here on Moon Lake." He put a night crawler on his hook and sat back.

Jack Robin and I sat at the table by the camper and talked about everything from the fire department to our children. All of the sudden, Bummer yells, "I got one." He had caught a rainbow trout right there on Moon Lake.

Soon after we joined Bum fishing, we caught enough for dinner that night. The long ride back to Chicago brought us back to reality and the end to our fishing trip of 1972. We had a great time, and we will do it again.

On July 18th there was a great picnic in honor of Harry Beilawski and Gene Craven. The picnic was held at Eggerts Grove at 112th and Avenue C. A benefit raffle raised money for the families of the two firefighters and we had a great time.

In late July, there had been so much trouble in the ghetto that police officers were detailed to stay in our firehouse at 4600 Cottage Grove. When we went out of the house, police were assigned to follow Engine #45, Truck #15 and the 16th Battalion buggy to all incidents. The summer months passed with fire bombings and civil disturbances on the east, west, and south sides of the city.

Engine #45's firehouse was located in an area that was always under gang influence. The station was located between the "Black P Stone Nation" territory and the "Disciples" territory. In one week's time, the firemen saw five shootings in the immediate area. Often the wounded were brought to the station for first aid or transportation to the hospitals.

The only thing firefighters on Engine #100 heard was a loud

thud when they were responding to a routine rubbish fire. When they stopped, a gaping bullet hole just below the windshield showed that that they had miraculously escaped death.

In October, Jasper "Rocky" Neal submitted a lay-up report from his doctor because he had become very sick. The next day, an order by the Chicago Fire Department's doctor, Dr. Cari, read that all members of Truck #15 and Engine #45 were to report to 3525 South Michigan Avenue for tests.

We found out that "Rocky" had tuberculosis, which is highly contagious. It is an infectious disease and most commonly affects the respiratory system, and the skin may also become infected. It is caused by a specific bacterium that is usually transmitted from one person to another through the air. The test that was given to each member of our firehouse was what they called the Mantue Test and we also had a chest X-ray.

All relief officers that had been detailed to the house were also called to report for tests. All dishes, pots and pans were thoroughly cleaned, as was the firehouse. Chief Foley from the fire department shops said that all bed pillows and blankets were to be thrown out and new ones would be issued. "Don't throw anything out until we get new bedding," said Wilson. What a way to get new bedding. We were afraid to go home and tell our families, but the word spread fast. By the time we got home, they had already heard the news. It was a very hard time for all of the firefighters.

Sitting by the front desk after dinner, we were all enlightened by the stories that Lieutenant Steed had told us about going out to dinner with his wife. It had been their anniversary and he explained how to stay happily married when you're a fireman. "First thing that you must learn," he said, "is never come home unannounced, because if Momma has a visitor you could ruin a perfectly good marriage. You see a fireman works for twenty-four hours every third day, and if for some reason he was to show up very unexpectedly, there could be trouble."

Lieutenant Alletto said, "You mean if Conioto was in your house. . ."

With a big smile Steed said, "Well, I don't no about no Conioto, but in a black man's term, which I think you're referring to, he is Frankenstein."

We all broke out in laughter. Eddie Steed continued with his story about being out with his wife at a club on the north side. He had everyone's attention including Chief Deneen.

"The dinner was great and we had the best wine in the house. I had reserved a front row table for me and momma in the lounge where the band was playing. It was only a three-piece band with a singer, but they were good. What a wonderful evening. I was drinking Cutty & water and momma was drinking wine. As the band played on, I got a sense that this singer was just singing to my bride, swinging his hips in front of her and looking down from the stage at her. He was singing 'I wanna make love to you.' He didn't even look at me, and I thought to myself, it was nothing.

"I ordered us another round of drinks but he just kept singing to her. When I looked over at her, she had the biggest smile on her face, and was having a grand old time. Now, this is where I had a problem. I knew I had to pee soon, because of the six Cutty and waters that I drank. But, if you think for one moment that I was going to leave her side with, what did you call him Alletto, 'Conioto'? I would have peed in my pants first."

We were all laughing so hard that Bill Alletto was lying on the floor crying in laughter.

The speaker opened, "#45 and the group, a fire now at 4631 South Michigan." We all were still laughing at the story that Lieutenant Steed told as we raced westward on 46th Street. Michigan Avenue is a one-way street south bound, and as we rounded the corner you could smell the wood burning. There was a woman lying on the front lawn with her hair on fire and also her nightgown. We jumped from the truck and Lieutenant Alletto yelled to me to get the hand pump. We were now extinguishing the woman on the lawn. Chief Deneen called for a box. There were people screaming for help. The wind was from the east and blowing right in our faces.

Norm Doolan and Jack Robin took a 30' ladder down the gangway. Wags was raising the 100' aerial ladder to the roof. Firemen Nolan and Connors led out a 2 1/2" line to the second floor. Truck #15 took the second line (3") through the gangway to the rear of the burning structure. Monk spannered in with the 3" line and yelled to the front, "Send the water on the 3" line." Lieutenant Steed yelled down the street to Engineer Morgan to send the water on the 3" line. The back porches were fully engulfed in flames and Monk was waiting for the water on the 3" line. If he got the 3" line charged, a large portion of this fire could be extinguished in the rear of the burning structure. Monk yelled to me, "Dave, tell them to charge the 3" line, God dammit." As I started to run down Michigan Avenue toward Engine #45, I could see the 2 1/2" line filling with water. I yelled as loud as I could, "Send the water on the 3" line." Fred Morgan, the engineer, said, "You want me to charge the 3" line? Okay."

I returned to the rear of the fire building and now Monk and Lieutenant Steed had their water on the 3" line. They were struggling to hold the line, so I jumped over the fence to help. We put a wall hook on the fence and the 3″ line was now putting out a lot of fire. Monk said, "Dave, what took so long to get the water?" I just shrugged my shoulders.

All of the sudden we lost the water on the 3″ line and the fire was now communicating to the next building to the north. I looked down the gangway and there was a wall of water spraying up from our 3″ line. "We burst the line," I told Monk.

I told them to shut down, after running through the wall of water and getting soaking wet. Out in front I yelled to Norm, "We burst our 3″ line, have them shut down."

Norm replied, "I don't have the radio, the chief's got it, Dave." Back down Michigan Avenue I ran to tell the engineer to shut down the 3″ line. It was the second time I had run to the engine to tell the engineer to shut down.

By the time I returned to Monk he was in the alley and the rear porches had collapsed. The fire extended to the building to the north and I was informed that we now had a 3-11 alarm fire. Monk yelled, "What took so long?" I don't know.

The 3″ line was disconnected and the burst length was rolled up. The line went into SS-1, the snorkel squad. Some three hours later we returned to our quarters. The engineer said that he didn't know that the 3″ line had burst. "Someday we might have a radio and we won't have to yell so much."

Lieutenant Steed just laughed. "We won't get radios, we don't even have good hose. Oh well, just get ready for the next one."

October 30, 1972, was a day to be remembered by all the Chicago Firefighters that responded to the Illinois Central train wreck. The call to respond to 27th and Brewery came in at about 08:00 when the shifts were changing. Truck #15 and Engine #45 responded to the 3-11 alarm incident. Upon their arrival on the scene they found two train cars filled with early morning commuters going to work. An older model train had crashed into the rear end of a newer model, double decker train.

After some three and one-half hours of digging through twisted steel with axes, crow bars, porta-power jacks and the K-12 saw, the firefighters removed from the wreckage over eighty-five people. By the end of that day, forty-five people were dead and 120 were injured. The Illinois Central train wreck was one of the deadliest train accidents in Chicago's history. Like always, the firefighters performed the gruesome task of removing all the victims of this terrible crash and returned to their own quarters, only to be called to another incident.

The firefighters were tested again in the early evening of December 8, 1972. Just outside of Midway Airport, a United Airline Boeing 707 slammed into homes on the southwest side. Beneath the twisted wreckage, firefighters worked throughout the night uncovering forty-three dead. The astonishing thing about firemen is their ability to do things that some say is humanly impossible. We were not on duty Christmas Eve or Christmas Day. It was nice to be home with our families for this holiday season.

Finally, we were back in the "garage" as Norm calls it, and it was a good feeling to be back with the guys. Christmas was over and someone wrote on the blackboard: "Santa Sucks." Wags was in a rare mood giving the third shift shit about only having four runs the day before. It was cold outside. The temperature was four degrees above zero and the forecast was to be colder as the day set in on the firehouse.

"Make sure there is rock salt in the hand pumps." Lieutenant Steed said to me. He would be on Truck #15 with a wire from a coat hanger. You would fill a cotton glove with rock salt, tie the wire from the coat hanger around the glove and hang it down into the water of the hand pump. Next you would tie the wire around the handle. This would keep the water from freezing.

Captain Wilson was on his annual furlough and Chief Deneen was on a Daley off. Norm told Bummer, "I will make a pot of soup."

Wags said, "You don't know how to cook!"

Norm Doolan always had something to say and this one was, "Boy, I have been cooking since you have been pissing in your diapers." Bum is the cook and it didn't really matter what Norm or Wags said. He was shopping and he was cooking, end of story.

Wags and I were going to the roof today, so while Bummer went shopping, we checked the rig. If you were going to the roof then you checked to see if there is gasoline in the K-12 saw, you start it, and run the saw for about a minute. We looked at the ladders, axes, pike poles, and the hand pumps to make sure when the bell rang, we were ready. After all the equipment was checked, we cleaned the kitchen before the cook returned, and made our bunks on the second floor.

Before long the cook returned with the groceries. The engine got a run to check a box on 4602 King Drive. Firefighter Armstead was the acting lieutenant of Engine # 45. Firefighter Connors and Firefighter Nolan were on the back step. As the engine pulled out, the cold air reminded us to put on our long johns. Norm called them romance busters, but we still put them on. There was a young fireman from Engine #65 detailed to Truck #15 on this day. In the kitchen, you could smell the chicken soup that was boiling in the pot. Bum was cutting up the vegetables and I asked him what was for lunch. "Hockey pucks and noodles," he replied with a grin.

"They are one of my favorites," I told him.

Even at 4600 Cottage Grove, with soot-covered walls from the exhaust of the fire truck, the great smell of food from the kitchen, mixed with steam from the radiators, made a sort of cozy feeling on a cold ghetto day. Louie Buick had a way of making hamburgers with onions and green peppers blended into them, and a mushroom soup for gravy and large egg noodles with carrots as a vegetable. They were the best and there was always plenty for the guys to have seconds. The engine returned from their run and we ate our lunch.

The sounder clicked out 3-3-3-3. "Attention Department: All Chicago Fire Department firehouses will fly the American and the city flags at half staff in respect to former President Harry Truman, who died today at the age of eighty-eight. He was the 33rd President of the United States."

Norm said, "That's not a bad age to live to."

Wags said, "I could take that age."

The temperature had now dropped to -2 degrees below zero. We had a few runs, but nothing too big. Cliff Armstead said, "Daddy, the Hawk is out tonight."

The firefighter from Engine #65 said, "Who is out tonight?"

Norm repeated, "the hawk."

With a puzzled face the detailed man said, "What is the hawk?"

By this time we had all gathered around to listen to Cliff Armstead explain about the Hawk.

"The Hawk is the cold wind that blows off Lake Michigan and through the ghetto. Up and down the streets and through the gangways," he said in a low voice. "As it gets colder, the Hawk sneaks into the cracks of your house. Even though the heat is on full, you can feel it on your feet when you're sitting in your chair. When you're outside, even if you have a hat and gloves on, you start to feel the Hawk working on your fingertips and your toes."

No one can tell it like Cliff. He has the detailed man, hook, line, and sinker. He continued, "You think the Hawk just affects you? Oh no! He gets everything. You have a car out there?" The fireman nodded his head. "You probably think it is winterized, but it's not, because the Hawk plays hell on engines and batteries. Did you ever see the white spots on a cold engine? Well, that's from the Hawk. And when you try to crank it over and all you hear is ugh, ugh, ugh, then click, click, you're out of service Daddy, because the hawk has got you."

We all laughed when Cliff told the story of the Hawk because he put so much effort into the mystery. That night the wind was so cold you could feel your body shiver just thinking about holding onto a hose line. We all started to head to the bunkroom one by one, but first making sure gloves, boots, and coats were ready for the next run.

In the bunkroom, even though the windows were closed and the shades pulled down, some of the windows had small pieces of newspaper stuffed in the cracks to keep the cold out. We could still feel the cold. With the blankets pulled up around our necks, the only sounds we could hear was the hissing of the radiator and we thought to ourselves, the Hawk, maybe Cliff is right.

At 02:14 the speaker opened, "Engine #45 and the group, a fire." The bells rang, we jumped into our bunker boots and slid the pole. The firefighter on watch yelled out, "4115 South Vincennes Avenue."

As the doors opened and the blast of cold air hit our faces, we started out on to Cottage Grove. Around 43rd we could smell something burning. Wags was waving his hand. "We got a hit."

The temperature was about eleven degrees below zero, and fire was blowing out one window on the second floor of the structure. "Lead out a 2 1/2 inch line." Connors yelled, "and get the hydrant."

There was no one on the street and this was an occupied building. As we started to gain entrance into the front of the building, Engine #45 threw a stream of water up into the fire room, and until this day, I don't know how they got water as fast as they did, but in no time, the fire was darkened. A woman was running around the side of the building and water came spraying down on her. In an instant, her hair turned white. The water froze as it fell all around her. Firefighter Frank Connors said, "Lady, get the hell out of the way, the Hawk is out."

The black lady turned toward us and yelled, "The Hawk's momma is out."

We put the fire out and luckily it was only in the one room. We will never forget the lady or the way she said the Hawk's momma was out, and as cold as it was, we laughed.

After returning back to the firehouse, I thought we really gave that one a hit. Everyone did his job and we put the fire out before the second engine got there. There was a relief battalion chief in the 16th Battalion that night. Norm said that by the time he had his firecoat, helmet and boots on, we had the fire knocked. On the way back to quarters he said to Norm, "That was some good work those guys did at that fire."

"Yes! We have become real good at putting out fires," Norm replied.

We were like a seasoned combat group, and we knew our job. It was about 03:30 and the chief came into the kitchen and said, "Good job guys." That didn't happen often.

Fire blowing out windows on the third floor on a cold night.

Norm told the chief that being with us was like being with Allstate, and he cupped his hands together and said, "You're in good hands."

We all laughed and climbed the twenty-five stairs to the second floor bunkroom.

We closed out the year 1972, without one firefighter being

killed in the line of duty. This was the first year since before the end of World War II that a firefighter was not killed in Chicago in the line of duty.

CHAPTER IX

ON A BITTER cold morning, January 6, 1973, Engines #13 and #42 and Hook and Ladder #3 were given a still alarm to the Forum Cafeteria located at 64 W. Madison Street in downtown Chicago. The firefighters led out lines and, as always, quickly attacked the fire. Everyone said it looked like just another fire. After most of the fire was out, the firefighters went about overhauling and checking the walls and ceilings. Some of the engines were hauling their hose back down the stairs when suddenly, flames erupted on the second floor, quickly burning through a false ceiling. There was a crackling sound and then the roof came in bringing with it a crushing weight of steel, brick and plaster. Firefighters were burned, cut and had smoke inhalation. One firefighter suffered a heart attack, but they were the lucky ones. The search began for the trapped firefighters and in a short time they found the body of Firefighter Timothy Moran of Engine #25. After digging through bricks, the second firefighter was found. Firefighter Richard Kowalzyk of Engine #104 was pronounced dead at the scene. Rev. Father McDonald anointed him. The search continued. There was still one fireman unaccounted for and for the third time, in about two hours, Reverend McDonald was called into the structure. The body of Firefighter Alfred Stach was carried out of the fire building.

On January 10th at Holy Name Cathedral, hundreds of fire-fighters from all over the nation lined the street. Michigan Avenue and Delaware Street were lined with pedestrians and office workers, out for lunch, watched in silence as the caskets were placed on the three American-LaFrance pumpers. The drums took up a slow beat and the beat grew stronger as the procession moved slowly down Michigan Avenue. The mournful sound of the bagpipes could be heard for blocks. The three pumpers came to rest before the steps of the church. The three flag-draped caskets were ever so gently lifted and in a loud voice, Chief Foley called out, "Detail attention." Then, "Detail Salute," and the white-gloved hands of hundreds of firefighters rose to salute their fallen comrades.

In the church, the Reverend Matthew McDonald, who gave the last rites to the three men at the fire scene, said in his sermon, "The choice is not ours. It is true, but if we think it over a little bit we have to come to the conclusion that the best possible circumstance for our death is that we might be doing whatever it is we like to do. Especially if that work involves doing something for our fellow human beings." In the back of the church two fire department buglers sounded taps, first loud and resonant and then softly and subdued.

In the days that followed the funeral of the firefighters, the mood was gloomy. It was a hard time for all firemen. We were looking forward to Super Bowl Sunday. Don Staskon was going to have a party at his tavern. While I was at the party, my mother called me and told me that I had to meet my wife at Christ Hospital. I watched the rest of the Super Bowl in the father's waiting room in the hospital. The Miami Dolphins beat the Washington Redskins by a score of fourteen to seven.

At 03:27 hours, on January 15, 1973, my fifth child was born.

Thomas Michael weighed 6 lbs. 9 oz. When I got into the firehouse the next day, I gave Norm a cigar, and he said, "Dave, another kid?"

I replied proudly, "Yes sir."

Norm said, "Dave, do you know that even Oscar Mayer puts skins on their wieners." We all laughed, but I knew Norm was just kidding.

On January 19th, Truck #15 was called into the shops and when we got there a 1972 Mack, eight-cylinder hook & ladder with the number 15 was sitting off to the side. It had a Macidine engine with a 100 foot, four section aerial ladder, and as a bonus, it had a 150 gallon hale booster pump. We were like kids with a new toy. Some rumors went around that the newly assigned Lieutenant Jerry Power on the second platoon was responsible for the truck. Norm started the rumor.

It was nice to have a new rig, but as I said before, firefighters may ride on a more modern rig, learn new techniques and enjoy shorter hours, and more pay, but they will always live in a world of smoke and flame, falling roofs and collapsing walls. Firefighting is the most dangerous profession.

The sounder clicked out "3-3-3-3 Attention Department" and then an announcement over the speaker, "All Chicago flags and American flags will fly at half-staff in respect to former President Lyndon B. Johnson, who died today in Texas. He was the 36th President of the United States."

Monk said, "Dave, bad time for former Presidents. We don't even have a flag pole. Why tell us to fly a flag at half-staff?"

Norm said, "Hey Monk, take it easy on Johnson, he won the silver star in World War II. He was about sixty-five years old when he died."

Monk said, "How do you know all this shit, Doolan?"

Norm replied "I know everything. If I tell you a chicken eats snuff, look under his wig for the can." Everyone starts laughing.

Chicago has the world's tallest buildings and one of them is the John Hancock Center. It stands 100 stories in height, about 1,100 feet tall. From a distance it looks beautiful, but from a firefighter's eyes, when the firetruck pulls up to the front of the building, it is a nightmare. Especially when a fireman sees smoke pouring out the windows on the 78th floor. Firefighters from Engines #98, #42 and Hook & Ladder #3 experienced this when an arsonist set three fires on various floors of the John Hancock Center.

There is a saying, "it's fireproof", and we, as firefighters, know that's not true. The building's steel is protected by concrete that prevents very high buildings from collapsing when a fire rages inside. Why do you think they put the concrete on the steel? Because a fire is anticipated to occur, that's why.

A fireproof building is nothing more than an excellent furnace. The perfect furnace is also an incinerator for people and firefighters. The basic problem is that once this fireproof building is constructed, it is loaded up with combustible contents. It is not the building's shell that is the problem; it is the contents. People cannot be exposed to fire without harm. This is true of even the best firefighters, although they give it one hell of a try.

These brave men headed into what was an inferno. With 1 1/2" hose packs and forcible entry tools, they rode up to the 75th floor, and then climbed the interior stairway to the fire floor. After connecting the hose to a stairwell standpipe, they entered the 78th floor and took a fearsome beating from the heat and smoke. Firefighters were forced back many times from the furnace-like fire floor.

The fire was located in a plush executive office. Overstuffed furniture, paneled walls, plastic drop ceilings, and thick carpeting, all made for a severe fire. There was so much smoke and heat that firemen crawled on their bellies to get to the fire room. After the fire was extinguished, it took some seventy firefighters three hours to overhaul.

If we learned anything from high-rise fires, it was, get a lot of help as soon as you can, because of the comparatively short time firefighters are able to endure the intense heat and smoke. There will be more high-rise fires. It is only by the accurate determination of the causes of fires in high rise buildings, the reason for their spread, and the use of manpower and firefighting equipment, that knowledge will be obtained which can be intelligently applied in the prevention and control of future similar occurrences.

Mid-February it was still cold outside, but we knew that the sub-zero weather was behind us. Franny Donegan was cooking today, and collected the money for the food. We were sitting around talking to the firemen on the third platoon. They had ten fire calls yesterday, but most were false alarms. One was a 2-11 alarm on Pershing Road and by the time it was extinguished, three buildings had burned. They had a stairway that collapsed in the rear of one building.

There was a note on the blackboard: "dangerous back porches at 244 East Pershing." This was to notify other firefighters to be careful if they went to that address. Uncle Jack said he was going to make pies today, and gave Fireman Donegan a list of a few things he might need.

When this guy made pies, they were the best. He made apple, blueberry, and his famous lemon meringue, in which he used many egg whites. The pies were delicious and he made plenty of them. I used to say to myself, this big strapping man, you just would not think he makes pies.

Norm would often offer to help with the pies. Gallapo would reply, "No you won't, boy." Norm would say, "Boy, it don't say 'boy' on my driver's license." Gallapo said, "It should."

The speaker cracked, "Engine #16 and Truck #15, a fire at 4531 South Michigan." The bell rang and the chief was the first one out the overhead door. The truck started up and you could hear the roar of the diesel engine, but the firemen on Engine #45 were waving their arms because the rig wouldn't start. Oftentimes the starter motor sticks. Everyone ran over and helped push the engine out onto the apron, and with a little momentum, the engineer popped the clutch and the rig started. We jumped back on Truck #15 and were on our way to the fire. Who would believe it?

You could hear Norm's voice on the radio saying that we had smoke showing. With that, we were traveling fast down 46th Street. The sirens were very loud, and if you stuck your head outside, the sound would hurt your ears. Not to say anything about how loud the truck's horns were when Jack Gallapo was pulling the rope. Wilson was the acting chief of the 16th Battalion again, and ordered Engine #45, who even though we had to push start the rig, still beat Engine #16 into their fire, to get a line on the second floor. Up the front stairs we went to the fire floor. Wags threw the 100' aerial ladder to the roof, and you could hear Norm's voice on the speakers on the side of Engine #45's rig: "Battalion #16 to the Englewood. We have a three-story brick building about 50' x 100' with fire on the two; all companies are working. Office stand by," Norm says. Up on the second floor, we waited with an empty 2 1/2" inch hose line, hoping the water would come soon. Gallapo yelled, " Hold the windows punk, until we get water."

The line started to fill and we were on our knees. "Here comes the water #45," someone yelled in the stairway.

Nolan was on the pipe and he cracked open the 1 1/4" inch shut-off pipe. First the air blew out, then the water. A 2 1/2" line on the inside can put out a lot of fire. Gallapo said, "Come on kids, let's hit this, I have to make my pies." We started down the sooty, smoke -filled hallway.

"Get those windows out punk."

I said, "I am."

Gallapo returned with, "Your momma could do better."

As we pulled the ceiling, hot plaster, and wood lathe came crashing down on us. The engine hit it and steam was burning our faces. Gallapo said, "Come on, we have to get this so I can bake my pies."

"Fuck those pies," Monk yelled out.

As we made our way out onto the back porches of the second floor, Wilson was yelling to Wags to hold the roof, because we knocked this fire. Engine #16 washed down behind Engine #45, and Wilson said to pick up. The hose lines were lying in the street and Uncle Jack said, "How about rolling the hose. We will bed it in the fire house."

Norm said, "What do you mean, we? Do you have a mouse in your pocket?"

We all laughed.

Gallapo said, "How about the pies? Your momma is a pie-maker."

We re-bedded the engine and returned to the firehouse.

Fire blowing out the windows, as a fire fighter climbs the aerial to the roof.

Norm said, "I thought we were going to box it, Dave."

Back in the kitchen, Gallapo had flour, sugar, bowls, and everything else spread out on every table. He had his recipes on little pieces of paper all mixed in with all this other shit on the tables. Wags started in about how were we going to eat now with all this shit on the tables. "Well, no pie for you then," Gallapo says.

Wags says, "Stick your pies in your ass Gallapo."

Norm walked in and said, "That was Chief Conte from the 4th Division on the Marshall line. He wants to know what time to pick up his pies."

Now Wags started up again, "Why you suck hole. You mean to tell me that you called the 4th Division and told him you were making pies?"

I should have paid more attention to the way Jack Gallapo made his pies because they were great. We ended the day with twelve runs and ten of them were check the box alarms that were all false.

During the month of March we were called down to the fire academy for our annual physicals. The physical examination consisted of an eye exam, a chest x-ray, and a blood pressure test. As usual, Captain Wilson was the acting chief of the 11th Battalion and Uncle Jack went to the fire academy with Truck #15 on this day.

We had to report to the medical section, and fill out some paperwork. The nurse, Henrietta, was a good nurse, and at the time, was the only female to have a badge on the Chicago Fire Department. There was a black firefighter, Hugh Jackson and he was on Engine #45. He did the eye test, blood pressure test, and weighed you on the scale. If you were overweight, Hugh would take care of that. If your blood pressure was too high, Hugh would take care of that. If you couldn't see well, he took care of that too. The nurse would draw a little blood from your finger and if you wanted, she gave you a small cup of orange juice. Then she gave you another small cup, and you went into the washroom to pee in the cup. When you returned, the nurse would put a stick with some colors on it to see if you had any type of disease. After Gallapo returned from the washroom, he took one of the small cups of orange juice and put one of these sticks into the juice when the nurse was not looking. Then Uncle Jack said, "Henrietta, can I have some juice?

She said, "Yes, Lieutenant."

With that, Jack Gallapo took the juice with the stick and drank it, and the nurse yelled, "Oh no! Not that one! You drank the wrong one!"

We all started to laugh, but Henrietta was not too happy.

After, when we were leaving, she had to laugh to herself, thinking all firemen were nuts!.

We went over to the shops to pick up a new experimental 5' fiberglass pike pole, and new cases for our old chemox mask. Jack Robin said, "They look good in the compartment. Too bad they don't work in a fire."

As the spring of 1973 arrived and the weather got better, I looked forward to my annual furlough of twenty-three days off. Truck #15 had responded to some 500 alarms in the last two and one half months in which there were thirteen still and box alarms, three 2-11 alarms, and a 4-11 alarm.

Our union president, John Tebbens, submitted proposals for improvement in wages and working conditions to Mayor Richard Daley. The mayor recognized the hazardous job of the firefighter. He said we were not nearly compensated for our intense efforts to save the lives and property of all the citizens of Chicago. The union recognized that the city can never fully compensate the fire-fighters during this highly inflationary time, but all we wanted was fair and reasonable compensation. We wanted our longevity and in-step increases and a 5.5 percent increase under the cost of living rule. Firefighters suffered serious and substantial loss of pay during the years of 1972 and 1973.

The mayor of the city of Chicago was recognized for his understanding of the collective bargaining process and his accep-tance of the trade unions. A collective bargaining agreement for all firefighters was necessary to maintain and protect the dignity of our profession.

During the month of May, while I was enjoying my furlough, Sunday morning arrived and the shifts were changing at the fire-house. All of the sudden there was a tremendous roar. The explosion of the Levey Division Plant located at 4250 W. 42nd Street woke hundreds of people in both the city and suburbs. Firefighters were immediately dispatched. As the firefighters rushed to the fire, they had little idea of the fire they were about to extinguish that rainy Sunday morning.

The call went out for more equipment and within minutes the fire was designated a 2-11 alarm. Lead out was the call of the day as fire companies arrived on the scene. The fire grew to a 3-11 alarm, then a 4-11. Engine companies and truck companies came from everywhere, and hose was criss-crossing in a hundred directions. Flames engulfed the L Fish furniture warehouse and also the A&P Food store warehouse. Fire Commissioner Robert Quinn arrived on the scene and pulled a 5-11 alarm.

The flames, whipped by a strong northeast wind, sent smoke billowing some 500 feet into the air. The fire, now a 5-11 alarm with five special alarms, within hours was well under control. Although the ruins smoldered for days, it had been defeated. The best firefighting force in the world, the Chicago firefighters, had beaten the fire that had been described as a "volcano."

In later June, the gas man was looking for Engine #45, because one of the first fire companies that John the gas man took care of, was our firehouse. He wanted to get into the ghetto first thing in the morning and get out as soon as possible. I guess I couldn't blame him; he worked by himself. Jack Gallapo said, "John has been on the gas truck 7-2-2 as long as I can remember."

Well, as I said before, everyone gets a nickname, and even though the gas man was a fireman, his nick name was "Goddam John." Please let me explain how he got his name.

Early in the morning, about 09:00, we had received a fire call to one of the project buildings at 3939 South Lake Park Avenue.

After responding to this address we found that it was a false alarm. John the gas man heard us on the radio in his truck, and tried to call Engine #45. It went like this: "7-2-2 to Engine #45."

Gallapo said on the radio, "Is that you John?"

There was silence for a minute. "7-2-2 to Engine #45."

Gallapo said, "Is that you John?"

Again it happened and Gallapo called, "Is that you John?"

In an instant he yelled back, "Yeah Goddamn it, it's me!" That's why he is Goddamn John. Needless to say we got our gas and many laughs.

July 3rd, 1973, Truck #15 had a new man assigned named Mike Hill, and Engine #45 also got a new man, Tom Cunningham. The two candidates were assigned from the fire academy to the first platoon on Cottage Grove.

All over the ghetto there were gang signs painted on almost everything like the "stones run it" or "the black panthers run it." In the firehouses in the fourth division, some of the guys were organizing baseball games. Each firehouse put a team together for Saturday, July 7th, and Mike Donoghue was kind of in charge of our team. Mike was on the third shift and was assigned to Engine #45 as a firefighter.

Mike Donoghue's nick name was "The Pear" and he insisted on being in charge of running this baseball team. It wasn't easy for "The Pear" because he had many firefighters who opposed him. Namely, Patrick Devine, a firefighter on Truck #15, who worked with "The Pear" on the third shift. The game was played at Boyce Park at 41st and Union. I played for a short time in right field because "The Pear" and I were in the fire academy together. Sixteen-inch softball was a big thing on the south side of Chicago. Most of the guys had played sixteen-inch for years, but the best players were Rich Robin of Truck #15 and also his brother, Jack, of Truck #15. So, we had a very good team, and The Pear took the credit for organizing it. The third shift started painting slogans all over the ghetto: "The Pear runs it" like the gang slogans that are all over the ghetto, e.g. "the Stones run it," meaning the street gang called the Blackstone Rangers.

The phone company was installing a new pole behind the firehouse and at the top of the pole, the firemen wrote "The Pear runs it" in white paint. The slogan was now in all the elevators of the projects over the top of all the swear words and gang slogans. The gangs were probably wondering who the fuck The Pear was.

One night we had an incinerator fire at 4445 South Evans. While we were going up to the fire floor in the elevator, two guys from the projects said to each other, "Who's The Pear anyway?" We all laughed just to think that The Pear was famous throughout the ghetto. The summer was busy as usual, but one night in July, Truck #15 and the 16th Battalion were given a special duty alarm to assist the police at 4921 South Dr. Martin Luther King Drive. I never liked a call where we had to assist the police, because they always had something bad. This call was no exception. It was a hot night about 20:45 hours and we reported to Chief Murphy at the scene.

The 2nd District police officers informed Chief Murphy that the other tenants had not seen the woman who occupied the apartment on the second floor around the building for about three weeks.

After noticing a very distinct odor emanating from her apartment, they called the police. From the look on Captain Wilson's face, I knew this wasn't going to be good. He said, "I want a 30' ladder to that window on the second floor. I need a volunteer."

I asked Captain Wilson what he wanted me to volunteer for.

"There is no rush," Wilson said, Let's get you fitted in a chemox mask."

The chemox mask, otherwise known as the filter or canister mask, had a face piece with a rubber hose that connected to a canister that filtered out particles of smoke. The canister was used until it was hot indicating that it was expired. The chemox did not filter out a number of harmful and toxic gases and probably would not be much good on this incident. But like Wilson said, it was all we had and it was better than no mask.

As I climbed the ladder to the second floor window, I could hear Captain Wilson yelling to me not to break the window. "Try to force it open with your axe, and ventilate the apartment. Then open the hall door." The window to the apartment was not locked. With the blade of my axe, I forced open the bottom sash. I put my axe through the window and followed one leg at a time. The chemox mask was very cumbersome while trying to get inside the apartment. Once inside, I knew in an instant that the body of the missing woman was somewhere in this apartment. The smell was atrocious and was taking my breath away even with the chemox mask. I knew that all I had to do was find the door and I was out of this mess. I turned on my light, because it was dark, and I made my way through the first room. I tried to keep calm, and breathe slowly. I kept telling myself to calm down as I walk into the next room.

The first thing I spotted was a door that appeared to be the one that led out into the hallway. As I crossed the room toward the hallway door, there appeared to be some type of light to my left side. I shone my flashlight over in that direction, but my vision was blurred because of condensation on the mask lens. I stepped a little closer to the light. My curiosity got the best of me and I reached for the light. All of the sudden, hundreds, maybe thousands of flies came off the lamp shade. I jumped back. Flying insects were now bouncing off my face piece, neck, and arms. I had gloves, firecoat, and my hip boots on, and I knew I had to get out of this room. When all the flies came off the lampshade, the whole room lit up. There, right in front of me lying on a sofa, was the missing woman. Her face was eaten away. She was slumped over with her arm hanging down toward the floor. She was a big woman anyway, but now swollen to almost twice her size.

In front of her, on the floor between the sofa and a coffee table, was her dog. Most of the side of the German Shepherd's face and head were eaten away by the flies. I worked my way across the room to the doorway trying not to vomit into the chemox mask that did not work. Once in the hallway, the flies were all over me. As I hand-signaled to everyone in the stairway that I was going outside now, they cleared my path. I ripped the face piece off my head and was gasping for air. The fetid smell from the apartment filled the staircase. Once I caught my breath, I explained to Wilson and the other firemen what was up there.

We ventilated each window of the second floor apartment from the outside. If the window wouldn't open, then we broke the glass. The police went over to Provident Hospital for masks to cover our faces. They also brought back twelve cans of spray disinfectant to spray the apartment.

We got two salvage covers from the rig and unfolded them. The covers are twelve feet by fourteen feet. We moved the coffee table, and other furniture from the room and spread the cover on the floor in front of the sofa. With the shovels and pike poles we carefully removed the German Shepherd from the apartment.

With two salvage covers thrown in front of the sofa, we tipped the sofa over onto the covers, and the woman fell right on the floor. The sofa was set to the side and we wrapped her up and brought her down the stairs. It took all the police and firemen to complete the task. She was placed in the police wagon and transported to the Cook County Morgue. That smell stayed with me for days, and I ended up throwing my firecoat away. This was for sure one of the worst experiences I ever had as a firefighter. Mike Hill had just been introduced as a candidate to his first dead person.

As the summer months passed by, the fires still raged on without any change. There was no fire prevention in the ghettos of Chicago. We responded to each fire and did our job. We rescued, extinguished, re-bedded the hose, and cleaned our tools for the next fire. At each fire we got better at our job, and many times the chiefs would say, "Good job #45 and Truck #15, you made one hell of a stop." We knew what each other was doing at the fire. We worked as a disciplined team. Wags would raise the aerial ladder to the roof while the engine was leading out the hose. I would go in the front with the engine while Jack Robin was getting the K-12 saw. Franny Donegan would ventilate the back of the building. There was pride in this firehouse. In order to be the pipeman on Engine #45, on the first shift, you had to hang your firecoat on the hard suction. The first man into the firehouse, that had his coat on the suction was the pipeman. There were days when they would get in at 06:00 hours just to be the pipeman.

We had trust in each other and there was a bond. I am sure that other firehouses felt the same, but in 1973, we didn't know that any other firehouses in the city were as busy as ours.

We had no special equipment, just rubber hip boots, rubber coats (that in the summer was as hot and uncomfortable as being fully dressed in a steam room), and a 3 1/2 pound leather helmet. Engine companies went into the fire, took as much smoke as they could, then backed out, and many times were carried out.

Just like the infantry, the firefighters's job would always involve hand labor. Maybe someday, industry will come up with a robot that can crawl around a smoke-filled apartment looking under beds and opening closets. Maybe there will be an automated gadget that can take a hose up a twisting staircase, force a door open, then open the pipe on the floor. How about a machine that will raise a ladder, and wrestle a hysterical woman out of the second floor window. They will never replace the infantry we know as the firefighter.

After roll call in August, we responded to a fire in one of the many abandoned buildings in our district. This one was located at 435 East 45th Place. We could hear Norm's voice reporting to the Englewood Fire Alarm Office that we had smoke showing in a vacant structure. As we arrived on the scene, fire and smoke were issuing from the second floor window on the north side. Engine #45 led out a 1 1/2 inch line up the front, and as they entered the building, the front stairs collapsed from under them, and Frank Connors almost went through the floor.

There had been many fires in this building, and today a couple of firemen almost got killed. We raised a 30' ladder to the second floor and the engine extinguished not one, but three fires all in separate rooms.

It appeared to be some type of set-up booby trap that the stairs just fell in when we entered the structure. When we returned to the firehouse, Captain Wilson said, "Get the housework done, because we are going to have a drill on operating in vacant buildings."

As we gathered around the table behind the hook and ladder with our coffee and cigarettes, Captain Wilson related to us the special hazards of these types of structures. Namely the one we were just in on 45th Place.

"I think it was a fire set by derelicts and vandals or perhaps someone who resented any type of public authority and tried to hurt firemen," Wilson said. "Why, I don't know. So, we will begin not to enter as fast as we have been. If a stairway feels weak, don't trust it. Wait for a ladder. Truckmen use your tools to test the step in front of you. Watch out for holes in floors, they are everywhere.

Here again, your sense of smell is important. If you smell anything similar to the odor of gasoline, get your asses outside.

"Lead out. Don't go back in without a charged line. The accelerant may be spread all over and ignite instantaneously and trap you in a room. You guys that are working on roofs everyday be careful on vacant buildings, there may be holes from other fires, and don't walk backwards. Don't get hurt. That was a close call this morning."

Norm said, "Hey Captain, you could get a job on Squad #51 on TV. They just had a special on a vacant building fire on the TV show Emergency. They put it on film."

"That's not what we do," Wilson said.

The Monk yells to Norm, "You don't really watch that shit on the television, do you?"

Norm replied, "No, I just heard about the show from my kid."

"Yeah ,right." Wilson said as he walks to the front of the firehouse. We all started to laugh about Norm, but Wilson was a serious as a heart attack about the many abandoned buildings in our district.

The third shift had a still and box on Bowen Avenue and three kids died. It just seemed like little children were always the ones who didn't get out of a fire. The National Fire Protection Association, NFPA stated that 11,900 people died in fires in 1972. The tragic part about it was that more than half of these deaths occurred in dwellings. The article also stated that a high percentage of the toll was represented by children. The United States went into Southeast Asia in January 1, 1961, and up until October 7, 1972, 45,882 men and women of the military died serving their country, and another 153,206 were wounded. In this same time period civilian fire deaths totaled approximately 144,000 and injuries from fires were almost 3,500,000. What attention did the fire victims receive? What attention did the firefighter get? None, but the forces against crime always get beefed up. Whenever there is a bad crime, the city says to get more police and not to worry about the cost.

Yet, the deaths and injuries occurring from crime don't even remotely approach those from fire. Firemen don't get shit. Never did . . . and probably never will!

As a killer of children, fire ranks higher than many well funded diseases. The tragic loss of life from fire exceeds by four times the deaths inflicted by polio. We became excited when we conquered polio. We must become excited about fire, because it too can be conquered, and we will never have to write the atrocious numbers down again of children that die in dwelling fires, year after year.

The bell rang. We had to check the box at 4445 S. Drexel at about 14:30 hours. Someone made a pot of coffee and we sat around talking. Through the rear door, one of the regular neighborhood gents stopped to sell us some used pants. He was a tall, black man about sixty years old. He said that the pants were fifty cents a pair and showed off the old and dirty pants to everyone sitting at the table. Most of the guys that were sitting there said, "No thanks." Then Rich Wagner stood up and put one pair up to his waist. He said they were nice pants and with that handed the black man $1.00. One dollar for two pairs of old pants. We knew that he was up to something. He reached down into the pocket of the pants and pulled out a wad of money. All you could see was the whites of this poor, black man's eyes. He immediately asked for the pants back. Wags said, "No, no, these are my pants. I just gave one dollar for them."

The old man was now pleading with Wags and said that he would split the money half and half. We were all laughing as Wags kept tormenting the old man. It took Wags about one hour before he could make the old man realize that the money was his and he was just playing a joke. Wags liked to kid around and did it a lot. Especially to the fire fans that rode the engine.

FIRE FANS

Fire fans have been around for a long, long time. Many firehouses around the city have had fire fans.

A fire fan or buff, is someone who is especially attracted to the fire service culture. Some are great people who are helpful and good friends to the firefighters. Others however, can be a real pain in the ass, and carry stories that are mostly untrue, and there have been a few fans that have been known to be fire setters. In Engine #45's firehouse we had good fire fans that were young and strong, namely Mike Fox and Bobby Hoff, who were fans of Truck #15 on the third platoon. Mike Fox's father was the captain of Engine #45 at the time, and was a good fireman, who was highly respected by all of the firefighters in our house. Bob Hoff's brother was a fire-fighter on Truck #15 on the third platoon. Ray Hoff was a good fireman and taught his younger brother to also be a good fire-fighter like their father.

Battalion Chief Thomas Hoff was killed in the line of duty on February 14, 1962, with Chief Robert O'Brien of the Fire Prevention Bureau, while working at an extra alarm fire located at 1365 E. 70th Street, when the building suddenly collapsed. We had a fire fan on the third platoon, William Phillips, who was nicknamed "No Jaw" because when he was a boy he was hit by a coal truck, and as a result had lost most of his jawbone. William Phillips was a twenty-year-old black man, and a very devoted fire fan who was helpful during fires and also around the firehouse. There was many incidents around the firehouse that "No Jaw" had been involved in, but the one that stuck in my mind the most was when he owned a black Cadillac. During the funeral proces-sion of Jim Ward, several firefighters were in No Jaws car, and he told us that he was almost out of gas. With that he turned out of the procession and into the gas station at 111th & Cicero Avenue. I think Rich Wagner told him that if we missed any part of the cer-emony at the cemetery that he would kill him.

No Jaw jumped from the car, put two dollars worth of gas in the Cadillac and we caught up with the procession just as they were turning into the cemetery. It would have been awfully embarrassing that part of the honor guard was missing because we had to stop for gas! At the time, it was serious, but afterwards we had many laughs about No Jaw running out of gas.

Probably one of the most interesting things that happened involving a fire fan was the day we met Bob Josefson, a fan that rode on Squad #3 in Engine #61's firehouse, when Squad #3 was in service a few years ago. It was said that Bob Josefson was in the undertaker business in one of the southwest suburbs.

One afternoon in November, in the back of our firehouse on Cottage Grove, Bob Josefson explained to us that he had an idea that could make us a lot of money. We all gathered around the table behind the Hook and Ladder #15 drinking coffee and listening to this new deal. Bob Josefson stated that in the business of undertakers, funeral homes, and caskets, there was a growing need for the protection of caskets that were being transported on airplanes from one state to another. Caskets that were being loaded onto airplanes with the remains of someone inside, were being scratched and dented. The cost of the loss was becoming enormous, not to say anything about how the family felt when they received the scratched or dented casket at the airport with their loved one inside.

Norm looked at me and his eyes were wide open. "Dave, this is it! We will be rich!" As Josefson continued to explain that he couldn't do this by himself, but with some investors, and some special help, we could build an "air-tray" with a cover to protect the casket from being damaged.

Well after talking it over for a short while, the members of Engine #45 and Truck #15 were now in this new business of making "air-trays." On November 30, 1973, we all bought ten shares of a new company called "Fliteline Caskets."

Bob Josefson had us hook, line, and sinker. He rented a storefront on the northwest side near O'Hare International Airport. Soon we were making "air-trays" and believe it or not, they were selling. Only a few guys were doing all the work. Namely Wags, but Josefson wanted more. He rented a showroom on South Ashland Avenue, and purchased about twenty-five steel caskets to sell to undertakers. This was the downfall of "Flightline Casket Co.", and our new company was bankrupt by late February. It was a good idea for a while, and we only lost $30.00. and some of our valuable off-duty time. One of the most memorable things that happened to our casket business was on February 14th, St. Valentines Day. A few of the boys as a joke, delivered a casket to Louie Buick's house and set it up in the living room. It took many years for his wife Lorretta to forgive him for this sick joke, that he wasn't even involved with. All firemen are very unique, but a casket company, that takes the cake, I think!

In late November, there were rumors that Commissioner Quinn did not like the officers getting so close to the firemen. We heard that all the officers were going to switch shifts. Captain Alletto was detailed to Truck #15 for the day. We had a good day with only about five runs. Two were fires, and a couple check the box false alarms. I had second watch and about 03:15, I was relieved by Fireman Armstead. The Marshal line rang on the joker stand, and it was the Captain of Truck #11 at 35th and Calumet Avenue. He related to Cliff Armstead that the chief had missed a run to 4120 S. Prairie Avenue and an elevator was stuck with people. Cliff thanked the captain and rang the bell two times for the chief. Norm was first down, and Cliff told Norm that they had an elevator with Truck #11. The Chief went out the door with lights and siren, but Truck #11 had already returned from 4120 S. Prairie. Cliff had misunderstood the captain of Truck #11 and sent the chief out on the run.

In the meantime the speaker opened and gave Engine #45 an auto fire at 39th and Vincennes Avenue. Norm and Chief Deneen were now waiting for Truck #11 to arrive at 4120 South Prairie. Engine #45 was now returning from the auto fire, and discovered a raging fire at 323 E. 43rd Street. Lieutenant Steed was screaming over the radio for a full still, and trying to tell the Englewood Fire Alarm Office that they had two stores fully involved in fire! The office now told Truck #15 to respond to the fire at 323 E. 43rd Street. Norm and the chief were still waiting for Truck #11. Upon our arrival on the scene, Engine #45 had two big hose lines on the fire and they were sitting in the middle of 43rd Street on the double yellow line. Captain Alletto and I climbed a 26′ foot ladder to the roof of the store next to the fire building. Captain Alletto looked the scene over and ordered me to tell Lieutenant Steed to get a box. I was yelling at the top of my voice, because we didn't have a radio. "Lou, Lou, get a box." He was shaking his head no.

I climbed down the ladder to the street below and ran up to Steed. "Get a box."

He said, "No, that's the Chief's job."

I turned and looked up at Alletto. "He said 'no, its the chief's job.' "

All this time, Norm and the chief were waiting for Truck #11. Alletto raced down the ladder and said, "Eddie, get a box, we need help."

"No, no, that's the chief's job to pull a box."

Captain Alletto jumped into the front seat of Truck #15 and yelled into the radio: "Englewood, this is Truck #15. Emergency! Give us a box!"

Now Norm and Chief Deneen g0t to the fire and ordered a 2-11 alarm, followed by a 3-11 alarm. on the Chicago Fire Department it is a courtesy to wait until the chief is on the scene to order the extra alarm, but in this case he didn't know that the chief wasn't responding. Talk about getting your wires crossed up. We were at the fire until 08:00 hours and were relieved by the second shift. From that time on they nicknamed Lieutenant Steed "C.J." or Chief's Job.

Winter was settling in again, and I surely wasn't looking forward to the cold weather. The day started out with a fire early in the morning, and then one after the next. We had about ten runs. Three of the runs were working fires. At 20:40 the office opened the speaker again. "Engine #45 and the group, you now have a fire at 811 East 43rd Street." The bell rang as the firefighters ran to get their gear on and the overhead doors open. As we approached the intersection at 43rd and Cottage Grove, heavy smoke filled the area. We had a hit! The wind was blowing from the northeast, and the smoke was so dense that the flashing lights could hardly be seen. People were now running in the street calling for help. Captain Wilson ordered us to get ground ladders to the second floor where people were hanging out the windows of the burning building. Some ten citizens were removed down ladders and Engine #45 led out their 2 1/2" hose line into the structure. Wags raised the aerial ladder to the roof.

As I unlocked the box where the K-12 saw was kept on the truck, you could hear Norm requesting a still and box alarm for more help. With the K-12 saw, an axe, and a pike pole I started to climb the 100' aerial ladder to the roof the three-story building. The smoke obscured the top of the ladder over the coping of the building, and on the roof I carefully walked toward the skylight. I knew if I could get the glass of the skylight knocked out, then the smoke in the stairway would lift out and rescues of trapped victims would be made a little easier. Thrashing through the glass with my axe, the smoke and heat billowed from the stairway. Wags was at my side yelling, "Where is the saw, Cos? I will start the hole while you pull the wainscot." The roof area was very large and Wags disappeared from view. Soon I could hear the sound of the saw cutting through the heavy, tar-coated flat roof. It was very hard to breathe because of the smoke, but I knew that if I got to the edge of the roof, I could get a clean breath of air.

Finally the wind blew in a different direction, and I made it to the coping on the east side of the roof. Looking down at the street, there were fire engines and hook & ladders everywhere. Wags yelled over the sound of the saw, "Get the top cut."

With my axe I swung as hard as I could through the thick roofing material. I was exhausted. I'm not sure how long we had been working at this fire, but it seemed like a week. Wags put the saw to the side, and gets his axe. The stripping ladder was in the shops for repair, so we had to pull this one with the picks of our axes. Wags put the hole right over the fire. The perfect spot, but dangerous to us if we didn't get out of the way. As we pulled back the roofing, and the 1" x 8" wooden boards, the smoke and heat billowed up into the clear night sky. Wags yelled, "Let's push the ceiling down with the 1" x 8" boards."

Down on one knee I pushed the ceiling of plaster and lath down into the fire room below. The fire, smoke and hot gases blew straight up and into my face.

I fell backwards grasping my throat. I could not catch my breath. I crawled away from the now burning 4' x 4' hole in the roof. Wags came to my side. "Are you alright?" I was choking and I thought my face was burned. Wags helped me to the aerial ladder. He knew I was hurt.

Slowly, I descended down the ladder to the ground. Captain Wilson saw that something was wrong. He rushed to my side, and helped me off the turntable of the hook & ladder. Wags was on the ground, and told the captain what had happened on the roof. "Get an ambulance," Wilson told Norm, "Cosgrove is hurt."

I was moved in Chicago Fire Department Ambulance #35, to Billings Hospital at the University of Chicago. I was diagnosed with heat and smoke inhalation and remained in the hospital the rest of the night. I was laid up for about six days before returning to duty.

It was one hell of an experience and a very close call. The end of 1973 came to a close, but the month of December went out with a bang with many extra alarm fires.

Within the year of 1973, four firefighters died in the line of duty.

Chapter X

ALSO, THE RUMOR was true about the officers changing shifts. Captain Wilson and Lieutenant Steed went to the third shift. Lieutenants Jerry Power and Ed Rickert were now on the first shift. Getting used to the new officers was not as bad as we thought.

Both Rickert and Power were good firefighters, and knew the job. Captain Fox was promoted to chief, and the new captain of Engine #45 was Dick Scheidt. The winter was hard on the equipment. The overhead doors were broken and had to be raised by hand for two weeks. The engine was out of service several times for various reasons, but mainly because it is old. It seemed like every day hoses were bursting at fires. Everyone just went along with what we had to work with and did the best they could. Lieutenant Rickert was a stickler about housework. The brass was always done, and so were the windows on window day. We had worked with Rickert about five working days in January before we got a hit.

We had small fires, but only hand pumps and the hard line were used to extinguish them. Bummer said to me, "This guy Rickert is nuts. He is always running around. He won't get into an elevator in the project because he got stuck in one for an hour.

Now he runs up the stairs and I can't keep up with him."

One day in mid-January, after about eight runs, we were watching TV in the kitchen after dinner. The speaker cracked, "Engine #45 and the group, there is a fire at 550 East 51st Street."

As we pulled up to the scene, nothing was showing, but there were people outside. "Get the pumps," Lieutenant Power yelled.

As we climbed the stairs with our hand pumps to the third floor, there was smoke and it was pretty heavy. We were still on the stairs just starting to crawl into the smoke with the hand pumps when all of the sudden you could hear Rickert yelling, "Lead out, lead out!" Bummer was next to me and there were maybe three guys behind us. The next thing, I felt someone banging into me, and then he was gone.

As we started to back out, we could hear Rickert yell, "Lead out!" But now he was down on the second floor.
Bummer looked at me and said, "Dave, wasn't he in front of us?"

We both started to laugh and Bummer said, "I think he ran over my back."

The next thing we saw was Fireman Cunningham, whose nickname was now "the Waterhead" and Dad Rickert coming back up the stairway with the 1 1/2" hose line. The fire was in the rear of the third floor apartment. Chief Deneen pulled a box on the fire, and we pulled the ceilings on the third floor and opened the roof. We had the fire extinguished in about two hours. Back in the firehouse, Bummer asked Dad Rickert, "How the hell did you get past me, and then back up the stairs with the line?"

Rickert said, "We had to lead out, and you were holding Cosgrove's hand in the hallway, so I went around you."

Bummer said "No, no, you went over the top of us!"

We all started laughing.

Norm came into the kitchen and told us we had two details the next day. One detail to Engine #39 and the other one was to Truck #8. He said to check the detail card and Fireman Donegan said, "I already did."

Jim Nolan took Engine #39 and I went to Truck #8. The first shift was heavy with manpower, and we had two details every day. If the detail card showed you were up for the detail, no questions asked, you took the detail. Although no one wanted to be detailed out, because they were afraid they would miss something, we went anyway.

Truck Company #8 was located at 2534 South Throop Street, just southwest of downtown. This firehouse was one of the newer houses. It was in a nice area with good parking. The firehouse was the headquarters of the 21st Battalion. The firehouse had Engine #28, Truck #8, Ambulance #19, and the chief's buggy. There was a big kitchen, a large bunkroom with plenty of beds, a handball court, and a steam room. This was a country club, I thought to myself. As the day passed, I looked around at the extra equipment.

There was a full change of hose hanging in the hose tower, and maybe ten lengths of hose rolled neatly on a hose rack. There were extra axes in a storeroom. Why did they have all this extra equipment? Engine #45 had just enough hose to complete the amount needed to bed the engine, with maybe a few extra lengths to spare.

Engine #28 and Truck #8 were not very busy, but when they did have a fire, it was usually a big one. Their district had some industrial buildings, as well as commercial and residential areas, with a lot of old multi-dwelling and three-story buildings.

As the months went by, big changes were happening on the

Chicago Fire Department. The officers changing shifts was the first major thing. Then an order came out that there would be no more trading of Daley Offs. If a day off was needed there were two options: take a day off and have your pay docked (a firefighter's pay for one day was $134.00), or you could forfeit three days of your furlough. The fire commissioner said the men were abusing the trade-offs, but I think they were cutting back the manpower and saving money.

In late February, we received some brand new fire hose (yellow). They said it was experimental hose. It was lighter in weight than the hose that we were using now. The couplings were made of some type of magnesium, and supposedly were stronger than brass couplings. Well in no time we found out that this hose was lighter, but when leading out in a stairway all it did was kink up when the engineer sent the water.

At one fire on the third floor, the engine started to advance the line, and a kink in the yellow hose on the second floor landing occurred. There were three firefighters who had to bail out of the third floor window because the kinks caused it to burst. From that time on, Captain Scheidt said, "Keep that yellow shit out of the stairways, because all it does is kink up on the inside of buildings and there's a good chance it will burst.".

I was now in my sixth year on the Chicago Fire Department, and it seemed like a very long time ago since that first day I entered into the fire academy as a candidate. With all the fires, I now considered myself a seasoned veteran firefighter.

I have stood as an honor guard at attention next to the caskets of my friends. I have made the funerals of many fallen comrades. There were days that I asked myself why I was in this hazardous occupation, especially when the city takes firefighters for granted by freezing their pay and stopping pay grade advancement. I had been in the ceramic tile trade, and it was a good profession. The most hazardous part of being a tilesetter was getting hit on the head from a falling piece of ceramic tile that I had installed on the ceiling in a bathtub area. The answer to my question was a simple one: I just loved being a firefighter. The work was hard, dirty, and often times thankless, but when you carried the lifeless body of a child to safety and they were revived, the reward was much greater than money. There was a feeling of great satisfaction1

Sunday in the firehouse was always a good day because there were usually no big housework projects like the brass or windows. We did the basic housecleaning like the kitchen, the rigs, and made up our beds. Bummer was cooking and he was making Sunday breakfast. The usual bacon, sausage, hash brown potatoes, and eggs. There was plenty of coffee, and for dinner we were having turkey with dressing, and mashed potatoes with gravy. As the day went along we had a few runs, but sometime in the afternoon we had a chance to read or take a nap. The Chicago Bears were playing the Packers on TV, which also helped make the long twenty-four hours go a little faster. We drew for watches and I got second watch. Although it was the longest watch, or just seemed to be, it was 03:15 and I woke Fireman Hill to relieve me. I told Mike Hill that all was quiet and started up the stairs when the speaker opened: "Engine #45, Truck #15 there is a fire now at 4615 South Ellis.

I yelled at Mike, You are a bum luck S.O.B. I sat here all night without a call and you're not down here two minutes and we get a run."

We were out the door in less than two minutes. Norm and the chief were on the scene and reported a working fire in an occupied three-story building. Lieutenant Power ordered us to open the roof, and Wags started raising the main ladder to the roof while I pulled the outriggers out on each side of the rig. Mike Hill and Franny Donegan started raising ground ladders. Dad Rickert came running out of the burning structure and said, "We have fire on the first and second floor."

Chief Deneen called the office and requested a still and box alarm. The fire was burning in the basement and throughout the first and second floor. We definitely needed help. There were people in their nightclothes running out into the winter cold. Chief Deneen ordered a 2-11 alarm as Wags and I worked at getting a hole in the roof. Some twelve people were taken down ladders, as we started to make progress and brought this fire under control. After getting back down from the roof Wags told me that they took one woman out of the third floor. She was badly burned and didn't make it. We took our tools, axes, and pike poles into the building to pull the lath and plaster. The noise inside a fire building was incredible. Firemen were yelling, cursing, chopping walls, breaking windows, and the water was pouring throughout the building. After some two hours, we were ordered to pick up by the chief. After putting all the tools and the ladders away, it was time for a smoke, but all my cigarettes were soaking wet. I knew Norm always had dry cigarettes. I said, "Hey Norm, how about a dry one."

"Sure Dave." As he extended his package toward me, Wags jumped in and grabbed one too. We were sitting on the front of the chief's car looking at the burned out structure. When a Chicago Police Officer approached us and starts asking questions about how the fire started. This was when Norm was at his best. The officer said, "Do you have a cause for the fire?"

Norm replied, "Yeah, mice with matches."

The cop looked at us and started laughing. He started to walk away shaking his head and saying, "You guys are nuts."

Norm said, "The guy who lived in the basement apartment fell asleep with a cigarette and when he awoke, the bed was on fire. He was burned on his arm and a little on his face, but he will be alright."

The cop said ,"Did you get his name?"

Norm said, "No, but Ambulance #38 transported him to Michael Reese Hospital."

The cop now asked Norm, "You don't know what his occupation was, do you?"

Norm said, "Yeah, he was a test pilot for the "Mogen David Wine Company."

We all started laughing, and the cop just shook his head and said, "I should never have asked that question."

We picked up the hose and returned to the firehouse just in time to go home. I was looking forward to seeing my friends tonight. Every two weeks throughout the baseball season, I met with the "BULLS." This was our baseball club. We played fantasy baseball, had a few cold ones and talked about whomever was not there that night. I could forget about fires for a while on those nights.

Another big change was the election of our new Local #2 Union President, Bernard McKay. After a run-off election, McKay beat John Tebbens in a close race. Uncle Jack won his election and now was the union's 2nd vice president. Upon entering office, President Bernard McKay retired from the fire department for age and service because his campaign promise was to devote all of his time to his union duties..

When they got a fire in the Loop in a big building, it usually ended up to be a big fire. Loop traffic was totally stopped in all directions when fire broke out in a ten-story structure. The 5-11 and one special alarm tied the entire Loop for hours in late March. There were many tired firefighters that were relieved the next day by the oncoming platoon. Once again, the Chicago firefighters had effectively demonstrated how to battle a large building fire and come away from it a winner. Fire Commissioner Quinn, as usual, was right in the thick of the battle. No question about it!

A newspaper article about fires and fire deaths in Chicago had come up with startling conclusions. It stated that Chicago's fire death rate was one of the highest in the nation. Economy cuts in firefighter manpower and the number of men assigned to engine companies and truck companies had reduced the department's effectiveness in saving lives and property in the city of Chicago.

The Fire Prevention Bureau did very little to educate the most likely victims of fire, especially the black and Latinos from the ghetto. Reporters asked Fire Commissioner Robert J. Quinn about the assertions and the fires in Chicago's ghettos. Quinn said, "We don't have any ghettos or slums. All the people live pretty nicely in Chicago."

The truth of the matter was that a significant number of people who live in ghettos live below the poverty level. The buildings are overcrowded and are deteriorating. The winters are long and cold, and the heat must be turned up high. People live in buildings where double-locked doors and boarded-up windows are standard personal security equipment. The article made it very clear, the fault was not with Chicago's hard working and dedicated firemen. It appeared to lie with an uninformed leadership that worked harder to cover up or deny its failures, than to improve Chicago's record at saving citizens lives. In August, Norm said, "If you think you got trouble, how would you like to be in President Nixon's shoes?"

It seemed that some of Nixon's boys on a committee to re-elect the president were found to have broken into the Democratic National Committee offices during the 1972 campaign. Nixon said, "My fellow Americans, I deny ever having any involvement with the break in." But, those darn tapes, in fact, indicated that he tried to divert the investigation. Faced with what seemed almost certain impeachment, Nixon resigned as president on August 9, 1974.

Norm said, "You mess with the bull, you'll get the horns".

In November, Firefighter Patrick Devine on the third platoon, asked me if I could come in early to relieve him on November 16th. He said he was going out of town with his family. I told him if it was okay with Lieutenant Healy, because protocol mandates that you should have permission from your company's officer.

The time was approved and I came in at 04:00 hours. Pat was waiting at the door and said, "Thanks Cos, I owe you."

I said, "Get going, we will talk when you get back."

The firehouse was dark and the only one awake was the engineer, Bill Marshal. He said, "That was nice of you Cos, to come in early for Devine. How about some coffee?"

I said, "I'll have a cup."

As the engineer made a fresh pot, I put my gear on the right side of the rig and checked the hand pump out of habit.

Bill Marshal was a big, black man that lived in the Kenwood Community, a few blocks away from the firehouse. Rumor had it that he helped a lot of people who were down on their luck. As we drank our coffee, and talked about the fire department, it was just starting to get light outside. All of the sudden, there was banging on the overhead door in the front of the firehouse. We jumped from the table and ran toward the front. A black man was yelling about a fire and pointing in a northeast direction. As we looked, we could see smoke over the roofs of the buildings in the ghetto. Marshall said, "Cos, we got a hit." He then raised the overhead door.

I grabbed the Marshal line on the joker stand and dialed the office. I told the Englewood Fire Alarm Office that Engine #45 - Truck #15 had a fire somewhere in the 4500 block of Drexel Avenue. We rang the bell and were out of the firehouse in a minute. You could see the black column of smoke rising up into the new morning sky as we arrived on the scene at 4538 South Drexel Avenue.

Fire was blowing out of the third floor window of a U-shaped building. Standing out in front was the man that was pounding on the door of the firehouse, yelling to us that his kids were up there. Lieutenant Healy ordered Firefighter Rich Robin and me to try to get into the building. With our axes in hand, we entered the court-yard to the front stairs leading up to the third floor. Robin and I raced up the stairs. After several tries we kicked open the apartment door.

The living room was totally involved in fire. Rich said, "Wait for the engine Cos, it is too hot."

Down on the floor, I said, "I am going to take a look," and I entered the apartment. All of the fire was venting out the front window, so I made the decision to try for the rescue. The heat was bad and I made it into a doorway leading to the kitchen. Once in the kitchen, it wasn't as bad. The smoke was heavy, but I was away from the fire. I made my way across the kitchen floor to the rear door leading out to the back porches. That's when I realized that I had gone past the bedrooms. Backtracking toward the burning living room, and down a hallway to the left, the first door I opened was the bedroom. There they were, crouched down against the bed. The smoke wasn't too bad in the room, but by opening the , heavy smoke started filling the room fast. I told the woman that was holding onto her children that we had to get out of there right now. With that I took the infant from her and put him inside my firecoat. I grabbed another small child and told the woman to follow me out the back door. She had two other kids with her, about three and four years old. I told the woman to stay low as I felt my way through the dense smoke. I knew where I was going because I was at the back door a minute ago.

The woman was right on my heels, and we made it outside onto the porch and out of harm's way. I knew we had to get down the stairs and I yelled to her to follow me to the ground floor. The baby was crying as I handed him to the father. He was thankful and shook my hand as other firefighters helped with the rest of the kids. Fourth Division Marshal McCuen told Lieutenant Healy to write me up for the rescue. Timing was everything. If I didn't come in early for Pat Devine, someone else would have made the rescue. About thirteen days later, after several fires, we responded to a cold box at 4724 S. Vincennes at 03:09 in the morning.

A cold box alarm is when there are no calls made about a fire, but someone pulls the street box. When Norm and the chief arrived, they could see a fire down the street at 4811 S. Vincennes Avenue. The first floor was fully involved with fire and the chief ordered a box alarm. I was ordered to open up the rear of the burning building. With my axe and pike pole, I went up the rear stairway and Engine #61 was leading out a line from the alley.

As I ascended the wooden stairway to the third floor, smoke was emanating from the kitchen window. With my pike pole I smashed the glass, and heavy smoke poured out onto the rear porches.

I tried opening the door, but it was locked, With one good kick it opened, but not all the way. I was now pushing it, but the door would not open. Looking toward the floor I saw a hand. I said out loud, "There is someone in there." Then I was frantically pulling a woman out by one hand onto the back porches. She was still alive. As I pulled her down the stairs she was yelling, "My baby, my baby!"

Once we were on the second floor landing, she told me her baby was in the bedroom of the apartment. I yelled to Firefighter Mike Walsh for help as he was leading out Engine #61's line. I raced back up to the third floor and entered the smoke-filled apartment. As I crawled through looking for the baby, I heard a cry, and there he was on the floor. He wasn't a baby, he was a little kid about five years old. I grabbed him and started out, but I passed the doorway to the kitchen and came to a wall inside a closet!

Oh my God, please help me, I prayed. We have to get out, I thought, as I pulled him on the floor. I came to a tile floor and I knew it was the kitchen. The smoke was so heavy that my lungs were bursting and we made it out onto the back porches. I lifted the little boy up and ran down the stairs to the ground where firefighters from Engine #61 told me, "There's an ambulance in front." They transported the boy and his mother to Billings Hospital.

Chief Deneen wrote me up for the rescue and recommended

me for a high award. In the following month an investigation was made by Fourth Division Marshal James Conte of the rescues. Chief Conte wrote in a report to the fire commissioner: Firefighter William Cosgrove should not only be given recognition for his heroic efforts, but he should be given the highest award given by the Chicago Fire Department for this daring rescue.

The year of 1974 ended on a high note for me. It felt great to make the rescue of someone that might have died if we were not there. A rescue was about luck and being in the right place at the right time . . . no question about it.

CHAPTER XI

THE YEAR OF 1975 brought much uncertainty to the Chicago firefighters, but one thing was for sure, we still had fires, and a lot of them. The Chicago Firefighters Union was celebrating their 75th Anniversary, and Happy Birthday Local #2.

Bernie McKay and the officers of the union had one thing on their minds this year. That was to get a contract for the firefighters! All we asked for was an agreement in writing, spelling out our conditions of employment. When we could not agree on an issue, we wanted to be provided with binding arbitration to settle any unresolved problems.

The question remained: will firefighters continue to rely upon the word of city officials. Chiefs and firefighters had maintained a productive working relationship with the administration. In most cases, the current mayor of Chicago, Richard J. Daley, had given firefighters the attention and good wages they deserved. Whether or not this relationship could be maintained during these hard times and recession was a question for both the union and the city. That is why we needed a contract. The mayor's word was his bonded agreement. It might not be so with those who would follow him.

Many mornings in our firehouse, the engine or the truck prepared a mini breakfast. Monk would go next door to buy a package of hot dogs, and while the housework was being completed, and the cook was shopping, we would have some of the leftover food from the shift before ours, and the hot dogs would satisfy our appetites until lunch. Before the cook returned, we caught a fire in an abandoned building on 4515 South Oakenwald. Lieutenant Healy ordered us to ventilate the structure, but most of the windows and doors were covered with 1/2-inch plywood. If you ever tried to pull plywood off a window open, then you know that it's a bitch, unless you can get inside and knock it off with your ax. But if you have to work off of a ladder, it is very difficult to say the least!. Captain Wilson found a way of driving a steel bar with a point and a four-foot chain welded to the bar that made it easy to pull the plywood off the windows. A firefighter went up the ladder and with the pick of the ax, made a hole in the plywood. Two men on the ground with a rope attached, pulled the plywood right off the opening. It was a great tool that was used many times by Truck #15.

At this extra alarm fire was a new piece of equipment that the fire department had never used before: the new communications van. The unit contained the most highly sophisticated electronic equipment including a TV. Frank Connors said, "Yeah, so they can watch Bozo the Clown while we're putting the fire out."

"Who do they communicate with?" asked Monk. "We don't have any radios in the fire building."

Lieutenant Healy said, "They tell the office the progress of the fire. I wonder how much that baby set the city back."

Again it was Fire Prevention Week, and the night before the awards were to be given out, Second Deputy Chief Albert Prendergast came to visit our firehouse. He told Chief Deneen that Cosgrove was going to get the Lambert Tree for the rescues last year. The Lambert Tree Award was the highest award given to a fireman. I was told by Chief Prendergast to report to City Hall tomorrow in my full dress, class "A" uniform. The guys gave me a little bullshit about it, but most were happy about the award, and as for me, I considered it a great personal honor.

I was so excited about the award that I didn't sleep at all the night before. When I arrived at City Hall, there were many firefighters that were dressed in uniforms and we were directed to the second floor to the city council chambers. Out in the hall, the chief of personnel Walter Braun was getting everyone in line and inspecting our uniforms, shoes and hair to make sure no one who went before the mayor was out of uniform.

The Chief yelled to everyone to line up as our name was called. "Cosgrove, you're first because you're getting the Lambert Tree." As the names were called out, some sixty firemen got into line. The chief carefully instructed them to walk to the front row and take seats to the right of Cosgrove. From that first row, to the rows directly behind, they were to file in until all were properly in place and seated.

As I walked down the aisle to the front row, and turned toward the first seat, there was a fireman in my seat. I tried to explain that he was in my seat, but all he said was that he was told to sit there. Once again I told him, and he replied, "I was told to sit here."

By this time, everyone behind me was starting to move around me to take the other seats. Then the next guy was going to sit down, and I said, "No, no this is my seat."

He said, "No it's not! It has my name on it, look-Firefighter Edward Gniady.

"Well, until someone straightens this out," I said, "I am sitting here."

We all moved one seat over and all the names were messed up. The ceremony began with Mayor Richard J. Daley giving praise to the best fire and police Departments in the nation. Then the Carter Harrison Award was given to Firefighter Raymond Graan of Hook & Ladder #3, who performed a dramatic rescue in the Loop. I was called up next to be presented with two awards, a Special Honorable Mention and a Special Certificate of Merit. While I was shaking the hand of Robert J. Quinn, the fire commissioner, he looked right at me and said, "Are you Eddy's kid?"

"That's me Commissioner," I replied, "here's my badge," and I thanked him

His mouth dropped open and he said, "Oh!"

Everyone said Graan got the award because he played handball with the Commissioner. They told me to meet the fire commissioner for photos outside the council chambers, but I walked down the stairs and went home. One week later the Veterans of Foreign Wars with Ray Graan honored me. We sat in the bar after the ceremony and talked about what happened.

Raymond Graan was a good fireman that made a rescue of two window washers that were trapped on a scaffold. Graan went over the side of the building on a rope seventy-five feet down and secured it on the trapped men. It was a great rescue.

The year of 1976 brought the toughest times of my life. I was working at a fire scene at 5210 South Prairie Avenue when falling debris in the fire building injured me. I was taken to Billings Hospital and treated for a slight laceration on my arm, and also smoke inhalation. I was released from the hospital, but I could not return to work for about six days. I returned to the firehouse with my lay-up papers and put my fire gear in my car to go home. Unfortunately, I just remembered, I didn't have a home to go to anymore.

I was having marriage problems and my wife wanted a divorce. The days, weeks, and months that followed were terrible for me. I didn't care about anything but my children. I lost my wife, my home, my children, and my dignity. In June of 1976, I was divorced.

Not that much mattered to me about the fire department anymore. I went to work, did my job, and waited to see my children on the weekends. It was personally devastating.

Although one good thing did happen that year. Jack Gallapo, "my uncle," was elected President of Firefighters Union, Local #2. I knew one thing, that I would miss working at fires with my "Uncle Jack." He made working as a fireman fun and enjoyable. Firefighters were working without officers, and in many cases firemen were acting as engineers and lieutenants. No one had the right work clothes and the fire coats were all different types, with holes, rips, and silver duct tape holding them together. Fighting fires was getting very hard because of plastics. There was a new enemy called polyvinyl chloride or for short, PVC. When inhaled by a fireman, it caused a burning sensation that felt like your throat was closing. This was in addition to the usual headaches, dizziness, and nausea from smoke in a regular fire. The use of self-contained breathing apparatus was mandatory in fires with these hazardous chemicals. Now, plastics were in almost every home, office, factory, store, etc..

Respiratory distress could develop in firefighters up to two days after being exposed to these deadly agents. After years of exposure to smoke without masks, firefighters were known to have lungs of leather. But the material that was burning their lungs was cellulose material which results when CO or carbon monoxide, was inhaled by firefighters. A CO victim is usually okay after oxygen is administered for four hours, unless large and toxic amounts are inhaled. Today, plastics are capable of producing lung damage in almost any fire, even during the overhaul phase of a fire.

On the evening of November 21st, a fire broke out at the Commonwealth Edison Company's "Fisk" generating station. I heard on the radio in my car that firefighters were trapped. I had to give an estimate for a tile job to a fireman on Engine #39, at 1618 W. 33rd Pl. When I arrived at the firehouse, the engine was out at a fire. Listening to the radio in the firehouse, I soon learned that the fire at the Edison plant was a 5-11-alarm fire, so I drove to the fire. I met other firemen that were off-duty and they informed me that Wally Watroba, who was assigned to Engine Company #13 was trapped on top of a conveyor belt. They said the fire was on the conveyor belt and was sending burning coal from one structure to the next. Walter Watroba was in my class of 1969. I watched from a distance.

It was a bitter cold night and the wind was gusting at about twenty-five miles per hour. Wally's leg was pinned by a steel girder. After hours of waiting to free him, they had to amputate his left leg to get him off the burning building. Walter Watroba was dead one hour later, probably from shock. The funeral was attended by thousands of mourners.

It was about a month later on December 20th that the news spread fast across the city of Chicago and the nation. While at his doctor's office in Chicago, Mayor Richard J. Daley passed away. To the firefighters of Chicago, he was a man who always kept his

The late Mayor of Chicago Richard J. Daley

promises. If Richard J. Daley said, "All right, firemen will get a $2,000.00 raise next year," then you could take it to the bank. The mayor had a way of taking care of business, and it all just kept on working perfectly. Some would say the mayor made a big mistake by giving the order to "shoot to kill" anyone throwing a hand-held incendiary device into a building during the 1968 riots. Firefighters and policemen that were in that mess did not think that way. We knew the danger of working under those conditions.

This was his city, and no one was going to destroy it or any of the citizens who lived here. The mayor was a devoted family man who was able to bring all of the ethnic groups of people together in Chicago. He had a special gift for organizing everything in Chicago from the parks to the airports. The Chicago firefighters would miss Mayor Richard J. Daley. May he rest in peace.

As the year of 1976 came to a close, the firefighters lost three brothers in the line of duty.

Chapter XII

In 1977, my main interest was trying to figure a way to get custody of my children. Financially I was broke, and in order to get legal assistance you needed a lot of money. So, I went along with the weekend program of taking the kids to plays at the Martinique on Sunday afternoons. If there was no money then we went to the museums and Sears Tower, but all I wanted to do was be with my kids. My brother Pat lived in St. Paul, Minnesota, and worked for the Burlington Northern Railroad. He was the president of a ski club and invited me to come up to his house. Pat taught me how to ski downhill. Skiing is a great sport and it took my mind off of some of my troubles.

On my annual furlough in March, I went to Aspen, Colorado for one week with my brother, Pat. The mountain was just the most beautiful sight these eyes have ever seen. I could not wait to tell my kids all about it. I went on two other ski trips to the Upper Peninsula of Michigan.

On one of these trips, I met a girl named Suzi on the bus. She lived in Wheaton, Illinois, which is about thirty-five miles west of Chicago. It was a little too far away for me, but we saw each other every day.

With the death of Mayor Richard J. Daley, our president, Jack

Gallapo stressed the need to have a contract with the city. Firefighters always had the word of Mayor Daley in good faith and didn't need a contract. But now, it seemed like City Hall was always trying to change the working conditions of firefighters. The mood on this job was changing and the morale had never been so low. The conditions had worsened in so many ways. There had been stories of strikes in other cities. As we sat in the back of the firehouse, a detailed man from Engine #28 told us about the strike in Sacramento, California, in 1970.

The firefighters were asking the city for a pay raise of $60.00 per month and five paid holidays. Their strike lasted fourteen days and resulted in a court decision making it illegal for Firefighters to strike, and each man was assessed between $42.00 and $50.00 a month. They lost their asses. In Springfield, Illinois, the firefighters strike lasted eight days and four union officers were jailed for one week. The strike failed and the men went back to work without a contract. We all just laughed about what we heard because we knew there would never be a firefighters strike in Chicago.

We had used a self-contained breathing apparatus for a short time. It was a demand type and it was heavy, bulky and very large. When leading out a line into a fire building, first we had the hose on our backs, then this tank made of steel. Firefighters were subject to hard intensive work, and must climb in and out of windows and narrow partitions, not to say anything about raising ladders and performing rescues. Although we needed them, I guess we shouldn't complain about wearing this apparatus that was going to save our lives.

We had a new man on Truck #15. Firefighter Kinnerk was nicknamed "Joe the new guy" and he fit the name. Engine #45 had a new engineer, George Buckner. We must have had ten runs on this shift, six of them were hand pump fires on mattresses. After getting called four times in one night from your bunk, it almost doesn't make any sense to go back to bed.

Buckner had fourth watch, so we sat around talking about the weather because it was going to be a nice day. Saturday and I got the kids, and we were going to Illinois Beach State Park for the day. My youngest was Tom and he was three years old, and I had to carry him most of the day just to keep up with the other four kids. That evening I got a call from Suzi, from the ski trip. We started going out together and our relationship grew. She was a fourth grade school teacher and got along great with my kids. In the month of May the officers changed shifts again. Lieutenant Pat Healy was on the truck. Sometime in the early evening, Truck #15 got a special duty call for people stuck in the elevator at 3939 S. Lake Park Avenue. The car was stuck on the eleventh floor and we were unable to get on the other elevator.

It was a routine type of call that we had almost every day, but when we got up to where the elevator was stuck, people were screaming for help, and the door to the elevator was hanging loose on an angle. The car was stuck between the tenth and eleventh floors and there were about eight people inside. This was not going to be easy. We had to get down to the top of the broken elevator by climbing up on the elevator that we were on, and crossing over from one shaft into the other.

Carefully crossing over in the dark elevator shaft was not hard, but if you lost your footing, it was eleven floors down! I jumped down onto the broken car. In order to open the escape hatch we had to pry it off, because it was bolted down in two of the corners. Only one man could work because we had very little space with cables and the large motor that operated the doors. Once I was able to break loose one of the bolts that was holding the hatch closed, I bent the hatch door open. Inside the car were two women, one young man, and four children. All of them were crying. A ten-foot roofing ladder was used to let the victims climb from one elevator shaft to the other. One by one we lifted them out to safety . . . another job we could feel good about.

Usually a run for an elevator only took about a half-hour. This run had taken us almost two hours before we returned to the firehouse. The engine boys were giving us a razing about how long we were on the elevator run. We tried to tell them about lifting all seven of the trapped victims out of the broken elevator and across the top, but Connors said, "Yeah right, you guys went for ice cream or something. It never takes that long to get a few people out of an elevator".

There were a lot of different firemen in our house that were involved in outside activities. The one that stands out the most is Tom Cunningham, the "Waterhead." He was a skydiver. In a recent article in Firehouse Magazine, they did a story about the "Waterhead." Norm said, "You mean to tell me that you jump out of a perfectly good airplane for the hell of it? I think you need your head examined."

Lieutenant Healy agreed with Norm and the bell started to ring. The fire alarm office barked over the speaker, "Fire with Engine #19 to 3668 South Indiana Avenue. Truck #15, you're the still truck."

We were traveling north on Indiana Avenue. The main fire alarm office was now calling out on the radio. "Truck #15, main to Truck #15, we're getting information about people trapped in the rear."

"People are trapped in the rear of the building," replied Pat Healy in a calm voice.

There was a perfectly formed column of smoke rising upward and to the east. The wind was causing the smoke to whip around the corner of the burning building. "We need ladders in the back now," yelled the chief of the 10th Battalion. "There are people in the second floor."

We threw two 38' foot ladders and brought six people down. The fire was on the first floor and the hallway is snotty, as we made our way to the rear. Other companies were on the second and third floors. "Get the ceiling down in here so the engine can hit it!" Healy yelled.

Mike Hill and I were pulling with all our might as the fire crackled between the walls and ceiling. Firefighter Ralph Glover who transferred to our shift, yelled in, "Take a break while he steps into the burning room." Hot lath and plaster were falling down on us. We were almost done. The ceiling was now exposed and burning as we stepped out while the engine washed the room down. There was a lot more fire, and ceilings that would have to be pulled before this fire was extinguished.

The fire ended up becoming a 2-11 alarm and we worked until the second shift relieved us at the fire at 07:00 hours. From up the street came Jack O'Hare, a firefighter on the second shift, with a smile on his face. "Hey, we hear you dropped the hand pump on this one!" We all laughed.

As the summer months came and went so did the fires, and the officers changed shifts again. A new order came out that anyone, who wanted to be a trained EMT, "Emergency Medical Technician" could sign up at the academy. The course would be given at Wesley Hospital. A number of men would be trained as paramedic technicians. We talked about the new program for a little while. Some of the perks were that you could go to class on the day you were working. Most big cities had at least a basic emergency medical services program underway. "It is the way of the future," Captain Wilson said. "But, I don't have to think about being an EMT because I am not going to school to learn how to stick needles into people's arms. I was trained to be a firefighter, not a doctor. I hope that every ambulance in the city is manned by EMT personnel, so I never have to spend another day like the one I spent with Firefighter Mike 'White Dog' Walsh on Ambulance #36."

My brother Mike Cosgrove joined the fire department as an EMT and was assigned to Ambulance #14 at 71st and Parnell.

While working at a fire where two little kids died on the second floor, Firefighter Francis Donegan hurt his back chopping a hole in the floor, and he was transported to Billings Hospital by Ambulance #35. He was laid up on medical with a possible slipped disc. The next workday, at a 2-11 alarm, Firefighter Wagner hurt his back while pulling ceiling and sidewalls. He was taken to the hospital with two slipped discs in his lower back and was now also laid up.

It just seemed like every day someone was getting hurt at fires on all the shifts in our house. "There are a lot of fires day in and day out, and people get hurt," Wilson said. "We will run shorthanded again. What's new about that?"

The speaker opened and the Englewood fire alarm operator gave Truck #15 a special duty run:. "Man on the ledge attempting suicide at 4926 South Wabash Avenue."

Upon our arrival on the scene there was a boy who was going to jump off the third floor of DuSable High School. Acting Chief

Alletto ordered us to get the life net under this distraught kid. Firefighter Thomas Carmody who was detailed to Truck #15 said, "Hey Dave, I hope he jumps, because I never caught anyone in the life net before."

Carmody was detailed to the truck because of the lay-ups of Franny and Wags. We held the life net under this boy for almost an hour before the Chicago Police were able to pull him off the ledge from a window.

Later on in the year, bad news came to us that one of our firefighters, Donald Staskon, had passed away. Don was sick and had struggled with diabetes for a long time. He was a good fireman and we did have a lot of fun working together.

The cold winter weather returned, but so did Wags and Franny from back injuries. They were still slow moving around, because back injuries took a long time to heal. The year of 1977 ended with one firefighter who lost his life while responding to a fire.

On January 1, 1978, Bill Alletto was appointed as the Deputy Director of Fire Prevention. The officers changed shifts again, and we all were working with different chiefs. Howard McKee was our new chief. He was a good boss that had been around the 16th Battalion for years. His driver was Firefighter George Hensley who, in a short time, was nicknamed "Roger." He worked in well and was liked by all the boys on the first platoon.

Mike Hill got sick and was hospitalized at Christ Community Hospital with hepatitis. We were to report to the fire academy for shots because hepatitis was very contagious. The report we got on Mike was that he was in serious condition. One day, while responding to a fire at 4547 South Prairie, it was snowing and the streets were slippery. With our lights and siren blaring, a speeding car crashed into the left side of Truck #15 as we went through the intersection at 45th and Dr. Martin Luther King Drive. While driving an emergency vehicle we had been trained in safe driving. We slowed down at intersections without lights and sirens and watched out for other vehicles and pedestrians. But when some idiot was going too fast for conditions, accidents were unavoidable. More pressing than the accident was the vision of a burning building and the possibility of trapped victims. Although no one was injured, it was a bad accident, and we also had a working fire.

On a cold February day we responded to a still and box alarm at 3715 South Indiana Avenue. The structure involved was a very large three-story brick building with stores on the ground floor and apartments above.

It appeared the fire had started in the back on the ground floor. We fought this fire throughout the second floor, only to find out that it broke out on the third floor and burned the roof off. Most of the time when we responded to a fire outside of our still district, we usually were the first to pick up and return to our quarters. Well, this fire was in the 10th Battalion and we were on the scene for six long cold hours. While pulling ceilings on the second floor of the burning structure I met a good friend, John Joyce. He was a firefighter on Snorkel Squad #1. Snorkel Squad #1 responded to all 2-11 alarms in the city. We went back to when we were kids. My mother and his mother were friends. It was great to work with John at a fire. He introduced me to his lieutenant, Lieutenant Edward Gavin. He was on SS-1 for years and he had been to many fires across this city.

Not even four hours, later we responded to another fire on the same street, but a block south at 3814 South Indiana. We pulled ceiling and sidewalls on the second, third, and fourth floors of this abandoned building until 070:0 hours. When we left the fire, the lieutenant of Snorkel Squad #1 stopped me and said, "How would you like to get on SS#1?"

I informed Lieutenant Edward Gavin that I was not looking to respond to any more fires. At the time, Snorkel Squad #1 responded to all 2-11-alarm fires in the city. Two extra alarm fires was enough for me and all the guys agreed. The second shift relieved us at the fire. It was a good sight to see Firefighters Jack O'Hara, Bill Duszynski, and Bill Marx walking down Indian Avenue that morning.

Jack O'Hara yelled, "Okay, Cos, what did you guys do? Trip and fall with the hand pumps?" It was a joke that firemen say to each other. We all laughed. We went home with our asses dragging that morning.

There was a manpower crisis in the fire service during this time, and in many parts of the United States it was at an alarming low level situation, and was getting worse. The standards of the National Fire Protection Association (NFPA) called for a minimum of six firefighters, including the officer for each engine company and truck company. Currently, however, complements were closer to four men. The president of the International Association of Firefighters stated that too often there was one man on the back step of an engine company where there used to be three. You simply could not expect one man to do the work of three when you had a working fire. Too many chiefs were beholden for their jobs to the city administration, which told them they could not have more money for manpower. Some chiefs would say they didn't need any more men, they could do the job with two and three man companies. All of that type of talk was bullshit. If you were a firefighter that had responded to a fire where you had victims screaming and hanging out windows on the second floor, plus you were fighting a fast moving fire on the first floor, then you knew that even six men on a company was not enough manpower. Come on, we had all been there and the most experienced chiefs knew that this was bullshit!

One afternoon in late February, we followed Engine #61 to a fire at 4832 South Michigan. When we arrived on the scene, there were people on the second floor hanging out the windows. The chief requested a box alarm and then a 2-11. Cars were parked along the curb. I tried to raise the main ladder to the victims. Electrical wires that ran from one light pole to another were in the way. We didn't have time to get ground ladders to the victims and heavy brown smoke was now billowing up from the fire that was raging on the first floor. Chief McKee yelled to me to snap the wires with the main. I hesitated. Then he told me that there was no electricity in the lines until after 5:00 P.M. when the streetlights went on. I swung the ladder around and dropped it right through the wires. There were no sparks; we rescued four victims from what appeared to be almost certain death. It was good to work with a fire chief that knew about firefighting. We opened the roof and pulled walls and ceiling on all three floors, washed it down and returned to our quarters.

I started my annual furlough the next day, but I thought about the fire on Indiana Avenue, and the wires. I though to myself, what if Chief McKee was in the back of the building and didn't tell me to drop the wires. Oh well, I loved the new sport of skiing in the mountains. Suzi went to Aspen, Colorado, with me. It was good to get away for a while and forget about the fires. Well, maybe try to forget.

When I returned to the firehouse, the talk was about getting a contract. The guy that could get us a contract was Frank Muscare. It was election time for our union, Local #2, and Frank Muscare said he would work to get us a contract, better working conditions, more safety on the job, enough manpower, better salaries, and more protection for our families. "In order to get a contract we might have to revert to a strike," Bummer said.

"No, no not in Chicago. Mayor Bilandic will give us a contract," one of the guys said. "He likes the firemen."

In April of 1978, the firefighters in Normal, Illinois, went on strike for a contract and collective bargaining. The strike lasted fifty-six days and one of the main disputes was the city did not want officers to be in the union. When the firefighters refused a court order to return to work, many were sentenced to jail, and stayed there for forty-two days.

By May 1, 1978, Frank Muscare was the union president of Local #2 and he went right to work. Other changes were happening in the fire department. Robert J. Quinn, the fire commissioner had been very ill, and was replaced by Robert Albrecht.

The summer was like all the rest, hot and busy. Firefighter Jim Nolan was detailed to Engine #16, located at 4005 South Dearborn Street. They were our second engine to a fire, and we caught a working fire on 4220 South Calumet. The fire was on the second floor in the rear. Nolan led out up the back stairs with Engine #16's line, and Engine #45 led out their line up the front stairway. As we entered the burning apartment there was a lot of heat and smoke. I crawled to the window, pulled the curtains down and with one good swing of my axe, the window was done; I needed air. As we made our way through the smoke, you could hear someone yelling, "45, 45, shut down your line. We got it."

Bummer yelled back to Nolan, "Your momma's got it," and continued hitting the fire with the line.

Nolan yelled again and Bummer said, "No you shut down, we got the fire." Now the fire was almost extinguished and we could see a silhouette through the smoke and steam. It looked like Nolan in the kitchen of the apartment, and just then he turned and opened the pipe on us. Bummer called him a few choice words and he opened up his pipe on Nolan, and a major water fight began.

I was caught between these two nitwits, and I was getting soaked to the bone. "I never liked getting wet, that's why I am on a hook & ladder," I told them. We all just laughed and there was a strong feeling of camaraderie at that moment. We did a good job. All firefighters knew the feeling when everything worked right at a fire. You led out, the engineer got water and sent it to the pipeman. You made your way through the smoke and heat. Hot burning embers fell on you like a shower, hitting your helmet, back, and arms.

The next thing you knew, the fire was out. You gave it your all, and knocked the fire. Now wet, soaking wet to the bone, someone out in front told you, "Good stop guys." Good stop, with our faces dirty and a little burned and black lines around our eyes. The mucus was hardened under our noses, and our ears were filled with soot.

We looked at each other with a smile. "Good stop, you! Who's got smokes?" Without taking off our gloves, we took a light from each other's cigarettes.

On August 22, 1978, Frank Muscare and the union's twelve member executive board approved a draft of a contract for firemen. They demanded no more handshakes, it was time for a contract. The union negotiating team met each Monday at the Bismarck Hotel and awaited representatives from Mayor Bilandic's administration to begin bargaining. But they just waited, because city officials refused to attend the meetings.

In September, the officers changed shifts again, but Captain Wilson was detailed to Snorkel #3. It was a permanent detail. Rumor had it that he was sick and tired of being the acting battalion chief all the time. But Chief Deneen and Norm were back on our shift.

Norm enlightened me with all his old sayings and some new ones. For example, "Dave, did I ever tell you how fast I am?"

"No, you haven't Norm," I said with a smile on my face.

He said, "I am so fast that when I turn the lights off, I am in bed before the room gets dark." I don't know anyone that makes me laugh like Norman Doolan.

We could smell the chicken soup all the way up in the front of the firehouse, and it smelled good. It was a sign of fall and there was a chill in the air. Norm said, "Hey, when is the soup ready?"

Monk said, "It will be ready when we say it's ready."

Norm looked at Monk and then back at me and said, "Dave, look here. I raised a chick to peck my eyes out."

Norm was at Engine #45 when Monk was a candidate, and he always told us that he taught us everything. Bummer yelled, "It's soup; soup for the mooners. Get in there." Then the bell started ringing. We got a fire at 4610 South Evans. As we arrived on the scene, there was a fire on the second floor, and a little girl jumped out the window.

Engine #45 started leading out their hose. Truck #15 was in place and I started to set the outriggers as firemen were running toward the building. Lying in the grass and mud, the little girl was surrounded by the darkness of the night. Then I saw Norm kneeling over her as he tried to place an oxygen mask on her face and call on the radio for an ambulance. "Dave," Norm yelled to me, "she is breathing, isn't that great?"

"It sure is," I said as Wags swung the 100' aerial ladder over our heads.

He yelled, "Dave, get the saw, we're going to the roof."

On October 14th and 15th we all went to vote if we wanted to strike. I voted no because I thought somehow we could solve this contract stuff without going on strike. The ballots were counted and the rank and file voted against authorizing a strike. The count was close: 1729 against and 1664 for a strike. A short time later, the city budget was adopted without a word about contracts for the firemen. The administration never met with the union's negotiating team and it was kind of a slap in our faces.

The campaign for the upcoming mayoral election began. The candidate running against Mayor Michael Bilandic was a woman. Her name was Jane Byrne. Rumor had it that she was a commissioner of consumer services under Richard J. Daley and Bilandic until he fired her. Jane Byrne vowed if the Firefighters Union Local #2 endorsed her bid for mayor that she would get a collective bargaining and a contract for the firemen.

Some of the guys said a woman would never get elected as mayor of Chicago. I said if she gets us a contract she has my vote.

December 22nd, I was detailed to Engine #60, located at 1155 East 55th Street. Engine #60 is a good house with a lot of men. We had a few runs during the day and slept through the night. It had rained and then the temperature dropped to freezing. Everything had a coat of ice on it including my car. The second shift started coming in and I went out to start my car, and turn the defrosters on in order to melt the ice off the windshield. The ice was too thick and one of the firemen on Snorkel #3, Andy Kowalski, told me to take a bucket of lukewarm water and throw it on the windows.

So, I filled a bucket with warm water and carried it out to my car. All the guys from both shifts were watching as I carefully walked to the car. It was very slippery on the ice. I splashed one side of the car window and the ice ran off easily. By this time, Andy was coming out the door of the firehouse. I said, "Hey this works good," and as I walked around the car I slipped on the cement parking block next to my car. I went up in the air, water bucket and all, and landed right on my ass. The water spilled all over me and I couldn't get up right away. When I did, I looked into the glass windows where all the boys were laughing. I tried to smile, but I was hurt and I was also embarrassed. I went back in to the firehouse, put the bucket back and had some coffee. I told Andy that I thought I hurt myself, and he said, "You're young, shake it off."

As I drove home I knew something was wrong, and I was in pain. I took a hot shower and laid down. When I woke up there was a bump on my tailbone the size of a golf ball!

There was some last minute shopping to do because my kids were coming over for Christmas Eve. That night was very long for me and I didn't want the kids to know because it would have spoiled the evening. Suzi helped save the night by playing with the kids.

Christmas Day at the firehouse was one of the worst days for me, and I spent most of in my bunk. I was in the buggy driving Captain Scheidt, and I missed a few runs because Captain Scheidt knew that I was in a lot of pain. The next day I went to the doctor and was diagnosed with a pilonidal cyst. December 28th, I was operated on at St. Francis Hospital in Blue Island. It was a wide incision and the wound had to be left open to drain. This type of surgery heals very slowly and is very painful. I was told to avoid any direct trauma. I was released from the hospital on January 10, 1979. Dick Scheidt picked me up at the hospital and took me home. In the following days, I never even got out of bed other than going to the bathroom.

On January 19, 1979, Robert J. Quinn, the fire commissioner passed away. I was unable to attend his funeral because I was still in extreme pain from the surgery.

Robert J. Quinn was seventy-three years old and was the fire commissioner for twenty-three years. He was a forty-year member of the Firefighters Union Local #2. Robert Quinn was known throughout the fire department as a "fireman's fireman." Most people that knew him, liked him, but not everyone. But no one questioned his courage. All the way to the end of his command he would still respond to fires. He won the Lambert Tree Award for heroism in 1934. May he rest in peace.

I received a call from the boys. They wanted to come over. Norm said, "Dave, I will fix you some food or maybe make soup." I declined because I was still in bad shape, and wouldn't be any fun. Norm said "That's okay, maybe next week." A major snowstorm hit the city of Chicago on January 27th, dumping a record-breaking amount of snow-27 inches. The firemen were ordered back to the firehouse once again to fight fires. People were stranded all over and Mayor Bilandic took the blame for the way his cabinet members handled the snow removal. It was a real fiasco! They told me that we got two more candidates, Jim Kuknyo and Don Engelhardt.

On February 9, 1979, Rich Wagner called me. He said, "William, are you sitting down?"

photo courtesy of Chicago Fire Fighter

Robert J. Quinn

"Why," I asked.

He told me that Norman Doolan passed away as a result of a major heart attack.

"Oh no, not Norm." It was probably the worst news that I ever received. Norm was the life of our firehouse, and was liked by everyone on all shifts. He would be missed. We would miss the jokes and all the laughter that he provided. I would never forget him and I only hoped that I could remember all his sayings.

On February 10th, in the early evening, I went to the Blake-Lamb Funeral Home that was located at 5800 West 63rd Street. I went to pay my respects, but also to see if it was really true. Yes, Norm was laid out in his fire department dress blues as he would call them. Throughout the night people passed by to pay their respects to a good friend. The next night, I wore my Class "A" uniform so that I might get a chance to stand at attention next to his casket. Even though I was still in a lot of pain from the surgery, they could never have stopped me from attending.

February 12th, as I arrived at the funeral home, there was an engine company in front. Firefighters and officers were lining up to be next to stand honor guard for Norm. Standing next to his casket, I could hear him call my name, as he did so many nights in the bunkroom. I wanted to tell him, "Okay Norm, get up, let's get out of here."

It was a cold morning about twenty degrees, and the wind was blowing out of the northwest at about fifteen miles per hour. It was not snowing a lot, but enough to make the streets a mess. We said our final good-bye and the funeral started. There were a lot of cars. The pumper draped in purple and black with the number 45 on the side slowly pulled away, leading the procession past Norm's home located at 6638 West 64th Street.

As the funeral procession entered through the gates of the Evergreen Park Cemetery and pulled up to the chapel, we all took positions and formed two lines and the call went out. It was that now familiar "call of attention" followed by detail "hand salute" as the flag-draped casket passed in front of us. The snow was blowing and it was cold. We all returned to the Midway Lounge on 63rd Street for a memorial lunch. Norm liked the Midway Lounge, it was one of his watering holes that he always liked going to.

We saluted him, toasted him, and even roasted him. There were many laughs, and some tears, and we stayed late into the night, because that's just the way he would have wanted it. Norman Doolan was snatched away from us at the young age of forty-seven. Although he was not killed directly by fire, he had succumbed to the various side effects associated with long-term smoke inhalation. It was because he was a firefighter on all busy companies and we never had any fucking masks, that was why I was here today at his funeral.

The next morning when I woke up, there was such an emptiness. I was supposed to report to the fire department doctor for my weekly visit. I called into the medical section and told them I could not report. I was told to report the next day. In the weeks that followed I went to physical therapy and was getting stronger. I reported back to the firehouse in March. I was still not 100 percent, but I missed the guys and the job. Nothing ever seemed the same after Norm's untimely death.

In March, Jane Byrne told Chicago union leaders that city workers would get contracts if she was elected. She won the Chicago Federation of Labor Endorsement.

In May of 1979, my back problems increased, and I was forced to lay up on medical again. In June, I went on light duty at the fire academy. All the time I was on light duty, the fire department's main interest was that there was going to be a strike. The new mayor, Jane Byrne, promised to begin contract talks in City Hall with our president, Frank Muscare. I met Chief Conte at the academy, and he asked me to work light duty at the 4th Division

Headquarters at 4401 South Ashland. They had moved into Engine Company #49's firehouse. I agreed, because I didn't like the academy, and this way I was back on the first platoon. I met a firefighter that was on Engine #59. Firefighter Ed Tetzner worked in the fourth division until he could get on a company on the south side. We became good friends.

There were times that Chief Conte would ask if I would drive him on his driver's Daley day and furlough. Chief Conte was a good boss, and always helped a firefighter out, like Ed Tetzner, and me. I was detailed to Engine #39's firehouse for one month, because of a lay up and furloughs.

Frank Muscare, our president, and the many members of our union, Local #2, were working together and getting the job done. Our endorsed candidate, Jane Byrne, won the election for mayor, and she won big, mostly because of the mishandled snowstorm. She was called the "Snow Queen.".

Jane Byrne received 82 percent of the votes cast, which was the highest percentage ever in a Chicago mayoral election. "Brothers we're in, now we will get our first contract," Frank Muscare said. "Thanks to you guys."

In May, Mayor Byrne promised to begin contract talks in City Hall with President Frank Muscare. On May 25th, the crash of American Airlines, Flight 191 killed 275 people. Firefighters from Chicago and suburban towns next to O'Hare International Airport uncovered the bodies of the victims throughout the night.

It was not new, airlines crashing in and around Chicago's airports. Firefighters responded to many stand-byes at both O'Hare and Midway Airports every day. Two such crashes occurred on January 16th, 1967, and a United Airliner crashed outside of Midway Airport on December 8th, 1972. The task of recovering victims was a gruesome job, but firefighters were there and there was no panic, because we are always ready for anything. The city fathers always knew that.

The three airports that serve the city are the busiest in the world. About 2,000 planes land and take off each day from these three airports and firemen were always on standby. When something went wrong, you knew the firefighters would be there risking their lives.

Firefighters responded to rail accidents, and were trained to handle the many unexpected incidents associated with them. Chicago is the hub of railroads in America. There are more than seventeen major railroads that serve the city. At any given time of the day, hundreds of trains travel through residential neighborhoods, carrying bulk freight in boxcars and cylinder-shaped cars that are fifty feet long, filled with oil and many other volatile liquids. This creates a constant tension with firefighters. This, and the possibility that something could happen.

Firefighters are called to many major accidents on Chicago's expressways, that are heavily used by commuters from the suburbs. Semi trucks carrying more than five million gallons of gasoline and other hazardous material, daily roll along through Chicago on the Dan Ryan, Kennedy, Eisenhower, and the Stevenson Expressways and many of the major streets.

On a hot night in late June, we responded to a still and box alarm in the back of the yards at about 40th and Racine. The fire was issuing out the back of the structure. The young excited lieutenant jumped out of the front seat of the pumper, and yelled back to me, "I want two lines! Drop two lines!"

Without getting to excited, I said, "Hey Lou, there is me and you and the engineer on this fucking rig, and I can't hold two lines by myself."

With a dazed and confused look, he said, "See if you can get one line on the fire and I will make the hydrant."

When I first came on this job it took two or three men to hold a 2 1/2-inch line, and now we were doing the same job with only one man. It's no wonder that the injury level was so high. One man was leading out where there should be at least two or three.

Truck companies were now raising ladders with two men, when we needed at least four. The firefighter was taken for granted and had been for a long time. They forgot that he served in one of the most dangerous professions in the world. He had to combine physical courage with a high degree of technical know-how to deal with the many complex fire hazards. Training was as important as in any profession. We needed more men on the fire department, and rumor had it that a new class was starting at the fire academy soon. We hoped so!

On August 2nd, Mayor Byrne's advisers told union officials that a contract would have to await approval of a collective bargaining ordinance by the city council. Back in 1975, the International Association of Firefighters sent a young man to help us win this important battle. The city officials of many cities called him a carpetbagging, troublemaking, shit-steering union person, whose job it was to create a strike. Michael Lass was not a person who created strikes, and his job was to assist unions in achieving collective bargaining and contracts for firefighters.

Mike Lass was a thirty-eight-year-old that was born and raised in Evanston, Illinois. He had been a firefighter for eight years in Evanston. He was a member of Local #742 in Evanston, and he was in Chicago to help firefighters get a union contract.

On August 20th, Frank Muscare and the executive board

Why do firefighters need a contract? Three men for garbage and two men for saving lives.

began weekly meetings in the Bismarck Hotel; but city officials boycotted them. We call it stone-walling.

After many months of dating and going everywhere with each other, Suzi decided to move into my house. Her parents were not very happy about the move. People don't move into the city from the suburbs. Her mother said, "They move from the city to the suburbs." Suzi's mother was not real fond of the fact that she was dating a Chicago firefighter, divorced with five children. Suzi is a highly educated person with a Bachelor of Science in Education, and a Masters degree also in science in education. She loved teaching school to her fourth graders, but she still wanted to move into my little house in Chicago.

On September 9, 1979, Suzi and I were married at City Hall in Chicago. My brother Mike, was the best man and one of Suzi's girlfriends was the maid of honor. Her name was Elaine Castle. On that same Saturday evening, we invited our two families over for a party to meet one another; neither family knew that we got married that morning. We had a half-keg of beer, plenty of food and as the evening went on, people were feeling good. My brother Mike brought out a four-layer wedding cake with the bride and groom on top. Well, I am not sure who spoke first, but we sure fooled them all when we told them, especially Suzi's mother. There were no gifts, no cards, just a surprise; the way we wanted it.

The wedding was over. Suzi and I did not go anywhere on a honeymoon because of the trouble that was brewing on the fire department. Time and again letters were sent to City Hall requesting that the city's administration meet with the authorized representatives of Local #2 at the Bismarck Hotel. The city refused to attend. Stall tactics by the city, telling firefighters that they would get a contract soon, was the message told by the chiefs in the field.

Honor should not be bought so cheaply. We knew now that Jane Byrne's word was bullshit.

In the Bismarck Hotel, the executive board was drafting up a contract for the city and the board to talk about. Some of the main points were:

1. Local #2 as the sole bargaining agent for all uniformed members of the Chicago Fire Department below the rank of division marshal.

2. Hours of work for platoon duty shifts would be from 08:00 hours to 08:00 hours; bureaus of fire prevention, and all other forty-hour employees would be from 08:00 hours to 16:30 hours.

3. Paychecks would be due at 08:00 hours at their work place on the first and sixteenth days of the month. Overtime for anything over one-half hour beyond their regular scheduled hours, would be at time and a half. Recalled employees to duty would receive a minimum of three hours paid vacation; platoon employees would receive ten duty days off; Forty hour employees would receive four weeks.

4. Paid holidays (12); sick leave (12) months.

5. Seniority was defined by the length of time the employee had on the job. Vacancies must be filled to maintain manning of (5) on a truck and 5) on engines.

6. Grievance procedure, arbitration, hospitalization, dental, and optical.

7. Ambulances: one paramedic officer and one paramedic on each ambulance and cross training.

8. No acting out of classification, assignments and transfers would be filled on the basis of seniority.

9. Protective gear and clothing allowance of $400 per year.

These were some of the more important issues that we were asking for that were being enjoyed by firefighters in many cities that had a contract.

We had just heard about the firefighters in the city of Aurora, Illinois. City officials refused to talk to the firefighters about negotiating a contract. After talks broke down, the union took a vote, and out of 117 fire personnel, 112 walked out on strike. The striking firemen set up flying squads to assist in any fires in the city. About eight days into the strike, a fire occurred in an apartment building and one person lost their life. The next day the strike ended, on October 18, 1979. The firefighters returned to work with a contract.

Things were getting hot. Many firefighters were cleaning out lockers and taking personal things out to their cars. Rumors were flying fast from one firehouse to the next. If it came down to a strike, this job would never be the same again, was some of the scuttlebutt. The feelings were getting bitter, and emotions were high. Battalion chiefs were going from firehouse to firehouse asking each man what he was going to do if a strike did take place.

There were fires everywhere in the city and the undermanned fire companies were still doing the work the best they could.

Chapter XIII

We had waited long enough. We were in the eleventh month of 1979, and still we had no contract. The newly elected Mayor Jane Byrne attended an assembly of Local #2 members and personally thanked them for giving her their support in the recent elections. The mayor said she would fulfill her "promise" of a contract for members of Local #2. Here we were for over ninety days, sitting right across the street from City Hall, in the Bismarck Hotel waiting for Jane Byrne and her administration to meet with us at their convenience. But no, they were boycotting us. Why? They didn't want us to have a contract because it bound the city legally.

Well enough was enough, and President Frank "Moon" Muscare and the executive board of Local #2 approved taking a strike vote on November 27th. We would see what the membership would vote this time.

The next couple of days that followed were very interesting. All of the sudden new promotions came out, and lieutenant's and engineer's raises were being paid, which hadn't been happening for the past few months. All of the sudden there were some 250 promotions on the fire department.

All that time firefighters were acting in those positions. Engineers, lieutenants, captains, and chiefs positions in the city's budget were allotted for and paid for by the taxpayers of Chicago every day, but were not filled. Oh yes, the fires were put out by the best and under staffed without officers. Many lifesaving decisions by firefighters acting as lieutenants, captains acting as chiefs, were being made everyday. We wouldn't let "Her Honor" pay us off with 250 promotions that should have been filled a year ago. Her commitment was a contract in 1979. By the new promotions there was this divide and conquer philosophy. "Well, no one is going to divide this union," Muscare said.

The talk was now to vote. The word was out, and now was the time we had to make a decision. We were ready to negotiate a written agreement with the city of Chicago right now! The city wanted us to believe that our firefighters were the highest paid in the nation. But we knew that a firefighter first class, a newly promoted lieutenant, or an engineer would still make less than a first class firefighter in Detroit ($24,156). On December 15th and 16th, we all went to vote at the Chicago Plumber's Hall located at 1340 W. Washington. After the ballots were counted, 77 percent of 2,984 firefighters voting, (2,326 to 658), authorized the union's executive board to call a strike whenever it saw fit.

As the late Mayor Richard J. Daley would say in victory, "the people have spoken." A rash of letters were exchanged because of the vote. From Fire Commissioner Richard Albrecht to the union, to Mayor Byrne's letter to Frank Muscare, about now setting up a date and time for the commissioner and the director of personnel to discuss issues important to the firefighters.

The letter from Commissioner Albrecht to the firefighters stated that this was the first time the city had ever had to negotiate a contract and the city must develop ground rules for collective bargaining. There were very serious considerations which had to be addressed, like, Local #2 wanted to be the sole bargaining agent for all members of the uniformed force.

The commissioner wrote, "As commissioner, am I supposed to ignore the officers association and the engineers union? Nothing can be accomplished when there is always the constant threat of a walkout. The only way to negotiate is calmly, prudently, and efficiently." The letter back to the commissioner from Frank Muscare said that this was the only union that will be bargaining for all, and "we are calm, prudent and efficient and we will still meet you at the Bismarck, any time to discuss our contract."

Mayor Byrne had stated that we had not cared about the citizens of Chicago, and the property losses. Chicago was a great city, and any strike action would be attributed directly toward the firefighters if there were any fires or losses. Do you want this on your conscience? Muscare's reply was, "We won't have it on our conscience, because you promised us a contract. Chicago is a great city, Mayor Byrne, and we are the ones that are out there protecting life and property twenty-four hours a day, 365 days a year!".

Chicago is the second largest city in the United States and is the nation's leading industrial and transportation center. Trucks and railroad cars carry more goods in and out of Chicago than in any other U.S. city. The Loop, downtown Chicago with its spectacular skyscrapers, is where thousands of people live in luxurious high-rise apartments. About 310,000 people stream into the downtown area every day. We were the firefighters that manned the Loop. The first division, Battalions #1, #2, and #7 with thirteen engine companies, six hook and ladder companies, and Snorkel Squad #1 and two ambulance companies, we cared for this area of the city. Although undermanned we did the best we could to save the lives of citizens in the Loop.

The north side of Chicago is almost entirely residential. It stretches from the downtown area about nine miles, and north-west about thirteen miles. There are about 1 1/3 million people that live in this section of the city. We were the firefighters that protected this area. The firefighters of Division #3 and Battalions #3, #13, #20, and #27. We did this with eleven engine companies, six truck companies, one flying squad, and four ambulances. In this area on the north side there were many pockets of poverty, namely, the Cabrini Green Housing Project complex. Also within this area were poorly maintained, old buildings where fires occurred every day.

To the northwest of the Loop were the firefighters of the 6th Division and Battalions #4, #22, and #24, with seventeen engine companies, nine truck companies, two squads, and five ambulances. They protected this very large area of the city.

The West Side of the city lies west of the Loop, between Grand Avenue on the north and the Chicago Sanitary and Ship Canal on the south. About 510,000 people live on the West Side, nearly 60 percent of the residents are black, and about 9 percent are Hispanic, and the rest are white. The West Side firefighters were some of the busiest in the city. They were the firefighters of the 2nd Division., Battalions #15, #18, #23, and #28. There were fourteen engine companies, seven truck companies, one snorkel, and six ambulances. These companies served and protected the citizens that lived on the West Side of the city.

The south side is the biggest section of the city in area and population. It stretches about sixteen miles south of downtown, and all the way out to the southwest Beverly area and the Indiana border on the southeast side. Over 1 1/2 million people live on the south side. The firefighters of Division #4 and Battalions #10, #11,

#16, and #21 covered this area. There were fourteen engine companies, nine truck companies, one snorkel, and seven ambulances. Chicago's biggest public housing project is located on the East Side of the 4th Division. The Robert Taylor Homes cover about fifteen blocks along State Street and the Dan Ryan Expressway. Its 25,000 residents live in twenty-eight crowded buildings, where assault and robbery are constant threats, not to mention all the fires. To the west of the Dan Ryan Expressway is Bridgeport, the home of the last four mayors, and just south of Bridgeport is the Union Stockyards which has a history of its own with the Chicago Fire Department. At one time the stockyards supplied meat to much of this nation.

To the south and east are the firefighters of the 5th Division, and Battalions #8, #14, #17, and #19. There are seventeen engine companies, nine truck companies, two squads, and five ambulances. The 5th Division stretches all the way to the Indiana state line.

The far south West Side is where I was born, and raised. It is protected by the firefighters of the 7th Division, and Battalions #12, #26, #29, and #31. There are fourteen engine companies, ten truck companies, two squads, and five ambulances.

We not only cared about the citizens of Chicago, we were out there in the sub-zero temperatures and the hot searing temperatures of the summer, risking our lives, and all we asked was our fair share, a contract. The first meeting after the strike vote took place on January 8, 1979, to finally discuss our contract. The meeting was just a lot of no substance talk and another stall tactic by the city.

The Firefighters Union Local #2 and its members started to prepare for a strike by setting up offices across the city in the seven divisions. We could only hope for something to happen, and perhaps talks could begin to make some sense out of this mess. One of the biggest key issues in the negotiations between the city and the union was "political control" of the rank and file. The city wanted a contract that would give them control of the rank and file members of the fire department.

Finally! Mayor Byrne agreed to send Fire Commissioner Richard Albrecht and Director Charles Pounian to meet with Union President Frank Muscare at the Bismarck Hotel. Previously, Frank Muscare demanded that the city agree to begin contract talks; no more meetings, just contract talks. But, people said this session would be some bullshit exercise in public relations that would do very little to avert a threatened strike. One city official informed Mayor Byrne that she now had messed around with the wrong group. You know how most unions had a brotherhood . . . well, this union was a brotherhood because these guys ate, drank and slept together, and their strength was their brotherhood.

Ed Tetzner and I stopped for a beer at a place on Western called Tullys. There were a few other firefighters in the pub on Western, and the talk was strong about going on strike. Some of the boys were getting very loud saying, "Hey I just worked my ass off getting this bitch elected, because she promised if she was elected the firefighters of Chicago would get a contract." The news was on the TV in the bar and the announcer said that the first meeting between the city and firefighters would take place Tuesday at 2 P.M. in the Bismarck Hotel.

"Cross your fingers that this session with the city works," this guy said, "because otherwise we're going on strike." For the first time the word "strike" sounded so real. This couldn't be happening. Somehow it will be straightened out, I thought to myself.

I met younger firefighters that day. One of these firefighters was Philip Lamm. He went on about how the guys in his firehouse were all set to go on strike. He impressed me with the way he talked about his company. I told him that I was assigned to Truck #24, and how I was transferred. He told me that he only had about fourteen months on the job, and he loved being a fireman. I later found out that Phil Lamm was in the Vietnam War. He joined the United States Marine Corps in 1968, and was assigned to the 3rd Re Con Battalion in Vietnam. After a short rest and relaxation back in the states, he returned to Danang until returning home in June of 1971. He completed two tours of duty in Vietnam. He was awarded four medals and one combat ribbon, and the Cross of Gallantry!

On January 15th, union officials rejected the city's proposal to negotiate a contract, subject to provisions of an upcoming collective bargaining ordinance. President Muscare had said time and again that "all" the firemen, including the officers, would be in the union, but the city said no. The officers would be with the city as management, and the union would only have the firefighters. That wasn't going to happen. A short time later Muscare said that he wanted the first contract with the city to be retroactive to the last day of 1979. The union was proposing a ten percent pay raise. The city was offering six percent. In the face of a strike threat, Mayor Byrne rushed a collective bargaining ordinance to the city council. Some said it was a demonstration of good faith, but others said it was because she now knew that the firefighters would definitely go on strike.

"They are surface bargaining," Mike Lass said. "They want to legislate a contract rather than negotiate one." Snagged on the officers not being in the union, what the hell was wrong with this picture? Six of the eight members of the negotiating team were officers, including President Frank Muscare. At one point a big shouting match erupted between Frank and the city's chief attorney. Muscare charged that the city was on the verge of provoking a walkout.

The ordinance was prepared in late January by a committee headed by Alderman Martin Oberman of the 43rd Ward. The ordinance would require that police and firefighters disputes go to binding arbitration. A prohibition against strikes by police officers and firefighters was also one of the tenets of the ordinance which Mayor Byrne endorsed.

Back in the firehouse, the city started parking police cars inside firehouses, locked and unmanned in the event of a strike. Rumor had it that the police cars would respond to fires to help extinguish them if we went on strike.

Among the major points that had been discussed, the city proposed that all agreements covering wages for firemen would all be subject to conditions in Mrs. Byrne's new collective bargaining ordinance. Plus the city still refused to recognize the firemen's union as the exclusive bargaining agent. Dale Berry, attorney for the union, insisted that the city was engaged in stall tactics and was now trying to provoke a strike.

Rumors were flying fast about which firehouses were heavy on the strike and which ones were light. Men who had worked closely together for years had become buddies because of the intimacy of working conditions, like risking their lives together on a set of burning stairs, doing the dishes, and sweeping the floors back at the fire house. All firemen, that are off at home or wherever, have their thoughts back at the firehouse. Most of our day was spent checking with other firemen and calling the union hot line.

Most of the men that I knew felt the same way as I did. "If it comes to a strike, I'll strike. I voted for it and that's where I stand. I'll do it, if it's what we have to do to get a contract. But I'll tell you one thing, the job will never be the same again," I said.

I think it would take years for the job to recover, because the feelings would be so bitter. Guys who went out on strike risked everything, but they would never forget the guys who stayed on the job. I thought, If you don't back me up on this one, how can I trust you coming in behind me in some stinking, choking fire where my life is on the line? The Chicago Fire Department was once unified, but now firefighters, engineers, lieutenants, captains, and chiefs were diverse in their feelings about a strike.

On January 31st, negotiations between the city and the firefighters union broke down again over article #19, the provision proposed by the union which would make their contract with the city binding. The city officials maintained that any contract with the city of Chicago must be subject to a collective bargaining ordinance that was just passed. "The rank and file know that this is a deliberate stall tactic, and I will bring it to the Executive Committee," Muscare said.

The firefighters all came down from their divisions to join their buddies on the other side of the city for a rally at the Daley Center Plaza. We were chanting, waving signs, whistling, oath growling, and letting people know that we were the city's firefighters. We wanted to give City Hall a noisy warning that the threat of a strike was real and serious, and that it could happen at any time.

The rally really was noisy. The firefighters shouted, "Here comes the snow, it's time to go."
Frank Muscare yelled into a bullhorn, "She promised us a contract and we want one."

We walked across the street and up the stairs of City Hall outside the mayor's office. A group of paramedics were chanting "We're with the firemen 100%."

Ed Tetzner and I went back to meet up with some guys at Northeye's Bar at 58th & Pulaski. The mood was angry because the mayor would not come out and talk to us about the contract.

It just seemed like she was teasing us with this ordinance thing! We hadn't gotten to first base with the city. On February 1, 1980, the executive committee had enough. They took a vote to strike; eleven to strike and one against. The news media went nuts trying to find out when Muscare would make the announcement. Rumor in the firehouse was that it would take place on Sunday morning, February 3rd. All across Chicago, firefighters were cleaning last minute personal things out of firehouses. As we prepared for the worst, I didn't like the tension that was building up in the firehouses. One guy said that he quit the union and he would not go on strike. He was now alone and keeping to himself, making his own coffee on a hot plate. Everyone was disgusted with him. It's too bad, because he's the same guy that he always was, but no one trusted him now. He sat to the side all by himself in silence.

The guys would be split, and when you lived as close as firemen do, when you sort of survived on camaraderie like a great big family that meets every third day for twenty-four hours, you had to have that trust that only firefighters can give each other.

We all had to strike together as we would if we were fighting a fire. It had to be a whole team effort. When the fire was struck out we all went home. With the news of the executive committee vote, the city started marathon bargaining sessions with the union to avert the now planned and threatening strike. City negotiators

Chapter XIV

It was a cold morning and there was snow falling very lightly. The streets were empty and quiet. As my van traveled north on Western Avenue, all I thought about was the men that fought to get better conditions on this job for so many years. My father was a firefighter. What would he do if he was faced with this situation?

My brother Jim was a firefighter on the West Side, and my brother Mike, if for only a short time, had been a paramedical stationed at Ambulance #14 located at 71st and Parnell Avenue. Norm Doolan- what would he be doing this morning. I knew one thing: he would be with the firefighters and, as always, could make us laugh. Although, I'm not too sure that even Norm could bring any laughter out of this mess.

Engine Company #49 and Hook and Ladder #33 were not in quarters when I arrived at the firehouse, but there were a lot of firefighters out in front. We greeted each other and went inside where we were told to sit in the kitchen. I was called into Chief Conte's office. The chief told me that today he would need my support by not striking. I looked the chief in the eye and told him that I just could not work. It would be like abandoning family or a friend in need.

Jim Conte was a good man, and it hurt me to tell him, but he was a high-level chief in a management position, and even he knew that conditions had to get better on the fire department. In the kitchen of Engine #49's house, men were filing in and there were about seventy-five to eighty firefighters. The mood was somber throughout, knowing that in just a few minutes we would walk out the door, and for the first time in the city's history, the Chicago firefighters would go out on strike!

This was the time when each man had to evaluate his own situation and make a decision that would affect him for the rest of his life. Do I walk or do I stay? With that, one of our men, Peter O'Sullivan, stood up and yelled, "There's no sense in waiting any longer, it's after 05:00. I know we are supposed to wait until 05:15, but what the hell, I'm walking now!" With that everyone stood up and started filing out the door.

Ed Tetzner was a union steward, and he started to assemble the men out in front on the apron of the firehouse. How could we be on strike if we didn't have strike signs?

"We walked out a little early. The signs are on the way," said John Sheehan, one of the other stewards.

Some guys said, "Hey Engine #49 and the truck are returning from the fire at 5620 South Hermitage Avenue." The engine and truck pulled up and a loud cheer went up.

"Let's get the rigs back in service and we will all walk out together." Someone yelled, "The hell with the rigs."

The men said that we were going to be gentlemen about this and bed the engine. In no time flat, Engine #49 was back in service, and the men who had just returned from the fire on Hermitage also walked out on strike.

Ed Tetzner said to a reporter, Harry Porterfield, who just

arrived, "The lines are drawn in the sand. We are officially out on strike, and we need to get a barrel to get a fire started."

As the day began and it got light out, cars on Ashland Avenue began honking their horns in support of our strike, and the signs were given to each firefighter. We paced back and forth chanting, "We want a contract." Around the corner on 44th Street, Ed Tetzner was rolling a barrel yelling, "Let's get some wood."

Rumors were flying all over that the mayor and the fire commissioner wanted the strike to end within a few hours, but the hours came and went and we were still out. News from the union came to us about 11:00 hours that ninety-seven percent of the firefighters walked out on strike and the strike, so far, was very effective.

Mayor Byrne told the chiefs that were working, "You had better get your act together," and she was very critical of the fire department upper echelon, who failed to give her accurate reports of how many firefighters were working. The mayor told the news media that the city was in no immediate jeopardy because there were enough firefighters to protect it. Within one hour after the walkout, Circuit Court Judge John Hechinger issued a temporary restraining order requiring all firemen to return to their jobs.

The fire commissioner, Richard Albrecht, had issued a directive, informing all striking firemen back to return to work, and it was also broadcast on radio. But the order did not appear immediately effective because firefighters remained on the picket lines. My feet were cold and I now knew that in order to stay out in the cold I would have to get boots and warm clothes, because the overwhelming majority of firefighters and paramedics were staying out.

Jay McMullen, Byrne's press coordinator and husband, stated

to the press that the city expected half of the firefighting force to return to work by the afternoon as a direct result of the court order. McMullen also stated that no disciplinary action would be taken against those who complied with the order. Police officials called in all off-duty policemen and they were assigned to each fire station in the city. The police officers were told not to expect to go home.

Reports were coming in from everywhere and the news was any member failing to report to work would be subject to disciplinary action, including discharge. The city said that both O'Hare and Midway Airports were manned by firefighters, but the afternoon news showed only two people working at Midway, and no one was sure about the three firehouses at O'Hare.

The city had mutual aid pacts with several neighboring suburban departments that had agreed to cover fires between one and a half and three miles from their borders. There was a meeting at 19:00 hours at the musicians' hall at 175 W. Washington to give strikers an update on any progress.

At the meeting, the mood was defiant as the strikers filled the hall. Frank Muscare said, "She sent us a Valentine and we sent her one right back. I know for sure we won't be sweethearts."
A roar came from the crowded room. The walkout showed the city that we were strong and would remain strong; 97 percent of our brothers and sisters walked out on strike. We had solidarity!

The mayor said that any firefighter that didn't report to work by 08:00 hours would never again work for the Chicago Fire Department. Fire Commissioner Albrecht had ordered food for 1,100 people and we knew they were not all firemen. The meeting ended and Frank "Moon" Muscare said, "Let's all stick together out there."

Someone made a suggestion to start making shifts at the fire-houses and some of the guys could go home. Ed Tetzner and I returned to Engine #49's house where the men were in a good mood. We told the strikers what "Moon" told us and about the suggestion of two shifts. Ed and I would picket at night from 22:00 hours to 08:00 hours. I went off to the 4th Division strike head-quarters looking for Jack Gallapo.

I had coffee with Uncle Jack, Bill Alletto and a few guys from Engine #60's house. As the first day of the strike came to a close, I knew it would be another long day tomorrow. There were a very small number of people working the 120 some firehouses across the city. As a matter of fact, some of the firehouses were closed entirely. What was going through their minds with only two men in some houses and none in others? Battalion chiefs were driving engines to and from incidents if fires broke out. The chief would then go in and put the fire out. I don't think so. God help us all.

As the strike went into its second day, no immediate end was in sight. One thing was for sure, the press was having a field day with this story, and they were not taking the side of the strikers. Jane Byrne had all the newspapers, television, and radio stations in her pocket, as Mike Royko put in his column in the Sun Times. First of all, the strike was illegal. The federal mediator was sum-moned by the city and the union to meet in the Bismarck Hotel; at least, I thought, they were still meeting. City officials prepared to go into circuit court to seek contempt citations against the strikers for disobeying a court order against the strike.

The press filled the air with how much police protection was needed at firehouses, where reports of threats to non-strikers, and a big increase in vandalism was the big bullshit news. Mayor Byrne also said that she was setting up a special hotline for victims of threats or harassment from strikers. She was making the striker out to be a criminal. I just spent all night outside in the cold, and I knew that there was no vandalism or threats by any of the firefighters that stood defiant while others prayed around a wood-burning, fifty-five gallon steel barrel, that first long and lonely night. At around noon, word came that Mayor Byrne reportedly had agreed to compromise on who should be covered by the contract.

The city said that they had contingency plans with suburban fire departments, 140 new cadets from the fire academy, and supervisory personnel who manned slightly more than half of the city's fire equipment. The new cadets from the academy were told that if they didn't cross the picket lines, they could kiss their jobs good-bye. Meanwhile, streets and sanitation personnel were on twenty-four hour call to provide back-up assistance if necessary. One worker yelled out to the strikers, "Keep up the good work. We need the overtime."

"Yeah you guys are making overtime, and in many cases two and a half times our salaries," was the reply.

After some much needed sleep, I returned to 44th and Ashland, and was told to go inside the firehouse to pick up my pay check. I could not believe that the city would pay us while we were on strike. Inside the firehouse, there was a kind of silence, and someone said the chief wanted to see me downstairs. There were about four chiefs that told me that the strike was illegal and the union had misinformed us about the strike. The papers were being drawn up to fire me, they said, and I asked for my pay-check. All the doors to the kitchen were closed, and paper bags from some catering company covered the glass windows. I could hear noise and talking, but I had no idea how many people were in the kitchen. I was given my check and asked to leave, which I did.

Outside, there were some thirty guys all standing around the burning barrel trying to keep warm. The mood was strong, and in no time at all, I felt much better just being with them. An effort was being made to build a hut to block the wind. Wooden pallets were stacked to the side for firewood. Also, a second barrel was being set up in the back of the firehouse on 44th Street.

This firehouse was one of the newer ones, with a side entrance, and that's where all the deliveries to the firehouse were being made. So, we set up a picket line in the front and back.

After being paid, some of the striking firefighters, with money in their pockets, started drinking, and tempers started to flare. Every time we heard a new name of one of our brothers who was on the inside, there was a flare up, saying he could not be working, because he was all for the strike. But low and behold, one by one, we found out that some of our best friends and some excellent firemen were now our enemies. I wondered if they knew that 97 percent of us were on strike, and if the 3 percent walked out, it would be over? News came to the barrel from strike headquarters that the negotiations had broken down this afternoon, but they would resume tonight. The negotiations would now move over to the civic center to Circuit Judge John F. Hechinger's chambers. The Judge said, "Let's start over from the beginning," and moved back and forth from each side as the new mediator. Most of the time was spent with the union and our president, Frank Muscare.

Two more men came out of Engine #104's firehouse at 14th and Michigan, making it a 100% striking firehouse.

The third day came with very little progress made overnight in the judge's chambers and talks broke off early in the morning.

The city said that their contingency plan of paramedic service remained normal and was working. However, a Chicago Hospital Council spokesman said, "City hospitals haven't been notified as of yet what the city's paramedic contingency plan is." One ambulance crew that was at Rush Presbyterian Hospital told the staff that they were cadets in training to become paramedics, and the fire officials told them that if they did cross the picket line they could forget about being a paramedic. Word had it that any ambulances that were in service, were answering calls on the radio rather than working out of firehouses. I met with my brother Mike, to see how he was doing and also the strikers at Engine #54 and Truck #20 were holding up. Mike informed me that the Ambulance #14 was not there, but the firemen were and they were 100 percent out in that house.

Jane Byrne held a press conference where she warned the strikers that they would be fired and replaced if they didn't return to the firehouse by 10:00 P.M. and later extended the deadline to Sunday morning at 10:00 A.M.

Around the barrel that night, it was rather mild outside for February and the mood was getting tense. Firemen were getting a lot of flack at home from their wives and kids. The thought of losing their job was to some, unthinkable. What would I do? I was fifty-one years old and I had been a firefighter for twenty-two years. If I lost this job, who would hire me. Who needed an old man? "Keep your chin up. No one is going to lose their job," someone said. "This will be over soon."

We needed more wood so a few of us made a trip in my van into the stockyards, to a place that had agreed to supply us with old wood pallets. On the way back, I filled two thermoses with hot coffee at Dunkin Donuts. Bob Peterson stopped by with news from strike headquarters. "Stay strong," he told us, "and don't let anyone go back in by the 10:00 A.M. deadline."

We all knew it was going to be very hard to get this contract, they would try anything to get us back. She, the mayor, had lied to everyone about how many men were working and now the news media was finding out just how many were really working. They were ordering food for 1,100 people, but they were throwing most of the food away. It was good to hear any news during the night.

The fourth day of the strike began, and the day shift started arriving. We told them about what Bob Peterson had said and also about the rally at Daley Plaza.

I knew I was tired, but I also knew that the men who were locked up inside must really be exhausted. Rumors about the many arguments and fights among the guys on the inside were the talk of the morning. I went home to get some much needed sleep, but Ed Tetzner and I would go to the rally at noon.

Last night, Judge John Hechinger pleaded with the union and gave them an ultimatum. "Get back to work by 10:00 A.M. tomorrow or you will face contempt of court. You must understand I also have taken a sworn oath, like you, to uphold the law. I will do my job. It will be distasteful, but I must do it," the judge said.

Later that day, five striking firemen were arrested for blocking an engine that was backing into the firehouse at 80th and Kedzie Avenue. At the rally in the Daley Center, "Moon" told us that it would get tougher, but we wouldn't go back without a signed contract. Frank Muscare and the negotiating team went back to the judge's chambers.

Frank Muscare knew he could be held in contempt of court, and perhaps jailed. For the next three hours, the city and the union made a last minute try for some kind of agreement to end the strike, but the effort failed.

Shortly after 2:00 P.M. the judge ruled against the union's motion to dismiss the city's contempt request and they were told to return at 5:00 P.M. for a contempt hearing.

Frank Muscare told the press that yesterday the judge said if we went back to work then we could discuss the contract, but today the mayor said we had to go back to work and we might discuss a contract.

The Mayor told half-truths and outright lies in a press conference, and with her ugly blue polka dot dress on, she said that the fire commissioner would start hiring firefighters to replace the strikers.

The hearing at 5:00 P.M.. ended in a stalemate, and Judge John Hechinger imposed a $40,000 dollar a day fine on the union and its leaders for refusing to end their so-called illegal strike. Later that night at a mass meeting at the McCormick Inn, Frank Muscare addressed the strikers and said, "The Judge asked us to order all of you back to work, and the executive board all said no!"

Also at the meeting, Frank said we had to get the best contract we could now. "So, we're out and we're staying out!" The cheers for Frank and the negotiating them went on for ten minutes. It was back to the barrel, and we left the McCormick Inn. Out in the lobby there were flyers on tables. Eddie said, "Hey, look at this. It's a copy of a newspaper article on how much money these guys are making." A firefighter that normally makes $238.65 per twenty-four hours is now, with overtime, making $477.30 a day. A working engineer makes $520.34 per day. A lieutenant makes $562.76 per day and chiefs are making $732.58 per day.

Someone yelled out, "Well, that explains why a lot of these guys are in the firehouses."

When I got back to the barrel there was only one firefighter there, and he was cold. I had coffee in my van and he sat inside while I broke up some wood and got the fires going in both barrels, front and back. Soon there were some twenty guys outside with us, and we spent the night consoling each other. I went home that morning not knowing what the hell was going on any more.

Monday, February 18th, was the fifth day of the strike. Several hundred persons that were on the Chicago Fire Department's list of eligibility had agreed to temporarily replace striking firefighters. They were told to report to the gymnasium by Navy Pier at 08:00 hours. They were told that the city would accept them on a ninety-day emergency appointment, but later Mayor Byrne arrived at the gym and told them they were replacing the strikers permanently. A large fire broke out at 5450 South Michigan Avenue. Striking firefighters from Engine #61's house ran from about a block away and assisted the weary firemen who had been on duty for four continuous days.

While striking firemen were at home, all they thought about was what was going on at the barrel. Their wives and children asked them why they didn't go back to work. "Do you want to lose the job that you love? The mayor is calling in all the eligible people on the list. Can't you go back and do the right thing for us?" they would say.

It was so hard to answer, because we had made a decision. We had to get this contract. If we went back without the contract, there was a very good chance that we would lose everything anyway.

When you arrived back at the barrel with the men that were

in the same boat with you, there was a special sense of pride that you couldn't show at home to your wife or your children. In no time flat, your morale was back, because we gave strength to each other. There were problems. Guys had sick children, or parents that were old and needed help. Some even had wives that have cancer, but they were still out. What about this barrel? This garbage can that is set up on blocks of wood with holes punched through the bottom of the sides. What did this do for us, besides keep us warm?. All it did was make our clothes smell like fire and when we got into our van or car, then it also smelled.

When the north wind was blowing and you could hear a pin drop, because no one else was outside on nights like this, you stared at the bottom of the glowing can and thought about the better times you had as a firefighter. When I thought about it, I remembered Norm. Oh, how I wish he were here for this one. He would have said, "Dave, you're doing the right thing. Make this job better; get better equipment and working conditions."

The key issue in our strike was very much like all the other firefighter strikes in the state of Illinois. It was whether the officers would be represented by the union, or under the control of the city. Well, in Chicago, there were about 800 officers out of about 4,300 total men. Do you think that if the officers were not in the union that they would get the benefits of the contract that those in the bargaining unit would get? No, they would get a handshake, and in a bad year for the city, they would get a sad story about how tough times were now. We all should be in the bargaining unit, including the battalion chiefs, because we all had the same enemy: fire. In order to fight this enemy, we needed manpower and the right equipment. In order to get the five men on an engine and truck, we needed a contract. We had been working shorthanded for too many years. As the night became day and the day shift relieved us, all we could do was stay together and pray for an end to this nightmare. I said to myself, "Mayor Byrne be honest. Tell the citizens of Chicago that you don't have the situation under control. We know that there are only 313 professional firefighters working. Think about them. They have been locked up inside these firehouses for five days. Oh I guess they are good, but to protect the lives and property of three million people, after some 120 hours without a break, is asking too much of them. They haven't even been able to see their families. This is something that will blow, if they don't get some relief."

The Chicago Federation of Labor and the Teamsters Union voted to honor fire station picket lines, and bar their members from performing "struck work" usually carried out by firemen.

The mayor said that she would never negotiate with Frank Muscare again. More than 300 of the new recruits were given physical examinations and were promised permanent jobs. The mayor said she would ask the judge to enforce his order to remove the pickets. This again was a psychological ploy to play on the minds of the vulnerable firefighters and paramedics.

Local #2 offered the city a realistic plan to give fire protection to the citizens of Chicago by manning fire equipment and ambulances. Mayor Byrne immediately turned down the plan. But after looking at the men who fought the fire on Michigan Avenue on February 18th, it had become very evident that they were exhausted. The union told Mayor Byrne that the offer of the plan would still remain open to her.

All the Mayor was worried about were the "Goon Squads," that she said were terrorists. She called them the roving "Goon Squad." They were men who traveled to different working firehouses to try to get the candidates and working firemen to come out. "We know they want to," one fireman said, "but they can't because they are being held hostage."

The mayor was also concerned about the picketing, and she wanted it stopped, because her quest now was to break this union.

It was Tuesday, February 19th, the sixth day of the strike. Forced by the mayor's newest tactic, William A. Lee, the Chicago Federation of Labor's patriarch, attempted to contact Mayor Byrne in an effort to establish new talks between the city and the union. With the help and assistance of the Chicago Federation of Labor, Bill Lee's input was all we needed. He was a great and very powerful union man. The C.F.L. and Teamsters joint Council #25 could cripple city government by ordering the 12,000 municipal employee members to walk out. Mayor Byrne refused to return Bill Lee's phone calls, and for most of the day, was adamant about now refusing the many calls from Lee.

Mayor Byrne knew why Lee was calling, and she was not sure what her next move would be, because she couldn't get the C.F.L. mad at her. Lee and other labor leaders again threatened to cripple the city agencies by honoring all firefighter pickets if the mayor refused to reopen talks.

Finally, Mayor Byrne called Lee and said, "The men must return to work first, before talks begin. Judge John Hechinger allowed the Chicago Federation of Labor to join in the proceedings. Lee, along with Local 705 President Louis Pelck, the Plumber's Local Union, and Joseph Spingola of the Laborer's Union, met with Mayor Jane Byrne for some two hours. Sometime after midnight, the mayor and the union leader emerged from the long meeting. Byrne had once again, reluctantly agreed to start talking with our union negotiators.

Meanwhile back at the barrel, the good news spread fast across the city. The mood was good, firefighters said, and it was about time that the big union guns finally put the pressure on. Even the guys on the inside of the firehouses were excited, because now, maybe, there would be an end to the strike and they could go home to see their families.

Now that talks had begun, the worry of our jobs would end. We could get back to work, and the citizens of Chicago could once again have great fire protection. As the day shift strikers started to arrive at the barrel, this good news was well accepted.

It was Wednesday, February 20th, the seventh day of the strike. Today was my daughter Mary's birthday, and she was ten years old. I had a good feeling about the new meeting with the mayor and Moon. The union and the city's negotiators, along with the Chicago Federation of Labor, all returned to Judge Hechinger's courtroom chambers. Frank Muscare and the negotiators finally agreed to go back to work, but only for twenty-four hours without a full contract. But at the same time, we would be returning to the firehouses, the city and the union would begin around the clock negotiations. The union insisted on amnesty for all strikers. Bill Lee of the Chicago Federation of Labor put major pressure on Mayor Byrne, and she agreed to amnesty, except for those engaged in criminal or quasi-criminal activity. An agreement was formed. The men would return to the firehouses and the talks would begin.

A big rally was held at the McCormick Inn later that same night. Some 3,000 striking firefighters began yelling, "Moon, Moon," as they hailed Frank "Moon" Muscare when he walked to the podium.

Frank Muscare explained to the firefighters and paramedics that they could continue picketing firehouses, but should return to work by 11:00 hours Thursday.

Striking firemen put down their picket signs and non-striking firemen settled in for the last hours of the strike. After hearing the news that the union firefighters voted overwhelmingly to end their week-long strike, at least temporarily, the non-striking firemen who answered some 900 fire calls during the week, could express only relief, knowing their fatigue-filled days would be over soon.

In the north side division headquarters, at 3401 North Elston Avenue, Battalion Chief Robert Montgomery managed a smile. "I am very, very glad it's over," he said. "It really takes the pressure off. I can't count the number of fires we have fought."

The Chief said, "We all had decisions to make when the strike came down. Mine was to stay in, while others walked out on strike. I just hope we can be a team again, like before the strike."

Lieutenant John Leahy of Engine Company #62 on the south side, said that he was very worried over the agreements made in Mrs. Byrne's office. "Although I am pleased that it's over, I am not very happy about this amnesty that these treasonous firefighters will get. I don't think walking off the job should go unpunished," Leahy said. "I just hope we can work together again. It was a war, a war of nerves, and I know we won, because the strikers acted like cowards."

I said to myself, "That's his opinion and not mine or that of thousands of other firefighters."

On Thursday, February 21st, after 11:00 hours, the strikers started signing in at firehouses around the city. The mood was good, but some of the men were worried. I was sent back to

Engine #39 with Captain James Fox, Engineer Porter, and Firefighter James Robertson. We were glad it was over, because we are broke. The jubilation was unanimous. I was the cook, and spaghetti and Italian sausage would be the meal. We checked the engine out, because it hasn't been used in a week. The Marshal line rang; it was for me. "Cos? This is Bergdolld on Truck #8. Don't make your beds just yet!"

Bill Bergdolld was in my class when I came on the job. In fact he was the one that made the sound "EEE — OOOO," and he was a great firefighter. In a very excited voice, he said, "The city refused to meet with the union to discuss the contract because of some picketers." He also said that many houses did not open; they were locked out.

Within a few minutes I received a call from Bill Bracken, also a firefighter that I came on the job with. He said that he and Bill Alletto were in Engine #60's firehouse signing up when they heard the news that Moon was in jail. He also told me that his engine company #50 was being locked out. "We're back on strike!" Bill Alletto was so mad that he told some of the guys before we walked out, "Look in all the rooms and the basement. If you find anyone hiding, bring the son-of-a-bitch out bodily!"

The fire officials thought that if they let strikers back in the firehouses, after hearing the news about Muscare being jailed, that they might sabotage the fire equipment, so they locked us all out. I think what happened was after Fire Commissioner Albrecht's return to work order was refused because of picketers, the city called off talks, and both sides returned to Judge Hechinger's courtroom.

The union was told to follow Albrecht's orders about returning to work, and to take down the picket signs. The union agreed, but the city remained unconvinced. The city asked the judge to vacate the agreement because there was still picketing. Again, the city administration started to play the psychological warfare games.

Judge Hechinger heard the news, and found fault with both parties. The judge lashed out at Muscare, and reinstated the fines against the union. The judge charged Frank Muscare with criminal contempt of the court, and sentenced him to five months in the Cook County Jail. Cook County Sheriff's deputies took him out of the courtroom and delivered him to the Cook County Jail!. Five other firefighters on the executive board were also charged with civil contempt of the court, and were each fined $1,000 dollars.

Moon said, from the jail, that this was a deliberate and calculated plan. "The Mayor thought that I couldn't sell this to the firefighters, going back for twenty-four hours while the around-the-clock negotiations went on. When the mayor agreed to this, she was stuck with the agreement. So she had to get out of it, because she does not want to negotiate a contract with the firefighters."

As we got all of our personal equipment together at Engine #39's firehouse, all I could think of was we couldn't go back out in the cold again. Soon two police officers came through the front door. They said they had orders to lock everyone out, unless we were going to stay in. This was bullshit. What was going on? One of the cops tried to calm me down. He said, "Take all the time you need. You don't have to leave right now." Ed Porter looked at me and said, "Let's get the barrel burning again."

Captain Fox wouldn't come out with us, but within a few hours we had the barrel burning and Jimmy Robertson ran and got some hot dog rolls and a bottle of Ten High Whiskey. We ate the Italian sausage and Fox came out later.

Bill Cosgrove, the author, in front of Engine 39's fire house.

It was the longest night that I have ever spent. We had no idea what we were going to do. One thing was for sure: we were going to keep that barrel burning. Ed Porter and I went to 44th and Ashland to find out the news or anything of interest to the strikers. No one knew anything about what was going on. We then went to 4th Division Strike Headquarters at 4956 South Halsted. There were a lot of mad firefighters milling around there.

The most important thing was that we had to stick together. We would all find out as soon as we could. We had to stay strong and not let anyone go back in the firehouse. As the north wind blew on that cold night, we just huddled around the barrel trying to keep warm.

On Friday, February 22nd, the news wasn't good. Mayor Byrne thought now that Muscare was out of the way in jail, that she would end the strike her way. The executive board sent a news release stating that all union members had now left their firehouse and resumed the strike. William McClennan of the Firefighters International Union would arrive in Chicago later today. Local #2 made a formal appeal to the entire labor community to come to our assistance and support us against the city's union busting tactics.

Michael Lass was the staff representative for the International Association of Firefighters. He had been unsuccessful for several years in trying to get a contract for Local #2. Lass said that this was a fully organized, fully orchestrated, fully coordinated, union bust. With the utilization of the courts, Mayor Byrne and the city did not want the firefighters to have a contract, Lass was convinced, because it was a major threat to their patronage system.

Instead of having sponsors and your clout as a vehicle for transfers, assignments, and promotion, what would be in place would be the right of seniority, which was the core of every trade union that it usually enjoys in any collective bargaining relationship.

The principles that would be negotiated in a collective bargaining agreement could and would be the end of the patronage system on the Chicago Fire Department. The heads of the four Chicago Federation of Labor Unions, called Mayor Jane Byrne, and a special meeting was held in Marina City for some eighty minutes. I sure would like to have been a fly on the wall to hear what they had to say to her. Later they met with our union leaders for some two hours. Together the CFL and the firefighters union leaders returned to City Hall without Mike Lass and Dale Berry, the union's attorney. The talks began at around 15:30 hours and continued until 23:00 hours.

try to convince them to come out and join us on the picket line and bring an end to this protracted strike," Bill said.

The crowd cheered and yelled as we all left the amphitheater. For one of the first times, I felt the true meaning of just how many firefighters were on strike. They came from the far northwest side of the city. Firefighters came from Engine #119 and Truck #55 in the Norwood Park community and from Engine #102 and Truck #25 in the Edgewater community.

There were firefighters from the West Side, Engine #96 and Truck #29, from the Austin community; and from the far southwest side, Engine #92 and Truck #45, from the Mount Greenwood community. The firefighters of Engine #97 were also there from the Hegewisch community. If Jane Byrne watched this rally on television, then she also would know the true meaning of how many firefighters and paramedics were on strike. We stood united for a just cause. We wanted a contract!

I never felt more pride in my life than I did that night with the thousands of other firefighters that left the International Amphitheater.

It was February 24th, the eleventh day of the strike, with the spirit high from the rally. Fire union officials leveled new attacks on Bill Lee of the Chicago Federation of Labor. They wanted to call an all out strike and cripple the city, because the mayor was not willing to talk to our negotiating team. The mayor said that she would agree to amnesty, except for those engaged in criminal or quasi-criminal activity. Quasi-criminal means to some manner, or to some degree, of criminal activity.

The union said that when we went back to work there would be total amnesty or we wouldn't return.

They had a new name for a fire engine. It was called "Task

Force 42" and the commander of this task force was none other than Bill Foran. His fire department superiors in City Hall called him "Wild Bill." He lived up to his name when he took Task Force 42 all the way down to City Hall from the south side firehouse where he had been holed up since the strike began. He wanted to meet with the mayor, but was told to wait. Foran shouted at reporters, "The chief of the uniformed force runs the fire department, not some lunatic like Frank Muscare." Foran finally met with mayoral aides, because the mayor was too busy that afternoon.

The talk around the barrel that night was all about "Wild Bill" Foran, and how it was only a matter of time before one of those recruits got hurt following "Wild Bill" into fires. "Just look at what his bull-headedness brings on, like what the media has seen at the few fires this week," was one of the comments. Rookie firefighters and bone-tired non-strikers scrambled about in a frenzy that would have been comical had life and property not hung in the balance.

As the barrel burned into the night, one firefighter took new wood from the pile, and said, "We deserve a contract. The citizens of Chicago deserve fire protection. Both are possible if the mayor gets off her high horse and starts talking sincerely with the union negotiators".

CHAPTER XV

On FEBRUARY 25TH, the twelfth day of the strike, there were no talks set for the day. The mayor told the union, in a press release, either accept or reject the memorandum of agreement that the city and the labor leaders presented, because it would be the last offer from the city. Mayor Byrne's negotiating stance with the union came under attack from Alderman Martin Oberman of the 43rd Ward. Oberman told reporters at City Hall that everything she was doing was all calculated to prolong the firefighters strike. She wanted to destroy the union and scuttle the collective bargaining ordinance. "I believe she is going out of her way to make this strike worse every day," Oberman said. Five of Chicago's labor leaders also issued their own statement to the press, blasting the mayor, stating that Byrne was becoming the city's worst strike breaker in history.

In the CTA Transit strike, the Chicago teachers strike and now the firefighters strike, the mayor's first reaction was to threaten all union people with the loss of jobs, and to question their right to retain improvements they had made over the years. Maybe now the press and the politicians would rise in one voice and tell this mayor that what she was doing was all wrong. This was an election year and candidates who were running for office didn't want to get caught up in any protracted labor dispute.

Around the barrel that night firefighters could only think about how long it would take before she would start talking and bring this to an end. Another guy said to his buddies around the barrel, "I want to tell our union negotiators and Mayor Byrne one thing: this is bullshit. What are you people doing down there! You're all playing with the lives of a lot of people. My wife is so sick of this she wants to leave with the kids. Take this seriously please, because I am puking in the toilet at night, and my kids are crying because they think I will never be a fireman anymore. Start talking! Please."

I got worried when I heard that Mayor Byrne was deliberately prolonging the strike and using it as a psychological ploy to weaken the union membership.

It was February 26th, the thirteenth day of our strike. There were no new talks scheduled for today, but a new federal mediation representative from Washington would be flying into Chicago. Edward McMahon had been involved with strikes before, and had brought the opposing sides to an agreement. Firefighters welcomed him with open arms, but the city refused to meet with Mr. McMahon without even giving a reason. Some say he left because he knew she was using the Seaforth & Shaw law firm as advisors, and everyone knew they were notorious for their anti-labor stance and strategies.

There hadn't been any effort to end the strike since February 22nd, when labor leaders and the mayor met in the Marina City complex for two hours. In the past twelve days there hadn't been many fires in the city, thank God. As compared to an average day before the strike, there might be some two or three working still and box alarms, and a couple of 2-11 alarm fires almost every day. The city, and the make-shift fire department of older men and new recruits, had really been just lucky, The number of calls we used to respond to in a normal day weren't happening. Why? It was not as though I wanted to see all those fires break out all at once, but someone was just lucky. This city didn't have the right amount of fire protection, and this was being withheld from the firefighters, citizens of Chicago, and the media. The city said there was adequate fire protection and they knew that was bullshit!.

An independent expert analyzed the level of fire protection. He was Boyd Hartley, Chairman of the Department of Fire Protection and Safety Engineering worked at the Illinois Institute of Technology. Hartley said the key to effective firefighting was well-trained men, including an extensive training program. Without hands-on experience, you could have big problems. There were young men who had been holed up in firehouses and training without the necessary equipment, like in the fire academy. So, solutions in this city might not be so simple, not so simple as hiring a few hundred or a few thousand new men to fight fires. Firefighters, who had the great reputation, got to where they were the same way a fireman gets to the roof, one rung at a time.

It took years to build firemen who worked as smoothly as the best rigs on the department. A man who learned how to do it ten years ago, taught a man who was trying to learn. That man would take his teacher's place ten years later, because that's the way we did it in Chicago. You couldn't show a person movies, manuals, and war stories on how to be a firefighter. You had to be there to learn, time and time again, you had to be there.

It just seemed that whenever we felt the worst, it was because we were away from the barrel. Being at home watching the news or in the car listening to the news, made us feel like everything was all wrong. But when we returned to that barrel with our fellow firefighters, there was a sense of strength, of solidarity, being united again, and we were able to make it through one more night.

On February 27th, the fourteenth day, the fire commissioner, Richard Albrecht, made a final ultimatum. If the firefighters returned to work by 8:00 P.M.. there would be no disciplinary action. The biggest question was amnesty; who would get amnesty and who would not. The city said that no matter what happened, the seven battalion chiefs who went out on strike would be fired, because they were in management positions. Chiefs Mike Murphy, John McDonough, Fred Van Dorpe, John Wassinger, Ray Bleschke and Mike Wernick were the villains of the civic tragedy. Or were they men who had been driven into a corner by this double talk and broken promises over the years? Were they really irresponsible, ugly men who no longer should be permitted to lead firefighters into fires, as they had done for so many years?

I had known Chief Michael Murphy for many years. He, like many others, came from a long, family history of firefighters. His father was on the job. Chief Murphy's brother, Terry, was a firefighter on Hook & Ladder #20 at 71st and Parnell. From personal experience, I knew Mike Murphy to be a good and decent man, dedicated to saving lives and safeguarding property, and very often at the risk of his own life. I remember just before the strike, I met Chief Murphy at a 3-11 alarm fire, and he spoke with anger and shame that this fire should never have went to an extra alarm, but there was not enough manpower with which to fight the fire. When the division marshal asked Chief Murphy how he lost this one, he answered, "I did the best I could with what they sent me, Chief."

On February 28th, the firefighters ignored the fire commissioner's return to work order, and on February 29th, the 16th day, both the city and the union rejected a federal mediator's plan to resume talks on a contract. This meant that there hadn't been any serious talking in some six days, except that our union officials had made an offer to accept a labor contract that was very similar to the one that Mayor Byrne proposed a week ago. In the meantime, at 4th Division strike headquarters at 4956 South Halsted, Jack Gallapo was calling all local hospitals about an information meeting on March 1st at the Holiday Inn located at Madison and Halsted.

It was good to see Uncle Jack and also Bill Alletto that day. They were very busy coordinating 4th Division strike activities. We had a cup of coffee, and asked one another, "I wonder what Norm would think of how this is being handled?"

Uncle Jack asked me if I could help out with some picket signs that had to be put together for the big rally on Sunday, March 2nd at the Daley Plaza. Around the barrel, the men prepared for a long night. Bad news came to the barrel that Frank Muscare's attempt to be free from his jail cell was denied by the Illinois Supreme Court. Fire Commissioner Albrecht stated that he had now taken steps to discipline 280 of the striking firefighters, possibly by suspending or firing them.

The fire commissioner also stated that they, the city, had made a couple of mistakes with correct figures of how many men were working in firehouses. The city said they would hire 200 more recruits, bringing the number up to 1,132 that were now in training. Albrecht said that there were 616 experienced men now working with 227 recruits, for a total of 843 on duty! Also 106 paramedics were working with the support of 195 repair personnel at the repair shops. On a normal day in the fire department there were only 833 on one platoon. The outlook was very grim for us. Edward McMahon, the federal mediator who was sent from Washington, stated that he was convinced that the negotiating process was hopelessly deadlocked and with that, he returned to Washington.

The bitter cold wind was out of the north, and to make matters worse it began to snow. Angry and cold we huddled together around the barrel. It would be another cold, cold night. Some of us prayed, and some spit into the burning barrel. "Who do they think they are, playing with our lives?"

On March 1st, the 17th day of the strike, we were all summoned to gather at Michigan and Balboa Streets across the street from the Conrad Hilton Hotel. We were going to embarrass Mayor Byrne by jeering and booing Senator Edward Kennedy who was running for president against President Jimmy Carter in the upcoming primary on March 18th. About 1,000 strikers were there, and he knew we were there.

Kennedy tried to ignore our jeering, but when everyone started yelling, "we want Carter," there was a very worried look on his face. Before Kennedy arrived, Vice President Walter Mondale, also in the city for a campaign stop, left the Conrad Hilton Hotel and was cheered by striking firefighters while they waited for Kennedy.

This was an election year, and the big race was Senator Richard M. Daley, who was backing the president, and was running for Cook County States Attorney against Alderman Edward Burke. Burke was a supporter of Jane Byrne.

The union again made a proposal with significant concessions, but the city had stonewalled them. To let matters drag on with no action would only bring new bitterness, and not do anyone any good. The angry firefighters that were on strike called the working personnel that were in the firehouses, "scabs," and they wanted to get even. "They are taking our jobs away from us, goddamnit," one striker yelled. "I have twelve years on this department. All I want to do is get back to work and make a living for me and my family. Why is this mayor stonewalling us? I think she wants to bring us to our knees and destroy the union."

The mayor had promised her way into this dilemma and it would have to be largely up to her to maneuver her way toward a satisfactory solution. We all knew sooner than later this was going to happen. Six non-striking firefighters were injured last night on the West Side. A fire destroyed a two-story apartment building located at 4926 West Harrison. One of the men that was injured was one of the young recruits who had just come on the job. Two others went through a floor and fell into the basement. The rest of the injured suffered from smoke inhalation. A recruit firefighter about twenty-one years old, came out of a firehouse after his last alarm and joined the strikers on the picket line. He said that he had been a recruit since February 16, and had fought roughly six working fires. He said he was naturally scared in the fire building, and painted a very dismal picture of the type of training he had received. About the only instances of training he could remember were learning sessions in rolling up the hose and tying knots.

At a rally in a south side restaurant, wives of the striking firefighters made a statement that they were now in this fight. Grandmothers, mothers, wives and sisters said, "Enough is enough."

"Where are all the aldermen of this big city," one wife yelled out at the rally? "Their job is to represent you, the voters."
Another wife stood up and said, "Perhaps the people of Chicago

are not aware that this strike has been looming since the firefighters' civil service status was taken away a few years ago. Also, their retirement pension, which they have paid into for many years, is being threatened of being substituted for a lesser benefit under social security."

"Dedicated firefighters, their lives in jeopardy constantly, now have no job security and have been forced into a strike by the city of Chicago when the promise for a badly needed contract was broken. Now the city has spent huge sums of taxpayer money for the strikebreakers. The overtime that all city departments are receiving is so much a mismanagement of the taxpayers' money. Someone should be liable. The idea of no talks, because the Mayor won't grant amnesty, it is a sin," one woman said.. The women were given a standing ovation from the mostly feminine rally. They wanted the mayor to speak at the rally in the Daley Center Plaza the next day. She naturally declined.

I spent more time at the barrel than I did with my kids, and it showed. But, I hoped they would understand one day that I went on strike in order to make their lives better. They all remember the times that we worked and were not at home. Christmas, Easter, and Thanksgiving, so many of the important holidays, not only were we not in our homes with our families, but we never got any pay for being in the firehouse on those very special days.

At the barrel, we gave each other a sense of unity. It was cold out and the fire in the barrel was the only thing that kept us warm. If you faced it, you got warm on the front, and then you turned around and warmed your back, all night long. You kept moving so your feet didn't freeze.

Sunday, March 2nd, was the 18th day of the strike. As I returned home to sleep, my neighbors were going to church with their families. There was going to be a big rally today and I had to be there. Mayor Byrne had vowed to overhaul the strike-depleted Chicago Fire Department, and as far as she was concerned, the strike was over. Meanwhile, our executive board had asked Mayor Byrne to reconsider a federal mediator's proposal to resume bargaining.

The proposal, according to the mediator, and the union, was identical to the one made by the city earlier. Mayor Byrne flatly rejected the proposal by the federal mediator. Jane Byrne said the union was trying to control the entire fire department, and firemen would return to work on her terms, or not at all.

The overhaul needed to be done by an outside group to find out what was wrong and had been wrong for years. The management of the fire department was old-fashioned and needed to be modernized. The city had contracted Donald Jacobs, Dean of Northwestern University's Kellogg Graduate School of Management, to begin an in-depth study of the fire department's management structure. "It is a very sick department and has been disorganized for years," the mayor said.

Ed Tetzner and I arrived at the Daley Center Plaza. Several thousand firefighters and their wives and children showed that they were united. It was very cold out and there was a lot of anger within the crowd. Bill Reddy, acting vice president of Local #2 told the strikers that if we went back without a contract, we would be going back in on our knees begging, and they would keep us begging for a long time. As we listened in the wind-swept Daley Plaza, braving the twenty-four-degree temperatures for over two hours, the overwhelming majority of the strikers roared their solidarity.

At the same time the rally was taking place, just across the street Jesse Jackson had met with Mayor Byrne. She had agreed to let Jesse Jackson enter the conflict as an unofficial mediator.

At about 12:30, hours Jesse Jackson met with Bill Reddy and was immediately accepted as a mediator. After Jackson addressed the rally, he asked them to march on a prayer pilgrimage down Washington Street to State Street, and all the time the march went on they chanted "Jesse, Jesse," and returned to the Daley Plaza. In a prayer meeting, Reverend Jackson said, "Let us bow our heads in prayer. This is a serious and critical moment today. People's lives have been lost and their homes have been disrupted."

The rally ended with new hope that Reverend Jackson, as a mediator, can bring an end to this bitter strike. After the rally we stopped at a bar to meet with some of the guys. The gathering was located at 57th & Pulaski. They had hot dogs and chili for us. I sat with a good friend, Jim Carroll. He was a firefighter on Engine Company #107 on the West Side. We talked about the job and how much we loved being firemen. Jim said, "Cos, I can't lose this job. I worked too hard and too long to get it."

I replied to him, "We all worked hard to get this job."

Jim said, "I was a Coke driver, and waited over five years to be called. In February of 1971, I broke my leg and it was a bad break. I was in a cast for some four months. They called me for the job and I reported to the academy in a brace. After a few days, the fire department drill master, Chief Harold Prohaska, told me that I wasn't going to cut this work, and he sent me home. I had four kids, a wife, and a mortgage, and I didn't know what I was going to do. I called a friend who was a firefighter, and he told me to go see Commissioner Quinn. The next day, my wife and I showed up in the commissioner's office. I never knew Quinn or any politician. We waited for hours and around noontime, we were called into Quinn's office. I told the commissioner that I need this job, and he asked how I broke my leg in the first place. I didn't want to lie so I told him the truth, that I broke it roller skating and it was almost better. Quinn told me not to tell anyone about roller skating and to go back to the academy and do my best. After a week, Chief Prohaska again sent me home, saying I couldn't do the job.

Again, I returned to the commissioner's office, and sat there all day before he finally called me. Quinn said, 'Carroll, you have a lot of balls coming in here asking for help. I like that about you, and I am sure you will be a good firefighter.' Quinn picked up the red phone on his desk and gave the word, and he told me that he never wanted to see me again. Cos, now you see why I can't lose this job."

I said it was a good story that I would always remember.

When we returned to the barrel, I thought about what Jim Carroll and many other firefighters went through getting this job. Bill Bracken stopped with coffee and to tell us news that he heard at 4th Division Headquarters. If anyone in our family was going to have any surgeries or be admitted to the hospital, we had better pay one month of our insurance just to be we were covered.

Rich Diver and his wife, Joyce, had a baby boy. He was named Richie, Jr. He was 8 lbs. 12 oz., and there were cigars at the 4th Division strike headquarters.

Another firefighter heard that Chicago police caught one of Jane Byrne's new recruits with four small bags of marijuana at the police gym at 3540 South Normal Avenue. Also, the non-striking firemen received checks and were boasting about how much they received.

Bill Kugelman, chairman of the union's strike committee said he didn't know about the reorganization that the mayor had talked about. We didn't want to take control of the fire department; we wanted a contract. This was the talk around the barrel that night.

March 3rd was the 19th day that we have been on strike, and the sixth day that Jane Byrne hadn't spoken to the union. News spread of five persons who were killed in an early morning fire at 18th and St. Louis Avenue the day before. In another fire on the city's southeast side, the city said the response time to the fire was eight minutes, but it took them, the new recruits, over twenty minutes to get water on the fire. State Representative Carol Mosely Braun, who watched the recruits in action from her office across the street, said "They couldn't set up the ladders, and once they did, they were afraid to climb them. They didn't even enter the building, but instead quarreled among themselves about who was in charge." Carol Mosely Braun called for an immediate end to the strike, no matter what it took on either side. The fire that she watched was 7124 South Merrill Avenue, a forty-eight-unit apartment building.

The tempo of fires appeared to pick up in Chicago. Non-striking firemen fought fires at a warehouse at 1100 West Courtland and also at Armitage and Elston Avenue. On the south side, a fire took the life of a thirty-year-old woman at 8417 South Aberdeen Street.

The Chicago Police Department stated that they were taxed by the firefighter strike. They had canceled all furloughs, holidays, and put police officers on twelve-hour shifts. Police Superintendent Brzeczek stated that the strike was costing the police department about $270,000 per day in overtime expenses alone.

One young recruit worked for eleven straight days, and then quit. He told the media that they were not being trained because they didn't have enough people to train them. They were locking them in firehouse basements and in the bunkrooms, and brainwashing them. Mayor Byrne knew that all the fingers of this city were pointing at her for refusing to attend meetings with union officials. If she was not there, then she sent a signal to the people of Chicago that she didn't care about fire protection in Chicago. "This is union busting and the people don't like it," said Martin Oberman of the 43rd Ward. "She is concerned with what Adlai Stevenson, Richard M. Daley, and the political races say, not the firefighters on strike."

March 4th was the 19th day of the strike, and the city continued to boycott formal negotiations with striking firemen. City officials said their position remained the same: return to work and then we will talk. Bill Reddy, acting president of Local #2, who had been working day and night to bring the city to the bargaining table said whether illegal or not, we were trying to settle this strike, so we all can get back to work and the city of Chicago would have fire protection once again. The attorneys for the seven battalion chiefs pleaded before the Chicago Personnel Board that the city should not be permitted to take disciplinary action against them because of the strike.

Meanwhile, Reverend Jesse Jackson had met with more than fifty black striking firefighters to inform them that their support and the support of the rest of the black firefighters could be used as a bargaining chip to get talks going again between the city and the union. After meetings with the mayor and the union, Jackson began talks at the Bismarck Hotel.

Finally, talking began after some eleven days. The union made one of the first steps to negotiate in good faith by appointing the first black to the executive board. Landis McAlpin was a twenty-three- year veteran of the Chicago Fire Department, and also of Local #2. This was a good move for the union and Bill Reddy to win the support of some 400 black striking firefighters.

Firefighters Union lawyer, Dale Berry, started a petition drive urging Mayor Byrne to resume negotiations to end the strike. The drive drew support of Alderman Roman Pucinski of the 41st Ward. With the help of the communities in Chicago we could lean on the mayor to resume talks with the union. In a school hall at 7400 West Touhy Avenue, Berry told angry citizens that the mayor cared about one thing, "power," and she defied public opinion.

Back at the barrel, the talk among strikers was about the fires that were happening all over the city. Five people were killed in a burning West Side building and three of the victims were kids. When would this end? The recruits didn't have any training to rescue victims. They said about ten new firemen with clean ,black firecoats with clear yellow stripes, were the only ones battling the blaze.

One of the guys said, "I am concerned about the silly bastards. They are young and inexperienced."

Before he was done saying that, another firefighter yelled at him, "What's the matter with you? Silly bastards is what you call them? They are scabs, and they are taking our jobs away from us. Don't you listen to the radio or television? Do you read the newspaper? She is replacing us one by one, and soon there will be enough of those silly bastards and this strike will be over."

We all felt bad about the victims of the fires, but if we didn't get back to the bargaining table, we would be out of a job. Jesse Jackson was putting some pressure on the mayor and there was hope that he could start the talks once again. As more wood was thrown into the burning barrel, the angry firefighters tried to console each other. We had to stay strong, and the only way to do that was to stay united. But, it was cold outside, and the morale was down. The wind continued to blow out of the north, and my body was almost frozen. I thought to myself, if we are replaced, the experience that these firefighters have would be forever lost. It would take years to properly train the new recruits who would replace us. At one time I never thought it could happen, but now I just didn't know. I was scared, but didn't want to show my concern.

It must be said, and said plainly, Mayor Byrne was as wrong as she could be to continue stonewalling us. By doing so, she guarantees that the strike continued. Did she really want to bust this union? We had backed off many of our demands, saying we would accept a firm, no strike clause, and the binding arbitration offer that the city made weeks ago. The mayor had done a disservice to Chicago, as we did originally by going out on strike. By not talking to anyone, she was hurting the citizens, the striking firefighters and the non-striking firefighters, that were now exhausted after being locked up inside the firehouses across this city. Don't kid yourself, Mayor Byrne, this recent tragic loss of children was felt very deeply by all striking firefighters. We had felt this grief hundreds and hundreds of times before, because it was directly attributed to a lack of sufficient manpower.

I have felt the joy of rescuing people and so have many other firefighters who pushed themselves beyond their limits. It was hard to think that more lives could have been saved if there were two more men with us in the burning structure. This was one of the primary reasons for the strike. Men who appeared on the annual budget, but never on the engines and trucks. This had to be eliminated.

March 5th was the 20th day of the strike. I guess the mayor was now feeling the pressure. Communities across the city were outraged by the mayor's bullheadedness of not talking. The fires were not being extinguished and now there were more victims of fires every day. Mayor Byrne had still refused to talk to the fire-fighters, but had now agreed to meet with a top official of their International Union. International Secretary Frank Palumbo said that he would attempt to persuade the mayor to meet with union officials. The city's chief negotiator, William Hanley confirmed that Byrne would meet with Palumbo to discuss, not negotiate.

The meeting was planned for early that evening. The strike had gone on for twenty days, while the union refused to end it unless contract negotiations resumed, and amnesty was granted. The city refused to grant amnesty and demanded that the strikers go back to work before negotiations resumed. We were all acting like kids, instead of grown-ups, with our emotions sparked by hotheads on both sides of the labor dispute. They were indulging themselves in the cheapest of human emotions, "anger," instead of talking and working this out.

In the meeting between Mayor Byrne and Frank Palumbo, which took most of the day, the city proposed no reprisals of dis-ciplinary action against the rank and file firemen, except those responsible for criminal or quasi criminal behavior such as vio-lence or vandalism. The mayor promised to show mercy in cases of quasi-criminal behavior.

Mayor Jane Byrne demanded the following:

Loss of one day's pay for striking firemen and engineers.

Loss of two days' pay for striking lieutenants.

Loss of three days' pay for striking captains.

There was a recommendation of leniency to the city personnel

"Brotherhood of the Barrel" button.

board from Fire Commissioner Richard Albrecht in the cases of the seven striking battalion chiefs, the highest ranking fire department officers to join the walkout. The city earlier had taken steps to fire them.

The news was good. There were talks going on again. Jack Gallapo asked me to help out with making signs for the big meeting at the International Amphitheater. This could be it. Once the meeting was held, we could take a vote and the strike would be over.

At the barrel, there were new pins that came out for all of us to wear. They were called "Brotherhood of the Barrel" buttons.

The button depicted a garbage can burning with pieces of wood sticking out the top, and on the side it had the words "Brotherhood of the Barrel" inscribed on it. We were told to wear them with pride. We talked about the recent fires that occurred in the city and how some of our brothers were being accused of arson. I know we were mad and angry, but not mad enough to start a fire. There were stories in the newspaper on every page about the strike. We didn't know what to believe anymore. We all received a letter from Frank Muscare, in jail, about the contract and also about the upcoming union election. He was asking for our votes for president and to vote for the new team urging us to vote for them. But Moon left out four of the men who were now on the executive board, namely Jack Gallapo. I just didn't know how to feel about this. Jack Gallapo was the union's past president and had been active in the union since I met him. Bill Kugelman said that this was the wrong time to bring this up to the membership.

Chapter XVI

March 6th was the 21st day of the strike. The union meeting and rally was tonight and it would be a full house. The daily newspapers stated that Mayor Byrne called the firefighter's strike "a political strike encouraged by one of her foes, State Senator Richard M. Daley," and he was "behind the strike all the way," the Mayor said. Byrne said her problems with the Chicago Firefighters Union began after Daley announced he was running for Cook County State's Attorney nomination. Jane Byrne was supporting his opponent Alderman Edward M. Burke of the 14th Ward. She said as many as 1,400 of the city's 4,350 firefighters came from wards controlled by her political opponents: Daley of the 11th Ward; Cook County Assessor Thomas Hynes of the 19th Ward; Alderman Roman Pucinski of the 41st Ward.

This again was political bullshit of the first order! As a matter of fact, about three months after the strike, Bill Alletto met Richard Daley at a meeting and Daley mentioned that the strike was a terrible thing for both the people of Chicago, and the firefighters. Daley asked Bill Alletto what he did and Bill replied, "I was a twenty-three-day hard-core striker."

Daley replied, "I figured as much."

So if the strike was orchestrated by Daley, as Byrne charged, how come Daley didn't know what Bill Alletto did during the strike?

The strike was costing the city a bundle of money. Over fifteen million dollars in overtime had been paid to employees of the Department of Streets and Sanitation, the Department of Sewers, and the Chicago Police Department. Most the employees had been putting in twelve-hour days. City employees were paid time and a half for the first two hours above an eight-hour day, and double time for any time after ten hours.

The city was spending about 750,000 dollars per day for the overtime wages, including more than 250,000 dollars a day in wages for the police department.

The man in charge of putting out fires in Chicago was running short of men and patience. When asked by a reporter to show on a map what fire stations were in service, he replied, "The ones with the orange and green stick-on dots are in service." The reporter asked about all the fire stations with no dots. Chief Bill Foley just looked at the reporter and said, "If we tried to man too many stations, we'd be too spread out. We couldn't respond as an effective team."

Protocol was that police officers arrived on the scene first, because they were dispatched to the scene to report whether the call was bona fide or not. Police have criticized the fire department's response time, the reporter told Chief Foley. The police said that at a fire yesterday at 1434 South St. Louis, they waited almost fifteen minutes for an ambulance, and then transported the victims in police cars. "We are sacrificing a certain amount of response time to keep manpower up, because we're using a system of strike forces. So far it has been extremely effective," Foley said.

All but two firehouses on the West Side of the city were

closed. They put extra men in the stations at 1100 South California and 4666 West Fulton Street. On the south side of the city, they had task forces at 4401 South Ashland Avenue and 5955 South Ashland Avenue. In the Loop, one house was open at 55 West Illinois Street. On the north side of the city, the firehouses at 1625 North Damen, 1732 West Byron Street, 3401 North Elston Avenue, and 1723 West Greenleaf Avenue were open. The manpower was 984 firemen on duty, including 280 newly recruited trainees. The trainees were not going inside burning buildings; they stayed outside and handled ladders, hose lines, and that sort of thing, in a most inexperienced manner.

If you thought there was trouble with the fires, just guess what was happening to the ambulance service. Striking paramedics had been charging that there were only a handful of paramedics working and the rest were CETA Workers (Congressional Educational Training Act) who could, at best, only apply a splint, a bandage, and give cardio-pulmonary resuscitation.

"They can't administer IV's; they can't give drugs; they can't take an EKG; and they can't use the telemetry hook-ups to hospitals. It's back to scoop em and haul em," said one striking paramedic.

One Chicago Police Officer told reporters, "I'm a cop, not a paramedic. I'm not trained to save lives. I wouldn't know a heart attack from an appendicitis attack. Even if I did, I wouldn't know what to do about it."

Between a person calling 911 and then sending the police out to see if someone was really sick, and then calling communications that it was a bona fide medical emergency, they finally sent out an ambulance twenty-five minutes later. The officer said, "A person can die waiting."

Dr. Franaszek of Billings Hospital, said he was told by the fire department that nineteen ambulances were in service and had Advance Life Support equipment on them, but later found out seventeen ambulances did not have Advanced Life Support.

The International Amphitheater was full. They said about 4,000 people showed up to hear the outcome of the meeting with Frank Palumbo and Jane Byrne. Mrs. Bernadette Pavlik opened the meeting by explaining the viewpoint of a woman and a wife that was on strike. Firefighter Kenneth Cleeton followed with an excellent speech from a firefighter's perspective. A paramedic told the firefighters and paramedics that the city of Chicago was in direct violation of the federal labor law during this strike.

Bill Reddy, the acting president, was given a standing ovation for the job he was now doing. Reddy went down each and every point of the memorandum of the agreement. One by one he tried to clarify all the points.

As I looked around at the thousands of men, women and children with worried looks on their faces, I wondered, when will this end. The firefighters, dressed in heavy winter coats with hoods, were all wearing union buttons and Brotherhood of the Barrel buttons on their hats and watch caps. Their faces told the story: worried, mad with hate, angry, and not many smiles.

Reddy continued to read the proposal that called for the firefighters that were on strike to go back to work while the city and the union negotiated a contract. The union wanted full amnesty for all returning firefighters including the seven battalion chiefs, and the city wouldn't give in on that issue. The amphitheater went up in a roar. I think the roof might even had lifted a little, when the crowd came to their feet yelling and screaming about the proposal that the city gave to Frank Palumbo to deliver.

Someone in the crowd asked Frank Palumbo, if he had said to Mayor Byrne that he was going to ask Local #2 members to approve this memorandum of agreement. He answered, "no."

The acting president, Bill Reddy, called the meeting to the attention of a phone call from the Cook County Jail. It was Moon, and he was mad as hell. He again asked the members to vote no to this proposal. Frank Muscare said that if we accepted this proposal, then we would return to work begging for mercy on our hands and knees. The dignity that we had as firefighters would be lost forever, and the city still would not negotiate in good faith. We would not be given full amnesty and many firefighters would be dismissed.

The vote was taken and there were not many that went for the approval of the proposal. The vote was loud and clear: No! The angry crowd was standing and yelling, "Moon, Moon."

As I looked over to the East Side of the amphitheater, there sat my wife Suzi, now five months pregnant. She just looked at me with doubt in her eyes.

I had told her that I was sure that this meeting could end the twenty-one-day strike. Earlier that evening, Suzi was on the train returning from her job in the Loop. She overheard a young girl in the seat across from hers. The girl was boasting that her husband was offered a job as a fireman from the Alderman of the 15th Ward. Suzi, of course, had to tell this little brat that her husband was a fireman and was on strike. She further exclaimed that if her husband took the firefighter job, that he would be taking the food away from her unborn child's mouth. Other people on the train applauded Suzi. When she arrived at home and told me the story about the incident on the train, I broke down and said, "Thank you for that." Suzi then told me that she didn't care what occurred during the strike, she was in full support of me and she wanted to go to the amphitheater.

The meeting was called to order again by Bill Reddy. He introduced the Reverend Jesse Jackson, who was on the stage. As he walked up to the microphone in his mint green jogging suit, he drew loud cheers and applause from the striking firefighters. He asked the audience to rise in prayer to commemorate the lives that had been lost.

Seventeen people had died in fires since the strike began on February 14th. Jackson stated that he would meet with Mayor Byrne in the morning, and after the meeting, he would meet all of us in the Daley Center Plaza and we would march in a "prayer pilgrimage" in the Loop.

Bill Reddy thanked Reverend Jackson and asked everyone to be at the Daley Center tomorrow at noon. As the thousands of people left the amphitheater, they were angry as hell, and not knowing what was next. I met a good friend, Kenny Kelty. A firefighter for many years, he was disgusted as we all were. Ken told me how Bob Peterson walked into Engine #34's firehouse on February 14th, and said, "Okay guys, it's time to walk out on strike."

"I was detailed to drive the tiller of Truck #54," Kenny said to Big Pete. "I would rather go to war than walk out of this firehouse on strike. But I have to go out, because this is not only for our security now, but it is for all the young firefighters in the future." Kenny Kelty was in the United States Marines in the Korean War, and knew the true meaning of war.

I spoke to my good friend, Matt Moran, who was a lieutenant on Truck #15. As bad as everything was that night, Matt always was able to cheer me up. He said, "Cos, we have her (the Mayor) back against the wall," and with that we both broke out in laughter, because if anyone's back was against the wall it was the firefighters', and we both knew it.

We all left the amphitheater to resume picketing at Engine #49's firehouse. There were a lot of angry strikers, and they were yelling "Scab" through the closed overhead doors of the firehouse. Soon the police arrived and told everyone to get away from the front of the firehouse. Many of the police knew that what was going on was bullshit, and that the mayor was delaying this strike.

Two barrels were glowing with hot fires, and the men circled around them to keep warm. The ground was covered with snow, but around the base of the burning barrel, you could see the concrete. As we walked back and forth in front of this firehouse, the majority of the men left and we kept the barrels burning all night. Bill Bracken stopped to have coffee in my van. We talked about the rally in the Daley Center.

The word came out through the 4th Division Strike Headquarters that the mayor and her husband, Press Secretary Jay McMullen, had begun to solicit the city's Democratic committeemen for patronage workers to fill the jobs of striking firefighters. McMullen said such recruiting was no more political than fire department hiring under the late Mayor Richard J. Daley. McMullen also said, "I think most of the firemen were patronage workers anyway. If this is the case, it will cause more legal problems for the city. The Federal Court prohibits patronage hiring by the city and is ordering increased hiring from minority groups."

McMullen said the mayor was forced to take this action, because the city had exhausted the list of suitable candidates from the department's eligibility list of applicants. One fireman yelled out that it didn't make it legal. Now every chief's kid would get on because the list had been exhausted. As the night sky began to lighten, more strikers showed up to keep the barrels burning, and we went home for some much needed sleep.

It was Thursday, March 7th, and the 22nd day of the strike. Battling fires, one after the other, back to back, was pushing the city's non-striking firemen to the verge of sheer exhaustion.

One chief said on the morning news, "We have been fighting fires, about six in a row. Two of these fires had fatalities, and there will be more if the mayor doesn't end this strike pretty soon." The chief also said that the strike, and the loss of life had hit the minority communities the hardest.

A citizen told reporters at an early morning fire at 2732 W. Cermak that you could tell that the men who were fighting the fire were inexperienced. They tried to hold the hoses, but were being knocked around, and couldn't shoot the water straight. In another overnight blaze at 4616 South Champlain that was started by children playing with matches, two chiefs, three firemen, and two recruits battled the fire for three hours, eventually resulting in total destruction of the building. Reports like these were coming in all over the city of Chicago.

Uncle Jack asked me to come up to the union office before going to the rally at the Daley Center. Spirits were high at 54 West Randolph in Room 505, but you could see the tired look on the unshaved face of Bill Kugelman and many others. Uncle Jack told me that Jesse Jackson was now meeting with the mayor and would now be the mediator between the city and the union.

The phones were ringing off the wall and being answered as fast as possible. Two women sat in the outer office trying to answer all the questions that were being asked, and directing the calls to the union officials.

Jack Gallapo said, "Punk, if it wasn't for these two ladies," referring to Delores Rospenda and Marie Covert, secretaries of Local #2, "this union office wouldn't be able to function. Their dedication has been outstanding, for every day during the strike that you have been around the barrel, they have been here working for us."

Jesse Jackson emerged from the meeting with Mayor Byrne at City Hall. He went right over to the Daley Center and addressed about 1,000 strikers and their families. With Bill Reddy at his side, they led us on a "prayer pilgrimage" through the Loop about three blocks and back to the center. Bill Reddy and Jesse Jackson led the 1,000 strikers in the Lord's Prayer. The crowd dispersed and Jackson and Bill Reddy went to the Bismarck Hotel for a 2:30 meeting with city officials, in an attempt to reach a settlement for a contract. The mayor's press secretary, Jay McMullen, was critical of Jesse Jackson's involvement in the strike.

Mayor Byrne turned her wrath on Rich Daley and his political allies, when she accused him of playing politics with the strike. Richard M. Daley totally denied the charges and Cook County Assessor Thomas Hynes, a Daley backer, was also linked to the effort by the Mayor. Daley replied that it was absolutely irresponsible for Mayor Byrne to suggest that anyone would prolong the firemen's strike for even one minute to gain some imagined, political advantage. He said, "Her statements are outrageous and completely false. To have strikers and non-strikers try to prolong this would be political suicide and totally irresponsible!"

In the Bismarck Hotel, for over six and one half-hours, Jesse Jackson acted as a shuffling mediator between the city and the union. Sometimes they were together and then apart, but through it all, Jackson held them together. At about 9:00 P.M.. Jackson emerged from the meetings to meet the press. He made a statement that progress was being made between the city and the union. He said, "There is a good attitude between everyone. The period of not talking for so long created some strains in the beginning but we are beyond that part now. They have agreed upon the framework, and that is a very healthy step toward an interim agreement."

The most fundamental part by the mayor was that she had struggled for the right, as the manager of the city, to totally reorganize the fire department. She had stated that from the top to the bottom, the good oleo boys have run the fire department. Their management skills are the worst that she had ever seen before.

The union said that they would not interfere with the right to reorganize, but would like some input. Jackson also told the press that the city and the union had agreed on an affirmative action plan to get more minorities on the Chicago Fire Department, which was currently overwhelmingly white.

The Firefighter's Union today had agreed to a fact-finding committee that had been proposed by the mayor. Reddy said that we were always skeptical of the fact-finding proposal, because we were not sure if that meant binding arbitration on all remaining issues. After some heavy negotiating, they called a recess until 10:00 A.M.. on Friday. Bill Reddy and William Hanley, the city's negotiator, emerged from the meeting and said nothing to reporters other than they would be back in the morning. They were keeping closed mouthed about any progress that went on, because the press seemed to make something out of nothing, then someone got mad, and the talks stopped.

Meanwhile, out at the barrel, the mood was up-beat, because now, after some thirteen days, negotiators were meeting face to face again. The word was out that hundreds of potential recruits were lined up inside City Hall that afternoon. They were being sent in by their political sponsors to replace striking firefighters. One firefighter said, "Yeah, you know they can't keep the job, because the court ruled against that political hiring shit. They all could be in violation of federal law."

"You watch and see," one of the older strikers said, "these job grabbers will one day be our bosses."

A roar of laughter came from the other men standing around the barrel. "What did you call them?"

"You heard me. They're job grabbers, taking your fucking jobs, so stop laughing."

"Take it easy, Mike," one of the guys said, "they are only hiring them on a temporary basis, that's what the newspapers said."

"Yeah, right."

About 2:00 A.M., news came from strike headquarters that about eighteen guys assigned to one firehouse were being subpoenaed for arson. This was bullshit. They were using their political power to try to break this union, and it wouldn't happen.

It wasn't bullshit; all these guys had to appear before a Cook County Grand Jury. There was a very extensive investigation going on. One of the high-ranking cops had a brother who was a firefighter, and he said there were about seventy criminal cases that the police are investigating across the city.

Among some of the incidents were fires and criminal damage to cars and other property belonging to non-strikers. I knew that after twenty-two days, tempers would flare up. It was just a matter of time. If the talks that were going on right now broke down, there was a good chance that we would lose our jobs.

"Shut up and put some wood on the fire," one guy said. "No

one is going to lose their job." "Wait a minute, goddamnit. Don't tell me to shut up. Face the facts, man. They have steadily been hiring these, what did you call them Mike, job grabbers for days. We have been on strike for twenty-two days. I also heard that a lot of guys have been sneaking back in through the back doors. If they have enough guys inside the firehouses for relief, and can start sending people home, we are fucked, my union brother," I said.

Someone told us how much it had cost the city, or should I say, the taxpayers, for food to feed all the non-striking firemen and recruits. It had been estimated that the city had spent about $650,000 just to feed all the people that stayed in the firehouses, and also the fire alarm personnel assigned to the city's two alarm offices.

The Marriott Corporation had provided about 7,600 meals a day in Schiller Park, and Lee and Eddie's Catering in Elk Grove. Breakfast, lunch, and dinner were being served, consisting of pancakes, pork sausages, donuts, orange juice, and coffee for breakfast. Beef tips with Hungarian noodles and salad was served for lunch, and dinner was chicken cutlet, baked potato, tossed salad, and dessert. Plus, all the soft drinks and coffee they need.

One of the guys standing by the barrel said, "That's it! When we go back in, I am charging six bucks a man, and we will eat like kings!"

The news that we heard at the barrel was not always good. Danny Russel, the south side woodman, pulled up with more wood for our barrel. He said four more kids died in a fire at 6813 South Carpenter.

They said the fire was caused by a space heater that exploded. I sure hoped that the talks that were going to take place today would end this, and no more children would die.

As the morning sun started to lighten the sky, the men came to relieve us at the barrel. There had been twenty-one people killed in fires since the beginning of the strike. It was March 7th, the 23rd day of the strike. Hopes were high that negotiations between the city and the union would bring a contract. Alderman Edward Burke had lashed out at the city's striking firefighters and the outside agitators, who Burke said were causing us to prolong the strike. Burke had sided with the mayor on the strike, but this was the first time he had voiced an opinion. We had waited for twenty-three days for the alderman of this city to help bring an end to the strike, or at least speak out.

That night Mayor Byrne was on the news and made a statement that would cause the negotiating to stop again. She said, "The city is negotiating an end to the strike. It is not negotiating a contract. A contract is at least six months away. I have to be very honest about this. The department must first be reorganized, because it, the fire department, is very sick and has been for a long time."

Mayor Byrne's statement that the contract was a very long way off quickly erased the smiles and closed the mouths at the Bismarck Hotel that morning. Bill Reddy, who came to the meeting, was quite open about the negotiating, but after hearing the news about what the mayor had said, he walked out very disgusted. Jesse Jackson, with reference to the mayor's words, said he wished that both sides would please refrain from making such inflammatory statements at such a crucial time in the negotiations.

Jackson, in an effort to smooth out the mayor's statement, explained to the media that the difference between an interim agreement and a short-term contract was just a matter of semantics. We had agreed to the reorganization of the fire department that would take place in the next few months. There had to be some type of agreement between now and then. You could call it an agreement or you could call it a contract, but for the period in between, a new relationship would be established. A short time later, the talks resumed. The city and the union negotiators started hammering out the final agreement. The two key issues in the dispute were binding arbitration and amnesty.

As the talks progressed, sources close to the negotiations said there had been movement on both issues. Meanwhile, the city had announced a new round of testing for firefighter applicants. This news was making many striking firefighters very nervous about being replaced if the talks broke down. Chicago's top-ranking labor leaders made it very clear that if the mayor replaced the striking firefighters permanently, the union leaders (Bill Lee) would not retaliate with a large scale work stoppage by city employees. The pressure was on the firefighters' union leaders to come to terms immediately.

Besides arranging meetings for the union, taking care of many issues like insurance for the striking firefighters from the international, running the 4th Division strike headquarters, collecting money for Brotherhood of the Barrel buttons, and God only knows what else, Jack Gallapo had some personal obligations also. His son Robert Gallapo, also a striking firefighter, was getting married that evening. The reception was at the Martinique Restaurant in the Garden Room.

Uncle Jack had left notice at the union office and also at 4th Division Headquarters to call him if the executive board needed him or if any agreement had been reached.

An air of mixed tension hung over strikers and the firehouses in the city. As we walked in front of the firehouses trying to keep warm, the barrel glowing at the base and a small amount of flames issuing out the top, we waited for news from the Bismarck Hotel. We learned that Bill Lee, the president of the C.F.L., had rejected a personal plea from the president of the International Firefighters Union. William McClennan called Lee and asked him to please honor the firefighters' picket lines. Lee told him, "I can't do it."

One of the strikers said, "Hey, fuck Lee. He hasn't done one thing for us up until today. We don't need the CFL or Bill Lee."

Back at the Bismarck, in agreeing to fact finding, the union insisted that the size of the board be increased from four members to five, and that it be provided with a new chairman. Instead of the mayor's choice, Donald Jacobs, the Dean of Northwestern School of Management, another man was slated to be the chairman.

The chairman would be W. J. Ussery, former secretary of labor, and director of the Federal Mediation Service. The other members would be appointees of the city, the Chicago Firefighter's Union, and the Chicago Federation of Labor. The fact-finding panel would have a six-month period in which to make its findings and that period could extend for another two months. At that point, if the recommendations were not accepted, the issues would go to binding arbitration.

Affirmative action was agreed to, but Jesse Jackson insisted on spelling out affirmative action goals. Jackson recommended increasing the number of blacks on the force from 400 to 1200, and the number of Latinos from 60 to 600. These goals were a result of a 1979 court ruling of the justice department out of fairness, and the union agreed.

Amnesty, the final blow to the union's insistence on total amnesty, was again delivered by Jackson. He said, "I cannot agree to total amnesty because of the fire deaths." He told the union that if they did not agree, that all strikers must work a day without pay, and the seven battalion chiefs that were on strike were to be suspended without pay for four days.

If the union did not agree to this form of amnesty, Jackson said, he would encourage the approximately 400 black firefighters to break ranks with the strikers and they would all return to work. With those kinds of numbers facing us, the decision would be a tough one to make.

All the members of the executive board were called back into the Bismarck Hotel. After two days of talks, an announcement was made by the acting president of Local #2, Bill Reddy, and the city's top labor management attorney, William Hanley, that the city and the firefighter's union had reached an agreement at 10:00 P.M.

The union executive board signed the agreement, and Michael Lass gave it to Jackson, and just before 01:00 hours, he took the agreement to Mayor Bryne's apartment at 111 East Chestnut Street. The mayor signed the agreement. The executive board called a special meeting at midnight at the McCormick Inn at 23rd and Lake Shore Drive.

It had just stopped snowing when the news came to the waiting firefighters. There was relief and celebration around the barrel than an agreement was finally reached.

The McCormick Inn wasn't new to us. We had assembled there before, at a massive meeting on February 17th. The meeting at midnight didn't even faze the firefighters, because we had been out all night for the past twenty-three days. Eddie Tetzner pulled up in his black Chevy van. He said, "Cos, how about a cold one with the boys?" Ed had stopped and brought a cooler full of bear.

For the first time in twenty-three days of the strike, I had a beer with my brothers of the barrel. We then set out for the special meeting at the McCormick Inn.

It was midnight on Saturday, March 8th, the 23rd day of the strike. Firefighters from the southeast, the northwest, and all other parts of the city, started filing into the large ballroom on the second floor of the McCormick Inn. Everyone was happy and in good moods, because we were going back to work. We were tired, unshaven, and our heavy coats smelled of smoke from standing by the barrel. To me, we all looked great. We shook hands and hugged each other, because this was truly a celebration. They said that there were about 3,500 guys, maybe more, that packed the ballroom. They overflowed out into the hallway. We were united and there was a strong sense of pride that filled the room . . . but also a lot of bitterness.

The meeting was called to order by Acting President Bill Reddy. He started out by saying that Bill Kugelman talked with Frank "Moon" Muscare in the county jail. Frank said that he was angry that he wasn't here for the end, but he was happy the strike was over, and he wanted to be here for the finish. The firefighters jumped to their feet yelling, "Moon, Moon," and giving him a standing ovation. Bill Reddy started reading the agreement point by point to the membership. Reddy called for a vote, and the agreement was unanimously accepted. The formal ratification came at 01:37 hours, and there were no dissenting voices heard. All the labor lawyers said they might not call it a contract, but it was a letter of agreement, and it was just as binding as a contract.

Concluding the meeting, Jesse Jackson led us in a prayer, that the bitterness of more than three weeks would not be prolonged. One reporter asked us to voice our opinion on the agreement, and about the amnesty. A firefighter looked at him and said, "Who cares! We aren't striking any more. We're firemen again. That's really what counts!"

It's over!

Chapter XVII

Bill Kugelman met with Commissioner Albrecht in City Hall until about 03:30 hours, putting together a transition plan to get strikers back to work. Members of the second shift would sign in and remain on duty. The members of the third and first shift would sign in and be sent home.

The return to work went much better than when firefighters began returning to duty under the February 20th tentative agreement that fell apart and ended up in a lock-out by the city. The second platoon began returning at 10:00 hours for temporary assignments. Firehouses that non-striking men were in were left alone, and striking firemen were detailed until later to avoid any potential problems. Predictably, the returning firefighters were nervous, but overall they were glad to be back and ready to put the past behind them. The returning men said, "We got what we went after. Maybe not all of it, but hey, what the heck, you can't have it all in the first contract. We'll do better as we go along."

In the firehouses across the city, in order to get ready for a fire, it meant checking out all the equipment that had sat idle for over three weeks. It also meant getting the firehouse cleaned up, even though it wasn't their firehouse. The houses were filthy and had to be scrubbed out from top to bottom. It didn't matter to the returning firefighters what houses they went to, because we were used to being detailed. You can put twenty-four hours in anywhere with a contract.

The end of the strike meant time off for the weary, exhausted men who had been locked up for twenty-three days. They finally got to go home. One non-striker said, "They are a good bunch of guys out there, and we're still brothers. I haven't seen my family in twenty-three days. It has been lonely, sure. But they, the strikers, had more problems than we did in the firehouse. They could have been out of a job, and they had no money. We heard a lot of them are getting divorced, and if any of them needs money or the union needs to be bailed out to pay the fines, I will give toward those fines, because I made a lot of money during the strike."

One non-striker was leaving the firehouse on the north side. A reporter asked him for a comment, and he refused, because he said he didn't want anyone to know that he worked the strike.

As the day went on, the atmosphere was clearly evident that special firefighter camaraderie was back in the many firehouses. Joking and laughing was the order of the day. One firefighter said at the kitchen table, "Do you think it was all worth it?"

Everything takes time and this took us a little longer than we thought, but now we had some decent conditions to work under.

One thing was that any hopes that deep-seated feelings of animosity would fade quickly was just an illusion. The depth of these feelings between strikers and non-strikers no doubt would be a crucial element in determining how soon the fire department would return to normalcy. In one firehouse I was detailed to, the words "no scabs allowed in kitchen" were scrawled on the chalkboard. No one tried to remove it, and it stayed there all day. Similar "no scab" messages were hand-printed on the drinking fountain. Even though we were back in the firehouses, it would be a long, long time before things were really back to normal. In many cases it was just the silent treatment, and I didn't know how they could take it.

As the days passed, the constant arguing continued day after day. I heard about twenty firefighters became embroiled in a fistfight and shoving match during a shift change at a north side firehouse.

A Chicago policeman, a friend of mine, made a good comparison the other day. He said, "Between the men who stayed in the firehouses, and those who walked out, it is just like the Civil War."

When President Lincoln was elected, he was faced with plenty of problems. When Jane Byrne was elected, she immediately faced her share of problems.

President Lincoln told the southern states that he would reunite the union one way or another. Mayor Byrne told firefighters that she would not tolerate a strike by the firefighters. Both Byrne and Lincoln stood by their statements. Lincoln waged a bloody war and Jane Byrne waged a deadly game of cat and mouse with the firefighters. Just like the Civil War, the results of the confrontation would be seen and felt for years to come.

The bitterness of that war divided families, ruined friendships, and crippled alliances. Those same bitter feelings would persist in the wake of the firefighters' strike. The striking firemen were back to work, but the bitterness that they had would not magically disappear.

It's impossible to call someone a scab one day and embrace him as a fellow firefighter the next day. Time is the greatest healer, and in time, some of the bitterness would fade. But, for the majority of firefighters, things would never be what they once were.

The difference between Jane Byrne and President Lincoln is that Lincoln was shot before he could heal the wounds of the war, before they became infected with hatred. Mayor Byrne had a chance to heal the wounds of the firefighters' strike, but the big question was would she make that effort, or would she let them fester with hatred that would last for years, and generations to come.

When we went back to work, it just wasn't the same. We did all the housework, cleaned the kitchen, and made the bunks. But, the talk of the day was always the same. This guy did this and that guy did that, during the strike. There was bitterness in the extreme!

Often times I would think to myself about when the strike was called on February 14th, and the men who made the decision to work. I would really like to know their reason. Was it because of their great feelings of civic pride or dedication? I thought I was dedicated. Or rather, was it the fear of losing their jobs that compelled them to stay in on that cold morning?

The mayor had bribed them with paychecks of double time. If these men were truly dedicated, they would have worked for straight time and offered the excess of their fattened salaries to the firefighter's widow and orphan fund. It was a very profitable game to be a dedicated firefighter during the twenty-three-day strike. By staying in the firehouses as long as they did, they actually prolonged the strike. Just hear me out for a minute. Think for one minute if all firefighters walked out on strike on February 14th at 05:15 hours, the strike couldn't have lasted more than a couple of hours at the most. The city leaders would have been forced to bring this job action to a speedy end. Norm always said I was a dreamer, but what if. . . .

The city's comptroller, Raymond Coyne, said that the fire department spent more money on salaries, not less, during the twenty-three-day strike. Even though the department did not have to pay the strikers, many people, myself included, wrongfully assumed that the fire department was saving large sums in payroll cost.

Non-striking firemen were collecting double time while they worked. Firefighters who normally received $238.00 per twenty-four hours were being paid $477.00 a day, and after twenty-three days earned some $10,978.00. Non-striking lieutenants, captains, and chiefs were also being paid double time.

The news came out to the firehouse that our president, Frank Muscare, was released on Monday, March 10th, by Judge Hechinger, after the city agreed to the strike settlement. He had been in jail since February 21st.

Already the fire department was starting Mayor Byrne's reorganization, and the word was that there would be six districts replacing the seven divisions. All the battalions would be changed also.

The following is the "interim agreement" that I like to call a contract, because it makes me feel a little bit better about it:

The Interim Agreement
• The firefighters will return to work upholding a no-strike, no lockout agreement until December 31, 1980. During that time, remaining disputes will go to a three member fact-finding board for six months. If the board's recommendations are rejected by either side, negotiations would resume for two more months. After that, the issues would be submitted for binding arbitration.

• All firemen who participated in the strike will work one day without pay, except for seven battalion chiefs, who will lose four days' pay. the city will drop charges that could cost the chiefs their jobs.

• Firefighters will retain the rights and privileges they had prior to February 14th, 1980.

• The city will seek dismissal of its suit against the union, and ask for leniency with respect to contempt fines of $45,000 a day, levied for defiance of back to work orders.

• A strong affirmative action plan will be created to promote the hiring of all minority group members.

• The union's key demand to represent almost all offices as well as rank and file members will be submitted to the fact-finding board.

• For the duration of the interim agreement, there will be five men on every truck and half of the fire department's engines in 1980, and on the balance of engines in 1981. Currently there are four men on every truck and engine.

• Firefighters will have a new grievance structure, with the department handling the first two steps after the grievance is filed.

• The practice of assigning firefighters to higher job classifications without higher pay and benefits will end.

• A union demand that seniority be the controlling factor in promotions, assignments, vacation and other matters will be submitted to the impasse-resolution process.

I shall never forget the lives that were lost during the strike. I felt frustration and anger every time I heard about another person's life that was taken. The tragic loss of twenty-one victims was felt just as deeply by every striking firefighter. Firefighters have felt this terrible grief hundreds and hundreds of times in the deaths directly attributable to a lack of sufficient manpower. Although we feel bad about these fire deaths, we shall feel better that the strike was worthwhile. I know that someday we can read a news report and see that Chicago fire deaths are down 25 percent, because of more manpower, better equipment and working conditions.

We all paid one hell of a price for this agreement, but we held our heads high with honor. I sure hope when the young firefighters replace us, they can somehow appreciate what this struggle was all about, and the price we paid for it.

Late one night, I stared out the front window of a firehouse looking at the apron. I thought back to how we stood outside huddled around a barrel with our backs against the cold and the snow. I think about Norm and how simple it all was back then.

People will die today in fires across this country. Homes will burn, and millions of dollars in property will be lost. Yet on any given day, over two million firefighters will answer the call to duty, and put their lives on the lines for us.

They are:

The Noble Breed.

The Epilogue

On that cold morning, January 21st, 1990, I was hanging over the guardrail on Interstate 55 at Halsted Street, and I knew I was hurt bad. I was bleeding heavily from the right side of my head and had an intense burning pain in the upper portion of my back. It seemed that the fire department was on the scene in a minute. I was placed on a backboard and pulled under the very truck that just ran over me. I never imagined myself on a stretcher with firefighters and paramedics in their black coats with yellow reflecting stripes, walking around me. They lifted me up into Ambulance #19 and I was transported to Mercy Hospital. My wife was extracted from the van and taken to Michael Reese Hospital. I never lost consciousness and I worried so about Suzi; the truck hit her side of our vehicle.

I was taken into a trauma room in the ER. Father Thomas Mulcrone was waiting with the nurses and doctors to evaluate my condition. Father Mulcrone, the Chicago Fire Department Chaplain, tried to reassure me, but he also blessed me like I was going somewhere. The doctors told me that my back was broken, my heart had sustained contusions, my right ear was almost totally off, and I had five broken ribs.

After surgery and three days in the intensive care unit, I was moved to the upper floors of the hospital, where I underwent two more surgeries on my right ear. After twenty-one days, I finally saw my wife, after being taken home by my brother Mike. Suzi was black and blue and sustained a closed head trauma; her right ear was severed in two. Both of her knees were cut from glass, but we were alive and back holding onto each other.

I wasn't home very long and I was admitted into Northwestern Hospital where I under went a thirteen and one half-hour anterior-posterior spinal fusion on my back. After four days in the intensive care spinal cord unit, three of which I was on life support and received three units of blood, I was moved to the orthopedic floor. I received eight days of physical therapy, and after a total of twelve days, I was taken home by my brother, Mike.. After twenty-one months of therapy, I was able to pass the physical to return to the fire department. I was back to my old job of investigating fires in the Office of Fire Investigation. I was able to attend classes on the cause and origin of fires to increase my knowledge of fire investigation.

On June 15, 1995, while working at a fire scene at 2612 West Augusta Blvd., on the city's north side, I accidentally fell back-wards off the rear porch and landed on a stairway below. I was carefully taken from the stairway by Captain Richard Snyder and men from Engine Company #57, and transported to Northwestern Hospital by Ambulance #44, and two special paramedics, Anna Rosa and Scott Ronstadt. I was again operated on for the removal of my spinal stabilization from my back between the T-1 and the T-3 vertebras. The surgery took five and one half hours and that ended my career as a Chicago Firefighter. The doctor just looked at me and said, "Don't even think about it!"

One night in October 1997, I attended a promotion party for

three young firefighters that had been promoted to lieutenant. The party was at the Gaelic Fire Brigade located at 8404 South Kedzie Avenue. The Brigade is a large hall with a large horseshoe bar at the west end. Late into the night after many of the guys left, and many beers were had by all, Louie Buick and I were sitting at the north end of the bar. Just then two young firefighters approached us and offered to buy us a beer. "Sure Bum" told the young man, "but first you tell us who you are and where you're at."

They introduced themselves and Bum said, "What company are you on boy?"

He looked at us with pride and said, "Engine Company #122," in a loud voice.

I said to the young man, "Oh Engine 1#22, that's over east around 79th and Indiana. They do some work (meaning fires) over there. That's a good house."

The bartender yelled to these young firemen, "Who's your boss over there?"

The young fellow said, "Lieutenant So & So," as the kid blurted out the rest of the name.

Then there was silence and the bartender said, "He's a "SCAB."

The young man in defense said, "But he teaches us how to fight fires. Besides I was only seven years old when the strike occurred. I don't know what the strike was all about. I was just too young." Then he walked away from us. We all turned and looked at each other. He was only seven years old when the strike occurred; we laughed.

On my way home that night, I thought a lot about what the young man said about not knowing anything about the strike. I stopped at White Castle for a large coffee and three hamburgers.

That's when I knew that I had to write this book, so all the younger firefighters that come on this job will know how and what the strike was all about. The strike of the Chicago Firefighters Union in 1980 was probably the largest pivotal event in the Chicago Fire Department's history.

After the firefighters' strike the fire department underwent a complete reorganization. The old eight bureaus were broken down into six bureaus. Divisions were broken down to districts, and all battalions were moved around the city. But for the most part, the firehouses were still in the same locations. The pride of the job was somehow misplaced during the reorganization, and I often here that no one cares about the job any more.

Pride is never lost because the job is still the same, we all put out fires. The pride is to be on a company, as one of a unit. When you belong to an engine or a truck, you're on a company. When you do anything, you have to be a company! Plain and simple. If you have to make some small concessions each day for the sake of your company, then damn it make them. When you respond to a scene, demand respect for your company. I don't care from whom. Whether it is a poor helpless citizen, or the chief officer at the scene, you should know exactly what everyone on that rig is going to do, because you responded as a company, and you work as a company, so you know everything as a company.

Firefighters, most of the ones I knew, were thrilled to be on this job. Much of their pride was built around the notion that they did a job, most others were afraid to attempt.

Being a firefighter means being part of a special fraternity. It means eating together, sleeping together in the same bunkroom, and risking your lives together. Because you're one of 5,000 people in Chicago who put on the heavy black coat, you know the one, it has a yellow reflecting stripes, and they run into burning buildings to risk their lives to save another.

It doesn't make a difference to a firefighter if it is the life of the poorest citizen in a rat-infested tenement. They have as high a value as the occupant of the executive suite of a high-rise building on Chicago's gold coast.

The firehouse offers one of the last American strongholds for a certain kind of person. It's a place where all can speak their minds, and to some, it is their family, but to others, it is their second family.

In the firehouse, you can eat the way you like to eat, or say what you want to say, or curse if you want to say, "fuck it." But the most important part of the twenty-four hours at the firehouse is the cooking club. It is the heart and soul of the time in the firehouse. If a man is dropped out of a food club, it automatically puts a strain on everyone in the house. I don't know how it happens, but there is a strain. There is a separation in the camaraderie; it will affect your work at fires as a company. If you're "out," get back "in" somehow, even if it means transferring off the company.

The cooking club establishes harmony in the firehouse. Even with the amount of time during the day in which you may read, or just sit around talking or watching television, the kitchen is the hub of the firehouse.

The number of structural fires in the city has fallen steadily since 1980, but the number of ambulance assist calls has increased just in the last two years. As the city of Chicago begins to evaluate whether the fire department needs all of its 5,000 firefighters and paramedics, it's time to stay united.

The Fire Department's fighting force is 70% white, 21% black and 8% Hispanic. Women account for only 2% of all firefighters.

Today, the Chicago Fire Department is better integrated than it has even been. There are blacks and whites on the fire department and as a matter of fact, it has been this way for a long time.

Except for a new fire truck or new engine, color television, and now the new computer equipment to dispatch, firehouses across the city haven't changed much. But as I said before, you may ride a more modern apparatus, learn new fire suppression techniques, enjoy shorter hours, and more pay, but a firefighter must always live in a world of smoke, flames, falling walls, and ice-covered ladders.

This was never so true, as in the early part of last year when fire erupted in a tire store located at 10611 South Western Avenue. Firefighters Anthony Lockhart and Patrick King paid the ultimate price of being a firefighter. One was black and one was white, and I am almost certain that when these two firefighters entered that burning structure, there was no racism or discrimination between them. They were firefighters with only one enemy: fire! That's the way it should be, because we as firefighters depend on one another and always will.

Chicago Firefighters formed the Independent Firemen's Association on August 1st, 1901. In 1918, the association thereafter would be known as Local #2. The membership has grown from that tiny nucleus that first formed the association, to over 5,000 rank and file members of Local #2 today. William Kugelman is the president of the Chicago Firefighters Union today.

The 1910 Chicago Stockyard fire represented the largest loss of firefighter lives in the history of the Chicago Fire Department. Today in 1998, fund raising efforts are underway to erect a monument to the twenty-one Chicago firefighters who were killed in that fire on December 22, 1910. The plans call for a bronze memorial 125% of life size, created by artist Joseph Luiz Ramirez, and to be placed in a landscaped setting near the Chicago Stockyard Industrial Park. It will be backed by a "wall of honor" with all the names of Chicago Fire Department Firefighters and Paramedics who have given their lives in the line of duty in defense of this great city.

The non-profit Chicago Stockyards Fire Memorial Committee, comprised of firefighters and civilians, is raising money needed to create and erect the monument through private donations.

Contributions to this great effort may be sent to:

The 1910 Chicago Stockyards
Fire Monument Fund Inc.
117 North Jefferson Street Suite 204
Chicago, IL 60661

In 1969, the leather helmet, canvas fire coat, and rubber hip boots were all the equipment the firefighter had to protect him from the searing heat and flames. This equipment was bought and paid for by the firefighters, along with a class "A" uniform and work clothes. A small clothing allowance was provided by the city.

Today, a firefighter enjoys the convenience of a commissary where they are fitted in a class "A" uniform with two sets of work clothes that are made of fire resistive material. The fire turnout gear is the best that money can buy.

The "joker" stand that was such an essential part of communicating and dispatching a fire company, has now been replaced. The new system is a modern computerized method of dispatching fire companies and ambulances to incidents throughout Chicago.

Following the strike, changes and improvements came swiftly and steadily. The reorganization of the department was new, but in a short time many things became new.

Local #2 became the sole and exclusive bargaining agent for all uniformed members below the ranks of deputy district chief.

Wages: Employees shall now receive overtime pay at the rate of time and one half. If an employee is recalled to duty, he/she shall receive a minimum of three hours pay at overtime rate. An employee may be held over for a maximum of four hours. Any employee held over more than thirty minutes shall be paid overtime.

Vacations: Each platoon employee will receive two (20) day furloughs, which will include (5) duty days and one Daley Day. All (40) hour employees shall receive 4 weeks of furlough time.

Firefighters, Engineers, and EMS employees will select their furloughs on the basis of seniority.

Officers shall select their furloughs on the basis of rank and on the basis of seniority.

Paid holidays: Employees covered by this contract who work on any of the following (12) recognized city holidays shall be paid double time for all hours worked.

The following holidays are recognized:
1. New Years Day — January 1
2. Martin Luther King's Birthday — January 15
3. Lincoln's Birthday — February 12
4. Washington's Birthday — Third Monday in February
5. Good Friday — Friday before Easter
6. Memorial Day — Last Monday in May
7. Independence Day — July 4

8. Labor Day — First Monday in September

9. Columbus Day — October 12

10. Veterans Day — November 11

11. Thanksgiving Day — Last Thursday in November

12. Christmas Day — December 25

Seniority: Defined as the employee's length of continuous service since his last date of hire. Seniority lists are to be posted twice each year.

Vacancies and Promotions: Promotional vacancies within the bargaining unit created as a result of death, resignation, or retirement.

The employer must fill to maintain the minimum manning agreed to and shall be filled within 45 days of the last day worked. Promotions, which are required to fill vacancies, shall be made from established lists.

Grievance procedure: Any grievance or dispute, which may arise between the parties shall be settled in the following manner. Procedure steps and time limits.

No Acting Out of Classification: No employee shall be required or volunteer to perform duties of any other rank or classification.

Minimum Manning: 5 men on all trucks and 5 men on all engines.

The newspapers were filled with who won the strike, the strikers or the non-strikers. Many said no one won, because there was no contract. I do know one thing for sure. Before February 14, 1980, the city of Chicago had never paid me any overtime or time and one half for firefighting.

I am positive that I was never paid for not being in the fire-house on Thanksgiving Day, let alone being called to work on a holiday and being paid double time for something we always did anyway for our regular pay. Now we have twelve holidays paid.

Instead of having your alderman or a chief get you transferred or promoted, we now have seniority rights as our vehicle for assignments, promotion, furloughs, and even called back to work. It seems that seniority has put a stop to the patronage system.

Instead of getting your ass chewed out, and being sent to O'Hare Airport because you had a dispute with a chief, we now have a grievance procedure that can be settled by procedure steps and time limits.

Instead of being put in charge of the engine, no questions asked, there is no acting out of classification. Promotions are made from established lists.

Instead of two or three men on a fire company, all truck companies and engine companies will be manned with a minimum of five men on each rig.

I know that the newspapers print what they need in order to sell their paper. The letter of agreement that was signed by the mayor and the union was a contract. So, as far as who won the strike, I will let that decision be up to you. Who do you think won the strike?

Since the number of firefighters who are overcome by toxic smoke is so small these past few years in spite of frequent exposures, there are obviously some reasons why firefighters fare so much better. Maybe it is the equipment, like the self-contained breathing apparatus that allows a firefighter to advance to the fire, instead of lying on the floor inching his way closer to the fire. There are a couple of other reasons also. One is knowledge that is obtained by study, and the second is experience that can be gained in time. A new firefighter can be assured some protection by listening to their officers and seasoned firefighters.

At the time of this writing, Jack Gallapo, after years of service on the Chicago Fire Department, has retired and lives on the south side of Chicago. He has three sons that remain on the job today.

William C. Alletto was promoted through the ranks to deputy fire commissioner, and is the Administrator of the Bureau of Support Services, and remains on the Chicago Fire Department today.

Presently, I am a licensed private detective working out of my office located in downtown Chicago, as Bill Cosgrove Investigations Inc., 221 North LaSalle Street, Suite 2248, Chicago, IL 60601. I am conducting fire investigations for insurance companies, attorneys at law, and private citizens. I testify as an expert witness in the state and federal courts on the cause and origin of fire incidents.

On the very day that I started on the Chicago Fire Department, February 16, 1969, my son, Timothy Cosgrove, began his career on the Chicago Fire Department thirty years later, February 16, 1999. A third generation firefighter, he wears his father's badge #1825.

To the firefighters whose stories I was unable to tell, I am truly sorry. I know there are many fire stories that have been locked up for so long that would enlighten everyone who listens about . . . *The NOBLE BREED!*

A Prayer for Firemen

When they are called to duty, God
Whenever flames may rage
Give them the strength to save
some life, whatever be its age,
Help them embrace a little child
Before it is too late,
Or save an older person
From the horror of that fate
Enable them to be alert
And hear the weakest shout
And quickly and efficiently
To put the fire out
And if according to Your will
They have to lose their lives
Please bless with Your hand
Their children and their wives.

References

Chicago Newspapers:

Chicago Tribune
Chicago Sun-Times
Southtown Economist
Daily Calumet
Chicago Defender

Magazines:

International Fire Fighter
Chicago Fire Fighter
Fire House Magazine
Fire Engineering

Books:

History Highlights of the Chicago Fire Department, 1978
   Authors: Ken Little, senior fire alarm operator, Chicago Fire
   Department and Father John McNalis